THE
pram factory

THE
pram factory

The Australian Perfoming Group Recollected

TIM ROBERTSON

MELBOURNE UNIVERSITY PRESS

MELBOURNE UNIVERSITY PRESS
PO Box 278, Carlton South, Victoria 3053, Australia
mup-info@unimelb.edu.au
www.mup.com.au

First published 2001
Design and typography © Melbourne University Press 2001
Text © Tim Robertson 2001
The author asserts his moral rights in the work.

This book is copyright. Apart from any use permitted under the *Copyright Act* 1968 and subsequent amendments, no part may be reproduced, stored in a retrieval system or transmitted by any means or process whatsoever without the prior written permission of the publisher.

Designed by Ron Hampton, Pages in Action
Printed in Australia by Brown Prior Anderson

National Library of Australia Cataloguing-in-Publication entry

Robertson, Tim, 1944– .
The Pram Factory: The Australian Performing Group recollected.

   Bibliography.
   Includes index.
   ISBN 0 522 84983 0.

   1. Australian Performing Group—History. 2. Pram Factory—History.
   3. Theatre—Victoria—Melbourne—History—20th century. 4. Drama—
   Victoria—Melbourne—20th century—History and criticism. I. Title.

792.099451

Melbourne University Press gratefully acknowledges the generous contributions of the following people towards the production costs of this book:

Owen and Roslyn Beaton, John Bryson, John Cain, Meg Clancy, John Duigan, Carrillo Gantner, Bill Garner, Ian and Diana Gust, Lorna and Bill Hannan, Alan Lockwood, Dame Elisabeth Murdoch, Greig Pickhaver, John Timlin and the Bridget McDonnell Gallery and Neil Watson.

Foreword

IT'S A BRAVE WRITER who would tackle a history of that great explosion of the 1960s and '70s, the Pram Factory—the teeming events, theatrical, political and social, that changed forever Melburnians'—and by extension Australians'—idea of what theatre is, and what it might be. Here is the first book-length try, and a wild ride it is.

Tim Robertson was there. He lived it. In the spirit of that era he has constructed his version as a series of energetic and hilarious raves, and a gallery of joltingly vivid portraits. But this book is not an extravaganza of personal memory. Its free-associating style is grounded in massive research, countless interviews, and a sophisticated understanding of the history and theory of theatre.

It zooms magisterially, also, over a phantasmagorical landscape of one-night stands, communal households, offended writers, demonstrations, affairs, addictions, child-rearing, parties, smashed marriages, bump-outs, acid trips, collective meetings and pub brawls.

In the true tradition of the Pram, Robertson combines the intellectual abilities of a scholar with the imagination of a joyful lunatic.

Reading it is an experience full of surprises. Apart from working on *Betty Can Jump*, the first women's show, my connection with the Pram Factory was slight as well as short-lived—or so I have told myself, these past thirty years. Who would have thought—least of all *I*—that the first secretary of the Australian Performing Group was a certain Helen Garner? I have no memory of having served in this capacity, but minutes in my handwriting must exist and Robertson has unearthed them.

Points of view proliferate as to what actually happened at the Pram and what it all meant. Robertson has the audacity, here, to shape and date the stages, as he sees them, of the Pram's trajectory. That feat alone deserves respect; but though he is intellectually and chemically well placed to engage in the broadest sympathies, he is no respecter of persons, and will be excoriated from some quarters for his book.

A more faction-ridden organisation could hardly be imagined. By the time the mighty collective meetings were instituted, I had recognised my own bourgeois individualist tendencies and reduced my contact with Pram people to the merely social, but those meetings became legendary. People staggered out of them white-faced. They sat in the Lygon Street cafe then called Tamani, feverishly dissecting each other's positions and statements. To a detached observer it sounded both boring and weirdly fascinating—a kind of group masochism.

'In circumstances of egalitarian political correctness,' Robertson writes, 'the possession of performance talent could be a liability, seen as a threat. The naturals and those of proven track record had to exercise much tact and diplomacy for fear of being thought to be getting above their station.'

Even now, all these years later, it relieves something in me to hear that truth frankly stated.

But oh, the shows! The Pram, back then, was *where you went*. There was always, always *something on*. How many hours of our lives did we, the audience, spend in that primitive, many-spaced cavern of fantasy? How many tears (of laughter, perhaps, more than of tragic catharsis) did we shed on those rock-hard seats? How many times did we dance till the early hours of the morning, out there in the back theatre? How many night rides home, zooming through the streets and parks on our rusty, gearless old grids?

Tim Robertson's is the first full-on book about the Pram. It certainly won't be the last. But it deserves an honoured place among the histories, seething as it does with the moods, the beliefs and theories and indignations, the frenzied battles and the driven creativeness of those wonderful and fruitful years.

Helen Garner
2001

Contents

	Author's note	ix
	What was What in the Big World	xi
1	Preprambulation	1
2	The High Old Times of Tribe	14
3	On Drummond Street	22
4	Towerchildren	33
5	Cell Formation and Division	43
6	A Group Mugshot with a Partial Anatomy of the Group Head	63
7	Head fer the Hills (and Stasis)	76
8	Group Creation: Some Little Known Facts	88
9	The 'Pataphysics of Peter Cummins	116
10	Romeril's Art of Work	123
11	The Circus Way Round	128
	Appendix I: A Chronology of Productions	148
	Appendix II: Who was Who	159
	Bibliography	172
	Index	176

Author's note

LITTLE HAS BEEN PUBLISHED about the spring tide of creativity and democratic experiment in the performing arts that boiled around the Pram Factory in the Carlton of the '70s.

Pram Factory plays and playwrights are on the record, analysed and anthologised. The Australian Performing Group is the stuff of myth and thesis. We have been variously rated and berated as Idealists and Utopians, Regenerators of an Australian Idiom in performance, a Cultural Mafia, a Renaissance, a Sheltered Workshop. Many are the ideologically graven images, but there has been no general survey of the ground from the performer's point of view.

The following recollections of an ex-shareholding member of the APG are an attempt to evoke the milieu, its characters and their mindsets and to sketch the rise, processes, achievements, implosion and succession of a cultural phenomenon. They are based on my own experiences and interviews with other ex-members, the APG archives held at the Latrobe Library and the files of former collaborators. They remain partial impressions with egregious exclusions, and as they are the Reflexes of my Memory, I take sole responsibility for the Fallibility of that Engine.

To everyone who has helped me get it together, especially Louise Adler, Martin Armiger, Graeme Blundell, Sue Broadway, Meg Clancy, Jane Clifton, Tim Coldwell, Peter Corrigan, Peter Cummins, Kerry Dwyer, John Duigan, Laurel Frank, Bill Garner, Max Gillies, John Hawkes, Garrie Hutchinson, Sue Ingleton, David Kendall, Robert Meldrum, Barry Oakley, K. P. Pearson and Hannah at Black Pepper Press, Greig Pickhaver, Alan Robertson, Lindzee Smith, Bruce Spence, Suarupo, David Williamson—thanks for the mnemonic support, the raves, the dialogue and encouragement.

To Charmayne Lane I am indebted for your Perpetual Succour and Subvention to the Arts.

To my son Finn, thanks for the loan of your high itIQ.

John Timlin aided and abetted the erection of the Scholarly Apparatus, particularly the Who was Who and What was What. My gratitude to Bridget McDonnell and John and Michael Timlin for your chronic hospitality, creature comforts and footy in the hallway.

Ursula Harrison and Sue Ingleton's research contributed significantly to the Chronology of Shows.

For your forbearance in finding, trusting me with an extended loan of, and the generous permission to use photos you took and/or kept safe I am grateful to Lloyd Carrick, Ponch Hawkes, Ruth Maddison, Claire and Mal Dobbin, Jack Hibberd, Bill Garner, Jane Clifton, Max Gillies, Laurel Frank, Carol Porter, Tim Coldwell, Fay Stevens at Fruit Fly Circus, John Gollings, Don Whyte, *Herald Weekly Times*, Robin Leuba, Peter Corrigan and Meg Clancy.

Gratitude in extremis to Barry Dickins for the charitable malice of your singular noodle and nib.

Thanks, Benny Zable, for the bent diptych of the Pram Factory that covers the book and to John Timlin for permission to so exploit it. Also to Bob Daly and the estate of Arthur Horner for their cartoons. My thanks to Teresa Pitt at Melbourne University Press for your imprimatur and enthusiasm for the book; to Caroline Williamson for lending your informed and sympathetic faculties in a gentle reformation of the text; to Ron Hampton, who digs Grace, for the slick design. To the keepers of mss at Latrobe Library, Jock Murphy and company, I am grateful for your assistance and generosity.

As the Donors who provided the Subvention necessary to support Independent Publishing in Straitened Times I heartily thank: Greig Pickhaver, Bill Garner, Meg Clancy, Neil Watson, Carrillo Gantner, Dame Elisabeth Murdoch, John Duigan, Owen and Roslyn Beaton, Alan Lockwood, John Timlin, Bridget O'Donnell, Ian and Diana Gust, John Cain and John Bryson.

'Group Mugshot' appeared in *Overland*, Summer 1995. 'Romeril's Art of Work' was first published in *John Romeril,* edited by Gareth Griffiths (Rodopi, Amsterdam, Atlanta 1993).

What was What in the Big World

1965   Sir Robert Menzies declared in London that '. . . we are at war [in Vietnam]. Make no mistake about it.' ★ The Victorian Vice Squad seized D. H. Lawrence's *Lady Chatterley's Lover* for alleged obscenity.

1966   Sir Robert Menzies resigned, and was succeeded by Harold Holt. ★ The first conscripts embarked for Vietnam in April. ★ Violent anti-war demonstrations in Sydney.

1967   Ronald Ryan was the last man hanged at Pentridge. ★ Air Vice Marshal Ky, South Vietnamese P.M., was given a hostile reception in Australia. ★ Australians voted by referendum to count Aborigines in the Census. ★ P.M. Holt drowned at Portsea and was replaced by John Gorton.

1968   Aboriginal boxer Lionel Rose won the World Bantamweight Title. ★ Anti-conscription protests continued across Australia. ★ Comedian Tony Hancock died in Sydney. ★ Victoria's new National Gallery was opened.

1969   The US Consulate was stormed in Melbourne. ★ HMAS *Melbourne* cut HMAS *Voyager* in two. ★ Paul Hasluck was made Governor General. ★ Jack Hibberd's *Dimboola* opened, as did the rock musical *Hair*. ★ Equal pay for women was adopted. ★ A man walked on the Moon.

1970   Massive anti-war protests in Australia led by ALP's Dr Jim Cairns in Melbourne. ★ The Poseidon nickel boom collapsed. ★ Australian troops were hit hard by Viet Cong at Nui Dat. ★ Carlton won the VFL Premiership from Collingwood. ★ Melbourne's West Gate bridge collapsed. ★ Germaine Greer's *The Female Eunuch* was born.

1971   P.M. Gorton voted himself out and became deputy to Sir William McMahon. ★ Australian combat troops were withdrawn from Vietnam. ★ Gough Whitlam became the first Australian political leader to visit Communist China.

1972 — Gough Whitlam became P.M., ending conscription, recognising China, initiating Aboriginal land rights legislation and abolishing sales tax on contraceptives. ★ Shane Gould won five medals at the Munich Olympics, and Palestinians killed Israelis.

1973 — Attorney General Lionel Murphy raided ASIO headquarters. ★ Papua New Guinea won self-government. ★ The preferential tariff agreement between Australia and the U.K. ended, and the Queen opened the Sydney Opera House. ★ Gough bought Jackson Pollock's *Blue Poles*, and Patrick White won the Nobel Prize for Literature.

1974 — Whitlam appointed Sir John Kerr as Governor General and the ALP scraped back in at the May election. The ACT and NT Senates were granted representation. ★ Cyclone Tracy demolished Darwin. ★ Hawke's ACTU grounded Frank Sinatra in Sydney for sexist remarks about Australian female journalists.

1975 — Tirath Khemlani, a London-based money broker, was engaged by Mines Minister Rex Connor to raise $2 billion for a pipeline dream and became a nightmare for the ALP. ★ Five Oz journalists disappeared in Timor, and crusading editor Juanita Nielson disappeared in Kings Cross. ★ Malcolm Fraser persuaded G-G Kerr to sack P.M. Whitlam, who lost the subsequent election.

1976 — Douglas Nicholls, Aboriginal pastor and former Fitzroy footballer, became Governor of South Australia, and Pat O'Shane the first Aboriginal barrister in Australia. ★ The first Vietnamese boat people landed. ★ 'No fault' divorce was introduced, and random breath tests began in Victoria.

1977 — Sir John Kerr resigned. ★ Eighty-three people died in the Granville train disaster. ★ Whitlam handed ALP leadership to Bill Hayden.

1978 — The Hilton Hotel in Sydney was bombed during the Commonwealth Heads of Government Meeting, killing a garbage collector and a policeman. ★ Sir Robert Menzies died, and so did Johnnie O'Keefe. ★ Sir John Kerr was appointed Ambassador to UNESCO, and resigned on his first day because of pressure of work. ★ Galarrwuy Yunupingu was named Australian of the Year.

1979 — Don Dunstan resigned as Premier of South Australia. ★ Harry Miller's Computicket went into receivership. ★ Lillian Gasinskaya, eighteen, from Odessa jumped ship and sought political asylum wearing a red bikini. ★ Arbitration Commission established maternity leave. ★ Dr George Miller made *Mad Max*.

1980 — A Royal Commission found that Griffiths anti-drugs crusader Donald Mackay was killed by arrangement with a Calabrian syndicate. ★ Baby Azaria Chamberlain disappeared from a campsite at Ayers Rock.

⭐ 1 Preprambulation

THE CULTURAL SUPER-HERO of the '60s was the Group, the energy field of a set of individuals that created a charismatic surplus value, whereby the Beatles were more than the sum of John, Paul, George and Ringo. A Group was something to be, the exemplary organ, a source of power, proven catalyst of revolution and scientific discovery, lever to world fame and wilder sex. Individual talents thirsted for glory, rival ambitions went right on infighting; but now they were subsumed by, or flexed themselves in the name of, the Group. The Group had Authority when other forms and figures of it were out of order and exploded. The Groups that organised the anti-war demos, the Groups that performed at them and at the monster rock concerts, were potent inspirations. Eros on Fender throbbed the bass riff of the democratisation of apotheosis: Do it—anyone can make it—with a little help from your friends.

TV images of young unhuddled masses at Woodstock or on the streets of Chicago inflamed a desire to imitate, to put our bodies on the line and perform with the whole world watching.

> *Those images which yet*
> *fresh images beget*

were being received from Paris, Prague, London, Tokyo; but above all from Amerika. On the small screen all the elements of drama, moribund in theatre, seemed alive over there in the public domain. The fun, the danger and the crowds of a Big Time were there to be seized in guerrilla theatre around the marches, sit-ins, moratoria. The war was on the box, and with it we got the models of counterculture and the yanqui know-how of dissent.

We also got it in print through *Ramparts* and *Rolling Stone*, and we got it from a small but potent brainfood parcel that came from New

Guerrillas in the mass. Vietnam Moratorium, 1970. In an interval between agit-prop actions, hairy, wary performers in whiteface, from Tribe and the La Mama Group, check out the spectacle of pigs on horseback. (Don Whyte)

The head of hanging premier Bolte is paraded outside the Victorian parliament by Lindy Davies (in mask) and Tony Taylor (obscured), while Yvonne Marini embodies La Pasionaria. Albert Langer (bespectacled beard, extreme left) sneers approvingly. (Mal Dobbin)

Orleans—the quarterly *Tulane Drama Review* (now simply *The Drama Review*, based in NY). Many of its 120-odd pages were hard grits to chew. The rhetoric could be dense, abstract, deranged even, but it all went down. *TDR* had the word from the hippest and holiest of horses' mouths: Meyerhold, Brecht, Artaud, Brook, Marovitz, Littlewood, Chaikin, Schechner, Schumann, Barba, Lebel, Mnouchkine. And Grotowski, the wizard of Wroclaw, winning by a short head. It regurgitated manifestos galore, wild and whirling, or gnomic, in numbered clauses. Heavily into rite and ritual, the exploration and redefinition of performers and their relationship with audiences, *TDR* built up images of funky groups and productions that went to our aspirant heads. It functioned as a guru director at a remove; through it we were connected to far-out experiments like the *James Joyce Liquid* or the *Ontological-Hysteric* theatres. Those cats were high and we copied them.

Through the ironic lens of hindsight, *TDR* is a symbol of the American virus shot through an Australian theatre 'renaissance'.

La Mama is another. Its founder Betty Burstall recounts:

> When I was living in NY the theatre that most interested me wasn't Broadway or even off-Broadway. It was the Greenwich Village coffee house theatre which has since come to be known as off-off-Broadway. This coffee house theatre was then putting on the work of Joe Chaikin's Open Theatre, of Claude Van Itallie, Megan Terry and Sam Shepard. It made possible a new audience–actor relationship. It was informal, direct, immediate. It was also a playwright's theatre, a place where new ideas and new ways of expression could be tried out, where you could hear what people were now thinking and feeling. Its audience was small (50 to 100), its playing area was limited, its plays were short, its actors were unpaid and admission was low (US $1). When I returned to Australia I founded La Mama with the coffee house theatres in mind. La Mama is non-commercial, admission is 50 cents which covers the cost of coffee & the rent. My policy is to present new Australian plays, sketches, inter-media experiments, improvisations, happenings. La Mama has also put on regular readings of new poetry, programmes of new music & screenings of new films
>
> (July 1969, programme note for *Dimboola* and *The English Lesson* by the La Mama Company and *Programmes A & B* by Tribe)

Thus free spirits floating round Carlton/Fitzroy via Eltham were given a focus and a meeting place, and loose associations formed. Some were making experiments towards an Australian *cinéma vérité*, scratching an itch for a local *cinéma d'art* and doco. The new wave of low budget, performance-centred films, scripted and shot on the run by the young Cassavetes, Truffaut, Godard and Polanski, sparked the ambitions of David Baker, Vince Monton, Bea Faust, John Duigan, Gary Patterson, Margo Nash, the Burstall Boys, the Cantrills, Bert Deling, Nigel Buesst. Films like Brian Davies's *The Pudding Thieves* and *Brake Fluid* were cast from the La Mama mob. By the early '70s the cineastes had a place of their own in the Film Co-op round the corner in Lygon Street.

On Melbourne Sundays through 1967–68, enthusiasts with hangovers met to improvise with each other. The late Brian Davies brought an organising capacity, theories of group psychology and a yen to be a film director. Graeme Blundell came snapping, crackling, popping with a briefcase, the only performer to carry one, packing the latest *TDR*. Bruce Knappett, Lindy Davies, David Kendall, Kerry Dwyer, Geoffrey Gardiner, Meg Clancy, Anna Carmody, Peter Cummins, Alan Finney, Kim O'Leary, Robin Laurie, Rod Moore, Peggy Cook, Bill Garner, Peter Green, Lyndell Rowe, Martin Phelan, Lindzee Smith, Jon Hawkes, Paul Bailey, Tom Burstall, Bethany Lee, Jill Klooger, and Frank Bren, to name 23, came,

Melbourne *cinéma verité* street scene outside the old shot tower, now an interior enclosed by Daimaru. Doing the Godard thing while an unknown photographer readies the lens are L–R: Martin Phelan, Brian Davies, John Duigan (playing a director), Geoffrey Gardiner, Peter Cummins. The film *Brake Fluid* went on to win the Benson & Hedges award, the most prestigious at the time, pipping Peter Weir's *Holmesdale* and leaving Sydney filmies unamused. (Lloyd Carrick)

some more often than others, with their vigorous bodies and vernacular imaginations.

Later in the day the hippy yankeephiliacs and social surrealists would group around Doug Anders as Tribe, or by night might come a posse of poets, itching to perform, egged on by the Perfect Cheese, Syd Clayton, into wonders like *Um Jum Kun Aum Jum*.

Having set up La Mama as a workshop for writers, Betty Burstall remembers professional actors being iffy about the idea of working for nothing. There were no pros among the new performer spawn, these baby-boomers with tickets on themselves. Most had never left school. Dole bludgers from uni, used to living hand to mouth but used to getting something in both. Soon they were taking over the place. It became a regular performance lab—to the chagrin of the writers. Improvisation was unconfined and would burst outdoors onto nature strips and into the parks.

They liberated an old jukebox and freespiritedly ripped out the coin mechanism. Over the summer of 1968–69, 'Come On Baby Light My Fire' got a lot of play. They played it very loud and danced with a difference. They were separate, mad molecules in a throbbing critical mass, whirling and jigging, tumultuous and uncoupled. The embrace of the dance, union symbolised or foreshadowed, was undone. Woman was no longer held by Man. Man was no longer the leader of foxtrot, tango, jitterbug and jive. Both were now at liberty to move independently. Eye contact with strangers was facilitated. Dancers tended to disappear from each other into the music, each body electric with the bass. All making up the steps, kicking out the jams, streaming, shining now rocking with Miss Molly in the House of Blue Light.

A great notion of the transforming power of play had seized the children's collective fancy and they were knocking themselves out to make it work. Improvising. For the fun and principle of the thing, they played like children at being other people, played at being each other, improvising themselves into high old states, for 24 hours or more. They were playing against the war (at home). It was tough, sometimes, loading up the station wagon and going off to be Viet Cong or *Mr Big, the Big, Big Pig* and getting ignored or kicked and spat on for their trouble, but they were never so down they couldn't still get up and dance furiously to the Jukebox of Eternal Delight.

Stompin' at La Mama during workshops in 1969. Jukebox in corner under mezzanine. (Lloyd Carrick)

In 1969, after playing in and out of La Mama, the streets, parks and universities of Melbourne, this buzzing flux was invited to the Festival of Perth. They had the chutzpah to name themselves the Australian Performing Group. They culled those inconvenienced by jobs or family and went out West to act up. They took a mixed showbag of their wares: *Who* and *White with Wire Wheels* by Jack Hibberd; *The Front Room Boys* and *Norm and Ahmed* by Alex Buzo; John Romeril's *Chicago, Chicago*. They also demonstrated, in extremes of heat, the exotic form of Street Theatre. They were rude and hairy. They outraged some of the burghers of Tom the Cheap Grocer's fine city and received mixed reviews. Local girl Katherine Brisbane gave them a rave in the *Australian*, and the infant phenomenon, through brave new writing, coarse acting, animal spirits and streetlairiness, had itself a national profile.

★ Preprambulation ★

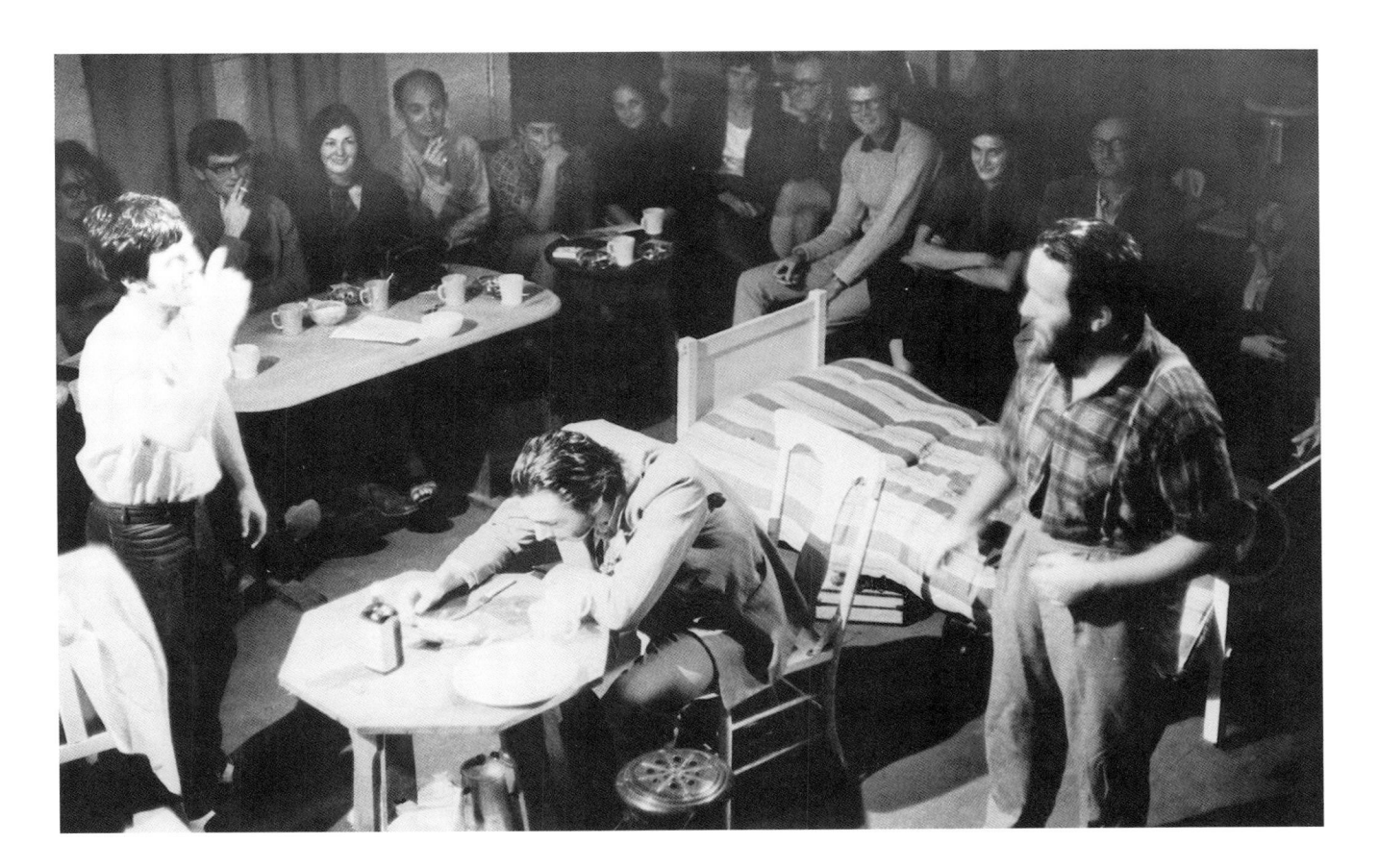

At the end of 1970 the APG went on another tour, to lotus-eating, sometime Lotus-racing Adelaide, city of churches. They went with Hibberd's anti-censorship farce *Customs and Excise*. This was a group Lost Weekend. It was a much smaller party. Kerry's V-Dub and Dr Hibberd's banger overlanded Graeme, Yvonne, Meg, Bill, Rod and the set. They crashed at Tim and Robin's at Devil's Elbow. Now the place has been bulldozed and it all seems like a dream.

I was a lecturer in Drama at Flinders University, long-haired, lordly, with an office and my name on the door. I had a fawning bank manager, super and an FJ panel van, and I was giving hedonism a run for its money. Robin Leuba was a salmon-backed madonna from Cunderdin (WA), with a French look when she wore her hair up. In those days she mostly let it hang down. 'What you will' was a good part of the law for both of us. We had met at the University of Western Australia. We had married in New York in 1967 and honeymooned in the Plaza and Chelsea Hotels because I was an instructor at Antioch College, Ohio (Elizabethan and Jacobean Drama a speciality).

Now, in the summer of 1970, I thought I was some crow-eating Hamlet summoning the players to Elsinore. In reality it was to Flinders University they came and Graeme Blundell had stitched up the deal with Wal Cherry and the Student Union. I did not yet know that this perky *wunderkind* and fixer was known as Mousie. I was unacquainted with

Anatomising mates: Jack Hibberd's *Who* at La Mama, 1969. L–R: Martin Phelan, Jon Hawkes and Lindzee Smith. In the audience, third from right is Ponch Hawkes, and second from left is the puckish playwright. (Lloyd Carrick)

Doing Amerika: John Romeril's *The Man from Chicago* at La Mama, 1970. L–R: Graeme Blundell, Margot Lindsay, Bill Garner, Bruce Spence, Rod Moore. (Lloyd Carrick)

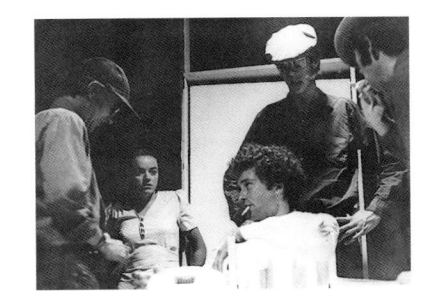

Crow-eating Hamlet with Fu Man Chu. The author at Devil's Elbow, Adelaide, with Jack Hibberd.

Jack Hibberd's classic short play *One of Nature's Gentlemen* or Graeme's definitive performance in it from which the name was nicked. I took pride in my nose for the coming thing. The nose I had followed to Romeril's *I Don't Know Who to Feel Sorry For* and *Whatever Happened to Realism?* at La Mama in 1969. The nose that flared at the legendary action of the actors busted for obscenity, accompanied to the Carlton watch-house by their audience chanting:

shitfuckcuntfartbuggeroffwillya!

I wanted a piece of that action. I had written, in collaboration with Flinders students, a splashy anti-censorship piece—*The Truth About the Protection Racket*—inspired by US Federal Theater Living Newspapers of the '30s and the contemporary Australian tabloid. Moonlighting as one of the *Toads,* a grubby, dada garage band under the spell of Frank Zappa, I had announced from a rotunda by the Torrens that I was Dr Mindfuck and these were my Follies. Resplendent in a cloak of feathers garnered from the zoo and laboriously fashioned by my wife, I had held up a plastic bag and sung:

> ***They call this stuff Mary Jane!***
> ***They say she drives men insane!***

Few in the small crowd of picnickers and passers-by paid me much attention until several uniformed police stormed the rotunda. Thus I too had been blooded in the cause. Cool it was in those days to perceive yourself part of the Free Speech Movement blowing in the wind from Berkeley California. Happy days when the burning questions were 'why don't we do it on the road?' or 'why can't I write it on my brow?' Fucking was the lingua franca of revolution, believing was seeing, we knew it all and wanted to tell it like it was.

Devil's Elbow was the last big turn on the grand corniche that switchbacked down the hills to the Adelaide plain, straight and proper. There the occasional semi, howling down in angel gear, would jackknife, and small crowds were drawn of a balmy night by the chance of a spectacular wreck. A shady track led from this venue to a weatherboard grange in a state of suspended collapse where Tim and Robin kept open house. The Kinks, Country Joe and the Fish, the Beatles, the Who, Big Brother and the Holding Company—and the Toads practising to become famous—all roared into the bush up the gully to the Eagle on the Hill. Heather, the barmaid at the Eagle, was our lodger. She claimed to have scored Keef, the Rolling Stone, on the Adelaide leg of the *Git Your Yayas Out* tour. There was a whiff of orgy about the joint. I liked to think of it as a regular Abbaye de Theleme, Crazy Castle and Big Pink all rock 'n' rolled into one. Hermann Hesse, Terry Southern, Bucky Fuller lay about with the Tibetan Book of the Dead and *The Whole Earth Catalog*, curling in the sun. The high jinks of Dr Timothy Leary, Aquarian role model, were held in high esteem, likewise Ken Kesey and the Pranksters. Augustus Owsley Stanley III, the populist synthesiser of LSD, was a hero. We aped their derrings-do. Arty Rimbaud was another icon for the Toads, who were in fact devising, with all their senses systematically deranged, a rock opera about his death and transfiguration; working title: *African Queen*.

We went tripping with the surrealists and Hieronymus Bosch, we were into the Tibetan Bardos and the paradoxical geometries of M. C. Escher. Psychedelia came in through the bathroom window along with the comics of R. Crumb, the cracked epiphanies of Marshall McLuhan and the electric entelechy of rock 'n' roll. We dug 'levels' and grooved on 'connections' and the word was 'Wow!' We 'grocked' on the star baby sequence in *2001*. While some of us were dropping LSD, Watson and Crick were discovering DNA and we felt we were discovering it right along with them. We were all over the no end of free rides in the Coney Island of the Mind. The Toads dug Bucky Fuller the most—'No legislation ever designed the potato!' If the human population joined hands it was only '9 chains to the moon!' Wow!

Notwithstanding sham enlightenment and brain damage, experiments with drugs remained a potent analogue for the sort of transport the performance arts could provide. The hubristic desire to reach the heights and depths of consciousness had its theatrical correlative in our desire to go beyond the conventions, to break taboos, to experience performance more vividly and viscerally, to amaze and astonish. The Trip became another Double of the Theatre, in the way the Plague was construed by Artaud. (Ah Toad, as we Toads pronounced him.) We were more than ready to enter the Magic Theatre of *Steppenwolf* to which 'the price of admission is your mind'. Goodbye to the superficiality of naturalism and the excessive rationality of the older Brecht. Hello again to an idea of theatre as that disorderly place of jeopardy and contagion the powers that be want to ban.

The players from Melbourne were pleased to be out of it. They unbuttoned, disrobed, fell about and forgot themselves: against the illustrated fridge; on the seagrass matting, surprised by Clipper the horse whinnying through the window; Chagall-like on the tar paper of the kitchen roof; with the magpies gargling at sparrow fart—characters in a bleached-out *fête champêtre*.

Scuse me while I kiss the sky!

Bill Garner, the headmaster's son, latterly a philosophy tutor and political trickster at Monash, living in an ambulance, and now, after Caravaggio, a curly faun on his haunches playing recorder in a purple haze of Salvation Jane.

Flame-haired, joshing, adversarial Meg Clancy, the Carlton publican's daughter, who had stunned the Flinders Drama faculty with a pre-emptive *décolletage* when she came to stand over us for the cheque, burning up in the Mediterranean climate. Old Bill the Slaught, the legendary drunken cocksman of Carlton, used to woo her as a 16-year-old schoolgirl, took her by tram to the Opera and to Vera's Slygrog after. Love in vain. Die-hard romantic, Meg took ship soon after her Adelaide jaunt with a loony anarchist lover for Catalonia.

Graeme Blundell, the undertaker's son, nuggety-muscly, motor-mouthed rover of the pack, buttering me up with a proposal of doing a living newspaper with the APG, juggling ideas like fiery clubs, dropping them now and again to break into the wheedling whine of Mousey.

Yvonne Marini, the butcher's daughter from Corinth whose dad spitted a lamb when Graeme married Kerry: tiny, tough and transcendental, tuning to the cosmic giggle, her violet aura shining, her long brown hair cloaking her with pre-raphaelite divinity to the knees. A ring-in to the original cast, she is remembering the lines she forgot in performance. Martin Armiger, Orpheus of the Toads, serenades her on a

APG in Arcadia. L–R: Bill Garner, Meg Clancy, Robin Leuba, Yvonne Marini, Graeme Blundell at Devil's Elbow, 1970.

golden Gibson guitar sought by repo men from a Hindley Street music shop.

Rod Moore, the randy pliant treasurer of the group, survivor of two '69 *Dimboolas* (the Melburnian Reception Rooms and La Mama) and one busted *Norm and Ahmed*. He wears long bodgie sideboards, lean as Landy, prickling with corny gags, thinking about putting the hard word on his hostess.

Jack Hibberd, the plumber's son, is there splenetic and snorting ferociously, smacking his lips over wine and words, a dandy larrikin, plucking at himself, at his shiny blackframed goggles, at the Fu Man Chewed moustache, at his crotch, sublimating his lusts into a vernacular translation of Baudelaire, bad-mouthing all others. He is watched by the smiling eyes of Jocelyn, his wife the biochemist, tacit, wry and wondering.

Wal Cherry was not there. Due to intemperate hospitality the performance of *Customs and Excise* at Flinders had been lacklustre. There was a certain unco hysteria. The laughter was punctuated, indeed led by the howler-monkey cachinnations of the playwright. The students had grown restless. Garner invited the audience to a turn at the Devil's Elbow. Wal, crafty old Brechtian hepcat in the black turtleneck sweater, evaded the visitors behind his famous foxy smile. Never the epicurean, he had a meeting to get to and he was leery of a group that discountenanced directors, a group that had declared for the autonomy of the performer. Wal came from the brave little art theatre tradition, American or European, director/guru led, cool and analytical, devoted to excellence, hierarchical and authoritarian.

For the APG, a director might stimulate, the writer might feed lines, but it was the performer, the worker, who was in control. The matrix of the theatre was the group of players who got the words and steps down, who with their voice and presence embodied the text (if there was one), who communicated the action to the audience.

Sporting a phallus, tottering on cothurni—doing Lear after a week's rehearsal from one prompt copy while putting up with Henchard the pennypinching manager—on tour with Molière or the Duke of Saxe-Meiningen's troupe—pretending to understand Stanislavsky—contradicting Brecht—racing each other off, getting it on, down through the centuries, players are primary. Foul-mouthed, disrespectful of any cultural authority but their own, the APG were messy and passionate and making it up as they went along. Their *modus operandi* was repugnant to Wal, with his professional values and cachet accumulated during the heroic struggle against creditors and indifference with George Whaley and the other actors in an isolated Robin-Boyd-converted church in Dorcas Street, Emerald Hill.

At Flinders, the Cherry system of realising dramatic performance, based on the sound historical principle of a Contract between performer and audience to provide a Significant Action, had become codified into an orthodoxy with a jargon. I had grown weary of marking beats and adjustments in tutorial papers on a given scene in Adamov's *Paolo Paoli*. I had begun assessing them according to Zen principles, floating them down the stairwell of the Humanities Wing. There were other signs and portents. A student had fallen asleep on stage during a Drama Department production of Brecht's *Galileo*. Wal had banned a slide of da Vinci's anatomical section of coitus in the living newspaper on censorship. A professor of Spanish had armed himself. The conflict was generational and Freudian. I needed a father figure to reject and Wal got the part. No more puritanism, no more *politique de papa*. It was time to drop out and do something. Having the APG about the house in the hills felt agreeably as if I was harbouring the guerrillas. Joining the APG would be a liberating rite of passage. The *I Ching*, when consulted, was thought to give its gnomic assent. I handed my resignation to Wal and he with a fatherly concern suggested psychiatric counselling. 'It's not the right move for you,' he said. I p'shaw'd. Now I pause and wonder.

The Toads set up the orgone boxes to lead the party into a crepuscular attempt to erogenise the gully. Barry Ball, their asynchronous drummer, passed round the Aztec biscuits out of the *Green and Gold Cookbook* with additional jimson weed and cantharides. The Jolly Girls, stout and froward backup singers, argued the toss of Christianity originating as a mushroom cult back and forth. Buzz the bass player quizzed a mighty red gum, one of 15 appearing to him in the likeness of Tlacol, the South American toad god, about the possibility of them joining the band. Hibberd and I were at a Baudelairean stand-off. His translation lacked music and I massacred the original with a vile accent to prove the point.

C'est l'Ennui—l'oeil chargé d'un pleur involontaire,
Il rêve d'échafauds en fumant son houka.
Tu le connais, lecteur, ce monstre délicat,
Hypocrite lecteur—mon semblable—mon frère!

(That's Boredom, eyes brimming with tears he can't keep in,
Dreaming of scaffolds as he smokes his hookah.
You know him reader, that delicate monster,
Hypocrite reader—so like me—my twin.)

The band drowned the recitation in a plasmic din, the lyrics might have been in Sanskrit:

Skin, skin, skin, skin
How do you fix to keep it all in?

Round midnight, sonar or chemical attraction drew some freaks over from the Red Angel Panic house in Beaumont. They helped themselves and denounced our guests as bourgeois imposters, johnny-come-latelies. Authentic radical alternative theatre in Melbourne began with the people who came to stay at their place, they said. That germinal cell, that full forward pocket of expanded consciousness was Tribe—thus was I advised by the dehydrated croak of a raven-haired warlock in crushed burgundy velvet—and I had better not forget it.

2 The High Old Times of Tribe

TRIBE HAD MANY MANSIONS. One had been a haven for visiting Sydney bohemians in the '30s and cracks a mention in Slessor's *Five Bells*:

> *In Melbourne . . .*
> *The sodden ecstasies of rectitude . . .*
> *At Labassa. Room 6 x 8*
> *On top of the tower; because of this, very dark*
> *And cold in winter.*

Times had changed since Joe, the Austral Lycidas, fell off the Manly ferry, greatcoat ballasted with bottles, descended to the bottom of the harbour and rose again as poetry. Rectitude was out, ecstasies were no longer sodden when Doug Anders(on) arrived from Brisbane in 1968. Doug was the very (for alphabetical reasons) first graduate of NIDA. His lifestyle was hallucinotropic yet ascetic; he had a gentle almost asexual air about him but with an attractive energy. He was lean and tan with flowing dark hair and deep dark brown eyes. That he and Tribe had Van Itallie's US-busted play *Motel* up and running added notoriety to charisma and advanced him toward guruhood. The organisers of the 1968 Monash Drama Festival—Jon Hawkes, Richard Murphett and Jane Clifton among them—booked *Motel*.

In 1969 Doug came back south to conduct classes in an old church in Mill Street, South Melbourne, and at RMIT. They were about Movement and Communication, redolent of Isadora Duncan, eurhythmics, yoga and the body electric. They were right behind the lyric from *Tommy* by the Who:

> *See me,*
> *feel me,*
> *touch me,*
> *heal me.*

A different drummer in Carlton Gardens. Vietnam Moratorium, 1970. (Graeme Blundell)

There were exercises, status games and whathaveyou from the *Tulane Drama Review*. The influence of the guru's guru, Margaret Barr, permeated the choreography of a version of *Carmina Burana*. She believed that in order to liberate the spirit of the dance a body best be naked. Which was fine with the young aspirants, rather more young women than young men. Intoning soft hypnotic litanies, Doug taught them how to relax, to allow gravity to drain the weight and tension from their prone bodies. Mellifluously he would suggest that they feel honey flowing over their face. They were drained and they flowed.

In February 1969 the classes joined up to perform *Saturday* at La Mama based on a script by Barry McKimm. It was an Artaudian approach to the Melbourne *Truth*. The RMIT class, including Carol Porter, Alison Ware and Lutz Presser, were the 'A' team and got to play people. The Mill Street mob—Fay Mokotow, Jan Bucknall, Mandy Pearce, Jane Clifton and Jude Kuring among them—wrote the script on blackboards up the back and played telephone boxes, police cars etc. as required. Bruce Spence, who was doing lights, played a cop, his debut on the Australian stage. Alan Robertson, whose Norton had been observed in pieces on a kitchen table, was brought in as a bikie. The climax was set in

The burnt-out corner of Faraday and Drummond streets, with Door of Perception bricked in. (John Gollings)

a Den of Vice at a Swiss Ski Lodge. Spence switched on the strobe, the Doors were turned up loud and everybody took their clothes off:

'5, 2, 1, baby, 1 in 5.'

Wild stuff, bristling with politico-sexual correctitude. Reclaiming the body in all its hairiness, letting it all hang out, saying Yes to the Eros their elders had denied, were high on Tribe's agenda. The public exposure of pudenda was undertaken as a political act and a confronting confession: 'OK, I've got 'em and I feel good about 'em and if I offend you I feel even better, 'cos that proves how uptight and fucked-up you are.' Baring all did much to bond the group, but some members did feel better about it than others. Some are born gropers. Some are hung up on the outer, armoured and un-Reichian, unable to go with the flow.

People were into explaining their bodies to themselves in unorthodox, esoteric ways. Along with the musclebuilding went a preoccupation with Eastern physiology. The *jaghana* was discovered where only a belly was known before. The subtle body was meditated upon. The image of Kundalini snaking through the chakras up from the cauldron of sexual energy located in the sacral/lumbar region exercised a fascination greater than Mao's Little Red Book. Not that anybody knew it at the time, the Chairman himself kept fit in congress with peasant girls. Sex and health were issues in the inner-city counterculture of Melbourne, for seekers given to overdoing it and wanting more. The consumption of muesli, if home made, was a virtue, a personal liberation from the imperialist supermarket. Macrobiotics was big but hard to live up to. After a night spent in tantric embrace, lysergically enhanced, figuring cosmic oneness, there were many who got stuck into the Kelloggs, white sugar and icy cold milk like there was no tomorrow. Or else apple juice with powdered yeast that went down like liquid struedel and was sworn by as one of many high vitamin-B lines of defence against the dreaded herpes when it arrived on the scene.

Tribe celebrated Love's Body by living together in cycles of carnival and collapse. They did not want to be actors, they wanted to live and learn, to experience, in the Jimi Hendrix sense of the word, to be in it all. They liked to get up and go. Gathering fresh cohorts from the *Motel* season at Monash, they took off to do the show in Adelaide. Twenty-five of them crashed at the rambling house and garden in Beaumont where Rob Tillet and the Red Angel Panic squatted. Networks of such hospitable 'head' houses stretched across the continent, caravanserai for the nomadic freak.

Having zapped Adelaide, Tribe regrouped at the old mansion in Toorak. It was shared by Anders, Joe Bolza, an intense and wiry mime recently repatriated via Amsterdam, and the members of their classes. They worked out physically and sensually, then worked up a scenario for the next performance/event/happening at La Mama or wherever. This could go on all night and into the next day. They would feed their heads, make mythopoeic connections and elaborate metaphors physically, groping towards their own thing. Which in some ways was but a homegrown version of Beck and Malina's living theater. Tribe was a spawn of both the radical Jewish consciousness of New York lofts and the performance communards on the West Coast.

In July 1969 they appeared at La Mama on the same bill as some people on the brink of declaring themselves the Australian Performing Group. A production of Barry Oakley's *The English Lesson* was sandwiched between Tribe's *Programmes 'A' & 'B'*. Tribe was right into sidestepping the tyranny of definition.

All around them a backyard renaissance in popular music was going down. Boppy little combos were peeping out of squalid band houses across the inner city. Insalubrious properties in Carlton, Brunswick and Fitzroy were fertile breeding grounds for groups like Daddy Cool, Co. Caine, McKenzie Theory, Spectrum ... Impressed by the success of rock impresario Bill Graham and his Filmores East and West in the US, local hip capitalists opened venues smaller in scale, similar in style and spirit. They were marijuana speakeasies with funky music for large young audiences into rock 'n' roll and roleplay. At John Pinder's T. F. Much and Much More Ballrooms of a Saturday night, high as Hopis after a convivial body painting session, Tribe would happen on in to 'interact' with the audience and put on a spot of freaky cabaret between the band sets.

Tribe celebrated Love's Body.
(Barry Dickins)

Tribe on the basketball court. L–R top: Di Fuller, Bob Daly. Second: Jan Cornall, Fay Mokotow, unknown, Alison Ware. Third: Jenny Jones, Jan Bucknall, Frank Starrs. Front: Mandy Pearce, Nick, Barb Bacon, Doug Anders (obscured head).

The Regent Ballroom, an incinerated cinema in South Yarra that had introduced the films of Fellini, Antonioni and the New Wave to Melbourne, was regenerated with venture capital from one Joe Monterosa (late of the Filmore Far East, supplier of rock 'n' roll to the Vietnam R and R trade). Fledgling filmmakers and sceneshakers Bert Deling, Helen Hooper and friends ran the place and booked the acts. Tribe had been kept on a retainer for the shooting of *Dalmas*, a shoestring *cinéma vérité* feature that Deling and Co. produced on the local drug scene. Tribe became the resident pranksters at the Regent for $200 per week, shared by a shifting membership of 15 to 20 people, artfully administrated by Alan Robertson. They would keep the crowd amused by playing in it and with it, rather than for it, inventing an instant dance craze like the Crabs, say. Macro structures were made out of willing bodies: *The Bridge Over the River Why*; the launching of the war canoes from *Coral Island*. Anything went.

The bands were as tight, as heavy, as trippy as their American models. They shared a desire to exceed the norm, to give more, to experiment. They wanted theatrics on top of the music. *Spectrum* for example, periodically bolted out of Gudinski's mushrooming muso stable for an arty muck-up with Tribe as the *Indelible Murtceps*. *Lipp Arthur*—later *Lipp and the Double Decker Brothers*, featuring the fabulous Lippettes—was another such music/theatre mix. Joe Camillieri, Ian 'Pudding' Wallace, Dave Flett, Fred Cass, Bruce Woodcock and Avril Bell were theatrically abetted by Jane Clifton, Barb Bacon, Bob Daly and Carol Porter (appearing as the Fantastic Tapdancing Crystal). They would dream up routines and scenarios to link original numbers such as *I'm Making a Sandwich for Jesus* or *Clouds Are a Funny Thing*. A goodly mix of loonytooning and a growing musical sophistication characterised the scene. Hugh

McSpeddon of the Leaping McSpeddons playing violin on top of a stepladder; Eric Gradman of the Sharks putting violin and saxophone together in a way that would have warmed the cockles of Captain Beefheart, had he been there. There was an everpresent urge to send up opera, after the manner of Frank Zappa and the Mothers of Invention, as strong as the urge to appear mother and buck naked. A tradition developed of writing it up in the kitchen tonight, to get it on at the gig tomorrow. *Godburst,* a rebuttal to the saccharinanity of *Godspell,* was one such thing of beauty and a joy for one night only. Cliffo ripped off a loose libretto from the Book of Job and the band worked it up. Job was played by guitarist Peter Starkie. 'Pudding', on sax, was God. A power strike assured that it was effectively candlelit. There was irony in that the butt of the jest had kicked off, off-off-Broadway, at Cafe La Mama, New York. Tribe's recycled Americana always had a larrikin spin on it.

Merely to laugh and let the good times roll was not enough. When Tribe put on *The Plague,* for instance, they took Joe Chaikin's injunction that the theatre should place the spectators before the idea of their mortality very seriously. They died horribly and variously in and on the audience for one and a half hours. The influence of the Open Theatre, the living theater and LSD sometimes closed down comic options. Outside cabaret/panto mode, their way was a total commitment to, and focus on, the heavy trip in their collective head. Tribe didn't go home

The inaugural gig at the T. F. Much Ballroom. The band: Fred Cass, Jo Camilleri, David Flett, Peter Starkie, Ian Wallace, Bruce Woodcock, Jeremy Noone with Doug Anders conducting. The fabulous Lippettes: Carol Porter, Barb Bacon, Avril Bell, Jane Clifton.

Our Dick (Bob Daly). Tribe in performance at La Mama, 1972. Under lampshade, Jane Bucknall; behind hat, Alan Robertson; in flippered extremis, Carol Porter.

The Ride across Lake Constance (Peter Handke). Euro-cool in the Back Theatre, 1973. L–R: Carol Porter, Jan Cornall, Red Symons, Janet Heywood.

after rehearsal, they would rather roll another joint and question the validity of it all. Then they might decide to drive to Lake Tyers to continue to combust the project with people on the Aboriginal reserve there, seeking wisdom.

The old Socratic bromide caught fire in the '60s. Heraclitean. Wham Bam. Seekers took off after it like Titan rockets, like disciples of Don Juan, the South American shaman invented by Carlos Castenada. Seekers after Knowledge that was dangerous, forbidden, attractive. Here was a grand role to play—someone on the Way, an Adept in an esoteric circle, a member of the Fellowship of an antipodean Castalia on a Journey to the East. Or North. Further. A bond existed between mental travellers who shared ineffable, restorative insights. The siren rubato of Grace Slick out front of the Jefferson Airplane laid it down in *White Rabbit:*

Go ask Alice,
When she 10 feet tall,
What the Dormouse said:
Feed your head.

Saying nay to Grace made you a Straight. Partaking of the lysergic host made you a Head, a Freak, one of a worldwide communion, scrambling down the rabbit hole, off on a psychedelic Children's Crusade, believing that uncles Hermann, Lao Tse, Pythagoras, Don Quixote, Baudelaire et al. (Ginsberg and Watts) were off with us.

The Way was littered with Acid Casualties on the Bummer of the lost soul. The quest for knowledge was a Faustian thing. To bend Marlowe, an Elizabethan head who would try anything:

Here fry my brains to get a deity!

By the end of 1972, after memorable fun with *Our Dick* by Bob Daly and *Punch and Judy* by Dame Sybil Thorndike, Tribe as an organism began to succumb to the law of entropy. Doug Anders went back up North to live in the country and become Doug Anderson again. (In the '80s he revived the APG group-created *Hills Family Show*.) Tribe's swansong was Handke's inscrutable *A Ride Across Lake Constance* in July '73. It was their debut at the Pram Factory, the second cab off the rank in the Back Theatre, it was scatted recliningly as jazz, very cool and internationalist, a stark contrast to *Dimboola* that the APG had put on in the Front Theatre a month before.

After dispersal, Tribe's DNA passed on into the ferment of shared living and working in the Tower of the Pram Factory, into the development of the Women's Theatre Group in 1974, into *The Great Stumble Forward* of 1975. After the fusion that became Circus Oz, it persisted even unto the next generation. A strong family resemblance is there for elders to remark in Desoxy, an avant-garde ensemble that devotes itself to bizarre and difficult pleasures.

⭐ 3 On Drummond Street

PART OF A GRID of working-class streets with ruling-class names—Lygon, Elgin, Rathdowne, Canning, Palmerston—Drummond Street, Carlton is broad and straight on Haussmann lines, fit for cavalcade and cannonade and green down the middle. *Mon Sejour* is a two-storied turn-of-the-century terrace, the facade lemon curd, the shutters and cast iron smudged white. Down a hallway hung with the framed posters for *Klag* and *Brainrot,* passing the photos of *Calm Down Mother* and *Marvellous Melbourne,* I enter the kitchen where Kerry Dwyer is feeding Nelly. Like the Victory of Samothrace she is but with an Irish head and her wings in the wardrobe somewhere upstairs. The Maud Gonne of the group, strong jaw, sharp chin, turned-up nose, flashing eyes with no-nonsense brows fringed with a helmet of (at the moment) short brown hair, she sits easy,

Carlton, summer 1972. (Laurel Frank)

her victorious breasts, one suck-shiny with a milk-blue vein like an asp, transfixing me. Graeme Blundell is on the phone and at the stove, cooking up spaghetti *aglio e olio,* the unpronounceable cheap filler of a house busy with an endless procession of drop-ins, petitioners, travellers, collaborators, visionaries and drunks. She rounds on him for insensitivity and neglect. He niggles at her high estimation of the soon to be staged *Joss Adams Show,* whose author has just left, when Romeril turns up off the plane from Turkey via the Khyber Pass with a block of incredible hash in his kick. Synchronicitously Colin Talbot arrives, paranoid about John Pinder, who has given the direction of his between-bands sketch for the next Much More Ballroom, *Love in an FJ Holden,* to this drop-out lecturer from Adelaide presently perving on the marmoreal breasts of Mama Kez, who placates Colin by introducing him to Peter Weir, down from Sydney directing *Drip Dry Dreams* with Graham Bond and casting a saturnine eye over the Melbourne rock 'n' roll cabaret scene.

'Bloody arrivistes', grumbles Colin. 'Kin sexist pigs', burps Jude Kuring, breaking into the kitchen with a life-sized puppet of a mother superior to embrace mother and child in a noisy foursome.

Ambition is the engine of the theatre. Graeme Blundell had it in the horsepower one needs to rise like the Bunyip out of Reservoir, found a theatre group and become its director. He dared to entertain this heretical fantasy of unilateral control when all about him were absorbed by the righteous glamour of the Group. Nimble as a dancer, shrewd-eyed and cheery, leatherjacketted against the backbiting that was to pursue him down the decade, Blundell was as fly as Philby. Any theatrical renaissance about to happen was going to have his name on it.

Kerry Dwyer felt the same way. She had gone about as far as you can go in student drama—all the way to the International Festival at Nancy. She had already tried to rally a group together (as John and Lois Ellis had tried, and briefly succeeded, with the Melbourne Youth Theatre). She vibrated to the notion of directing, of taking charge of action and agenda, and she recognised a coming man when she saw one.

After a certain lingering kiss at a La Mama New Year party in '69, Blundell and Dwyer vibrated together. A partnership was formed and sealed by the birth of Nelly. It was a ringleading one in the formation of the group. Their house was the group organising centre, their car the group car, their phone the group phone. Of course the partnership was doomed, like most within the APG ambit. Graeme and Kerry fell into a burning ring of fire, the one reserved for lovers who are rivals. In the union of Leo and Pisces, as Kerry often remarked, everyone knows the sun shines out of Leo's arse.

Jobseekers (i): Graeme Blundell as Crawfords punk. (Lloyd Carrick)

Jobseekers (ii): Kerry Dwyer inclining towards stardom en mini-jupe. (Lloyd Carrick)

Graeme had had a bite of the Big Apple. A scholarship had got him there in '71, and he had seen and met with the work and the people the rest of us could only read about. He kept a notebook of random running ideas for his report to the Arts Council that was the price of the trip. In New York he'd seen the fecundity of performance teeming in non-theatre buildings like the Space, a concept as much as a building, reserved for innovation, five stories of it, dominated by Joe Chaikin's Open Theater with a live-in, all-in lifestyle approach. He'd admired the business savvy of Joe Papp giving a new, young audience new plays, 'hate whitey' plays and Shakespeare at under $2 a shot at the Public Theater. He saw the gap between rhetoric and reality, the self-destructive, over-introspective urges, the fakes and the fact that the political/cultural momentum of '60s protest had died. He found a mentor in Rennie Davis of the San Francisco Mime Troupe.

The phone rang one day when Blundell and Lindzee Smith were about to go down to Alabama Street and pay Rennie a visit. It was Rennie on a wrong number. Sixties serendippy! They interviewed each other extensively. Blundell got a perspective and a critique of the American scene, as Davis pissed on the living theater—'guilt-ridden hysterics with a contempt for art'—and put down Chaikin, Schechner and Co. as well-intentioned moralists who wanted to salvage their souls in public. According to Davis, survival and success lay in getting out like Valdez and the Theatro Campesino, Schumann and the Bread and Puppet Theatre. 'A tight, absent-minded, somewhat shrivelled up little man with the mafia moustache, sharp square clothes and perpetual cigar', according to Blundell, Davis even had a critique of the inchoate APG: 'Yours is a theatre that exposes the hollowness of myths and attitudes without replacing them with any viable political alternative.'

After this encounter, Blundell drew up a very positive list of proposals in his notebook, among which:

> The importance of more discussion in A.P.G., not only political but also theatrical.
>
> Regular workshops in skills e.g. Circus. Forget the 'researching ourselves' nonsense, get down to practical alternatives.
>
> A much tougher approach to all people working with APG—intolerance of mediocrity and self indulgence. Demand ALL work as hard as the FEW— particularly if all are paid.
>
> Importance of MUSIC, SINGING/RHYTHM work.
>
> Literary advisors—people who remain objective in crises—McCaughey, Marg. Williams, Who else?
>
> Interaction with other groups—NEWSLETTER!!! Regular correspondence with overseas groups.

> Maybe set APG up like InterAction (UK)—separate but mutually interdependent groups working various areas—Political theatre—New plays/Writers theatre—Experimental—etc
>
> Importance of establishing certain areas that become permanent: workshop, costume, eating, office etc
>
> Institute various objectives in relation to women's movement!!! Talk to Kerry about this.

Kerry had the carriage, the straight back, the precise and supple body language of the yoga adept and *corps de ballet*. She could assume the asana of the Lotus and probably had been able to do so since she was a foetus. Her cartwheel was slomo and symmetrical. She was one of the elect, none of them male except Bob Thorneycroft, who could do the splits. An aura of the Lecoq mime workshop was about her even when she was throwing vegetables in a Carlton kitchen. Full on, she came out to avenge the Female Eunuch upon the Brotherhood of the One-Eyed Trouser Snake, pissing in each other's pockets, writing all the best parts and keeping all the power for themselves. Much before Buzo's *Coralie Lansdowne*, Kerry said no. No more playing beddable sheilas in minijupes with rising intonations, as per *White with Wire Wheels*. In *Marvellous Melbourne* she would not be party to the demeaning sexism of a bordello scene and told them where to put their feather boas and proffered breasts.

When the women drew apart the better to jump into a group of their own, the uniform they adopted was singlets and baggy shorts, army disposal adapted to sexual trench warfare, tie-died androgyny, workshop chic, or anti-chic, emphasising the physical strength and yin sensuality of bodies free to work.

Kerry had nailed Graeme but not his share of the action. Outside the APG circle, he was about town, networking away, getting the breaks. She was more often stuck at home. She deplored the machismo and pretensions of beastly Tim Burstall, the self-confessed Lawrentian, power playboy of the filmworld, husband of Saint Betty. Knocking around with Burstall, Al Finney and the boys in the film scene helped to put Blundell beyond the APG pale. Graeme shot *Alvin Purple* and wore him like an albatross for the rest of his Melbourne life. Kerry lacked Graeme's glib tongue but shared his happy magpie knack of picking up diverse talents and inviting them into the group. Their powerful pillowtalk, and Graeme's natural bent to do things off his own bat, bugged the bright, ambitious peers they gathered in.

Into their ménage stepped the gun from Adelaide, the head from the hills, in a cloud of patchouli from the Saturday morning fleamarket under the Front Theatre. It was difficult to concentrate on the blurred closetyped roneo of *Bastardy* by John Romeril. There was always someone round, always something up. There were all Graeme's books to read:

'The Fred Astaire and Ginger Rogers of Napier Street, Fitzroy.' Jude Kuring and Peter Cummins in *Bastardy* (John Romeril), Back Theatre, 1972. (Ian McKenzie)

books on groups and gurus and actors and spies, of science fiction and private eyes. There was the latest *Tulane Drama Review* to be browsed in the dunny, a deal of zombie grass to be sought in Box Hill and the night to be spent blasting off a slowmotion riposte to Len Radic's fatuous review of the Performance Syndicate's spellbinding production of *The Tempest*.

Bastardy, Romeril's squint at the local lower depths, is about the cycle of dispossession. A young black man (played by the legendary Jack Charles) comes to claim his mother, the old white whore, played with tatty majesty by Jude Kuring, a character workshopped at the old Champion Hotel. She comes home with a nasty john (Tim Robertson) and her son is murdered by her abject, methylated factotum (Peter Cummins). The play is set in a converted stables. The Paramount Pram Factory was originally built to house Freeman's Livery Stables, Est. 1912.

Dot Thompson, one of the comrades of the New Theatre who struggled with Brecht and socialist realism in makeshift circumstances, was the first to suss out the old Pram Factory on Drummond Street. It was a moribund storage place, housing a voluminous collection of props and scenery for the Melbourne Theatre Company. Blundell, employed by its director John Sumner at the time, came right in behind her. The trustee/lessor would have no truck with bohemian riff-raff so he talked the place up to John Timlin, Jack Hibberd and David Kendall at the Mayfair Hotel. Before long Timlin had renegotiated the lease for three years in favour of himself, Mr Respectable. The future administrator of the APG threw in with the others for the rent, $100 p.w.

The former pram factory at 323/325 Drummond Street, 'the cradle of dingo theatre', as it was in 1970. (Lloyd Carrick)

Thus was the southern, upstairs, half of the Paramount Pram Factory building liberated, as buildings were being liberated all over inner-city Melbourne. Especially in Carlton and Fitzroy, wild-eyed visionaries sought out shot towers, gasworks, shopfronts, pump stations, Lodges of the Ancient Order of Foresters, and saw the future. Everywhere the quest was on for the magic sweatshop, the unconsidered or derelict ground for transformation into groovy studio space. Like they did in New York, like Betty Burstall had parlayed Delmonaco's underwear factory into La Mama. The radicals of the *lumpenbourgeoisie* were burrowing into the ruins of capitalism to find *lebensraum* for cabaret. Crumbling mansions became grotty salons of creativity, delirium and dissent. Many denizens were ex-university back from abroad, malcontent and utopian, randy and into the whole cosmic cumquat.

Just such a group of young, hairy sexual and social activists spent Melbourne Cup Day 1970 in the back of the Paramount Pram Factory, reclaiming the Receival and Despatch Room. David Kendall had his money on Baghdad Note and the tranny was up loud, to which only a few objected. They were slapping white paint over the grime and rust of the elevator machinery that bulked in the ceiling. It all went a greyer shade of pale and was called the Back Theatre with no side bunged on. The Front Theatre was already de-mezzanined, scraped and sanded.

In 1970, performers take possession of the space (east end) of what will be the Front Theatre by improvising with Kim Novak. L–R: Max Gillies, Meg Clancy (back), Bill Garner, Evelyn Krape, Wilfred Last, Claire Dobbin. (Lloyd Carrick)

Graeme Leith, who would become the maker of that noblest of rots, Passing Clouds, had begun rewiring the place. Ian McKenzie, photographer and electronics head, improvised a rude dimmer board. Roof vents and access and plumbing were attended to, seats constructed. Timlin's weighbridge factory in North Melbourne became a school for welders, its billiard table a hotbed of theatre politics. With James McCaughey, the group got behind establishing the Community Arts Foundation to lend support to various cultural activists, themselves included. They organised fundraisers. They applied to the Drama Board of the Australia Council for a grant to run the workshop to create the first show at the Pram. They were in.

Since 1912, a little horse's head, a dawn Eohippus, had overlooked the growth of the traffic and the plane trees on the nature strip opposite 323–325 Drummond Street. Ears pricked up and mouth agape, collared by an upside-down horse shoe, a plaster morsel for the stone gryphons that reared above the Bardas building (one door up past the cyclone fence of Martin's Hire yard). It is now a trophy of the business interests which destroyed the premises to which it was attached. These were sturdily constructed of brick and bluestone with the entrance and exit of wheels and hooves in mind. Cobblestones led into Austral Auto Repairs P/L, whose name in red remained the dominant signifier of the place

The west end of the partly reclaimed storage space beyond which lies the squalid decrepitude of what will be the Back Theatre. Bill Garner (left) is setting up an exercise for his sceptical peers. L–R: Wilfred Last, Evelyn Krape, Claire Dobbin, Rod Moore (obscured), Max Gillies, Tony Taylor, Graeme Blundell. (Lloyd Carrick)

until the writing on the wall was demolition. Only towards the end did the name PRAM FACTORY appear in squat black capitals, the loops of the P and the R soon crossed to approximate the symbol for radio activity. PARAMOUNT PRAMS Wholesale/Retail was proclaimed from the flaking leeside of the tower. It was this old pile, held in common by the Australian Performing Group, which held it together. The building gave the group an identity in a squabble of individuals and factions.

Wooden stairs at either end of the building gave two-legged access to the upper levels. One from a bike-entangled portico went up to the Tower, and the other past a gimcrack box office to the Front Theatre. Double doors halfway down the building led up worn, wine-dark concrete steps to the same. Up these were hefted the dirty great seating modules from the basement to be bumped out down again. Up them plodded the actors loaded from lunch at Stewarts. Down them rolled or fell audiences disoriented by a novel relationship with the performers and a BYO licence during the bacchanalia of *Dimboola* and *Dudders*. Up them echoed the expletives of the ejected. Down fled audience members from a mystifying production of *My Foot My Tutor* by the fashionable Peter Handke, to be frustrated again by the door bolted against them. The acoustics on the claret-coloured steps were significantly clearer than in the Front Theatre.

Basement Niebelungen (i). Production manager Arthur Hines pops into the office. (Bill Garner)

Basement Niebelungen (ii). His successor, John Koenig, considers the Hamlet options. (Ponch Hawkes)

The Front Theatre (legal capacity 150; tickets $2.00, $1.50 concession) had the proportions of a shoebox with a dutch barn roof lined with varnished baltic pine, stressed with verdigreasy iron. Windows overlooked Drummond Street, and down the far end was all that remained of a demolished mezzanine that often became part of the constantly transforming performance space. A passage through to the Back Theatre had a dressing room/light storage on the right, about the size of a Murray riverboat cabin, and a hellish septic galley on the left abutted the controversial toilets. No amount of gloss paint could ever hide the truth once uttered by the amiable and supportive Mr Podlena from the Health Department: 'This place should be shut down. You'd need millions to bring it up to regs'. Like every alternative theatrical venue in the world, the Pram had an Achilles cloaca.

The Back Theatre was a bleak concrete chamber with high frosted windows, an atmosphere of rising damp and dust and room for about 75 persons. After the Flea Market was given the flick, the space below stairs that was not devoted to panelbeating was a workshop/paintshop/store/rehearsal/performance space. Down there was a hearth around whose fire gathered a fellowship of workers, idlers and handypersons whose task it was to realise the shifting concepts dreamt up by artistes in the spaces above. Chief among these heavy-smoking *niebelungen* were Arthur Hines, his much self-smitten pate hung with a hank of blond hair, a cross between Prince Valiant and Gyro Gearloose. After him there came the taciturn John Koenig, overalled and unflappable to his Dutch roots, giving the impression of Van Gogh as an engineer on the Santa Fe–Topeka Railroad. Laurel Frank, Alan Robertson, Greig Pickhaver and John Romeril also lurked there, amphibian worker/artists functioning in both worlds, able to make with their hands as well as loon with their minds. When the panelbeaters vacated in the late '70s, doubling the below stairs space, it spawned a subculture, a lumpen *demi-monde* of art, drugs and rock 'n' roll, over which the baleful aura of Mick Duncan and his bull terrier presided.

In the end Circus Oz inherited the bulk of the gear and lumber from the basement, and 20 years on, in another condemned workshop of filthy creation on Mount Alexander Road, I recognised bits and pieces, fragments of a continuum. Alan Robertson was still there amidst the detritus of performance. He was shaping a lump of iron into something on a forge of his own devising. His rusty helical curls were grizzled by time. Living and working hard and high had scribbled a grid over his freckled, kid-eager face. He was pondering ways and means to keep the shit

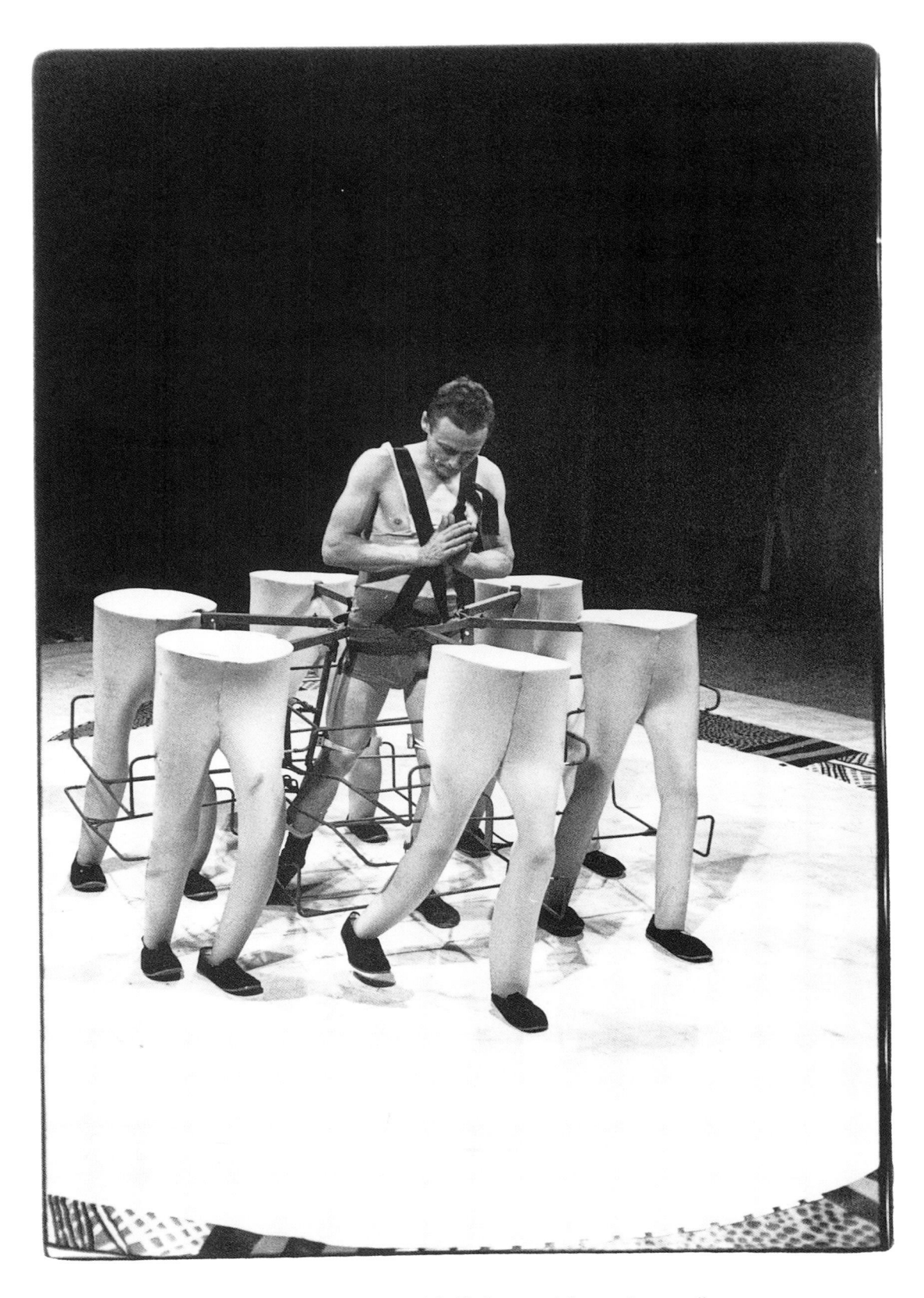

Alan Robertson, who learnt the craft of welding from John Timlin, prayerfully operating a small mechanical group, or People Machine, of his own contriving. (Ponch Hawkes)

together and move it on again. Laurel Frank, owl-eyed Athena, neat and deft, clear-browed as ever, was busy boxing costumes elsewhere. He produced a bottle of Johnny Walker, I rolled a joint, we raved. I proposed a toast to the Phantom Past and limned for Alan the Synopsis of an ill-made play in three acts to wit: *Drama on Drummond Street*.

The first act is about the democratisation of the process of bringing about dramatic performance. The fun of that process is as important as its rightness in principle. The writer is a collaborator with the performing group; the director is a mix of coach, umpire and crowd—but never captain. The action takes place in an ad hoc sort of a way around La Mama 1967–68 until the Red Dawn, the Leasing of the Pram Factory and the Advent of Rent.

Act Two is concerned with the Pramocratisation of Control. This happens when the group achieves a past, an address and the funds with which to secure a future. It is nasty, brutish and long. Personal politics mutate and multiply into factions and blocs. Once the performer/playwright complex wins credibility for the APG and the success of the plays is parlayed into grants, commissions and royalties, the struggle for worker control of information, of artistic direction and of the money becomes grim and earnest. There is backstabbing, betrayal and Hoopla galore. There is a *Great Stumble Forward* towards a more popular audience by some members finding no satisfaction running a theatre to service bourgeois Austral plays. Williamson splits to Sydney crying Maoist putsch. Blundell spins off to blend into the Sydney night to keep his files and plot revenge, seething like a Jacobean malcontent in a gym.

In Act Three, a house divided against itself collapses. There is inanition and brain damage. There is European weirdness, two-headed calves and Roger Pulvers. Theatrical talent leaks away or is discouraged, executive power passes to the new wave woman, absorbed by political correctitude and debt. Aborted from the ear of Zeus by committee, the new Ensemble writhes for a year. Lygon Court Developers moves in and works its own radical transformation: a Plaza del Shopping. A Writers' Theatre led by Hibberd and O'Hearn finds a home in the decaying but heritage-registered Carlton Courthouse next door. In a subplot before the catastrophe, the Performing Group, its ethos and practice, runs away to join the circus.

Jon Hawkes at an executive meeting in 1978. (Bob Daly)

4 Towerchildren

ONCE UPON A TIME at 323–325 Drummond Street, the Freeman family and retainers lived on the premises, above and behind their Livery Stables, decorously it may be supposed, in an atmosphere of horse. Two rooms were of ample dimensions, the remainder high-ceilinged but somewhat cramped. A passage to the right of the stairs led to a roof garden. The stairs wound on up to ascending eyries within the square bastion of a Tower. Decorums lapsed with the coming of the horseless carriage, and their home was subsumed by the *demi-monde*, became a house that did a roaring trade through World War II and a more discreet one in the Big Sleep of the Menzies era.

Come the '60s, the place was vacant and dilapidating. Ripening architecture students like Penny Brown and Sue Ingleton happened up on it. A freewheeling ménage took up residence. Romance flourished in whitewashed rooms as the old bordello was erogenised afresh to the very bathroom. Parties were legion and legendary. The Tower became a honeypot, a scene, Liberty House. The musk of rut osmosed into the rising damp, with the joss, the sweat, the jism from the opium smoking, the dancing, greek wrestling and whoopee of generations dead and gone. Spoof! The vision fades . . . A whole cycle of couplings took off from there to Europe, wedlock and ports beyond. After the nymphs departed, Eros redressed the balance with a bout of gay fecklessness. In the '70s it became the home of the Freak and the Psychedelic Bolshevik.

In 1971 Bill Garner was weary of a chequered, nomadic life in his crimson American ambulance and was looking for dissolution in a fixed abode. He had heard on the grapevine, probably the one in the Albion Hotel, that the lease on the Tower was up for grabs. He passed the word to John Timlin who, probably claiming he knew already, went off to Perpetual Trustees and grabbed it. A new and last generation of tenants moved in. Bill was in first and he chose the smallish north-facing room

The Tower, early '70s. (Lloyd Carrick)

Tower stairs. (Bill Garner)

at the top of the stairs, making him a slightly proprietary if reluctant concierge figure. Of Bill, a philosopher bum with an unending facility for confecting daisy chains out of ideas and images lying about him, the most distinct feature in my memory of this period is his belly. It was articulate with muscle like those on Roman breastplates. The *jaghana* of a jaguar, an inspiration to the potbellied hedonist. It had got that way through assiduous exercise of one kind and another, not least the practice of the yogic headstand, and in summertime it ascended or descended narrowly from baggy khaki drill shorts, which Bill was particular in

Tower kitchen freshly muralled, L by Carol Porter, R by Bob Daly. Figure in flying suit, holding paint can à la *Rolf Harris, is Carol Porter.*

keeping crisply laundered. Reynard the fox at the gate, inverted, he greeted Evelyn Krape the first time she ever came to a workshop, causing her to wonder fearfully if she too would be required to stand so on her head, expounding Situationism. Joining a gathering himself, Bill had a way of scanning above and around his proximate company, jesting with a grin, amiable but set, assaying the rest of the scene. If Garner was the gatekeeper of categories and cadres, of premises logical as well as physical, he held no keys and would entertain any notion for the fun of it. This anal anarch used to keep Boxes of History beneath the exhausted springs of his trucklebed, written in characters that breeze along sharply, openly, well above the line, as if doing handstands themselves.

Peter Dyke, who elected to perform the dispiriting task of keeping the APG books, set up his futon at the end of a blind passage, in what may have been the tiny quarters of the Freemans' maid. Next summer, back from California, Lindzee Smith and then a bit later Jon Hawkes (with Ted Heald from Oakland along for the trip) crashed for the night and stayed for the duration. Lindzee installed himself in the heights of the Tower; Jonno slipped in next to the kitchen, fitting choices both for the Tower Guru and its Vizier.

The kitchen was a high and poky space, and there must have been a larger one elsewhere in the Freemans' time to service their public luncheon rooms. It had an amazing expanding capacity. It seemed to be able to fit as many bodies as the much roomier People's Lounge one door down the passage. The kitchen was the central intelligence headquarters of the Tower and Environs. Of a Friday night, a seeker could find a supper show or a band or even a circus being hatched round the table, assorted liaisons, deals, political attitudes aspired towards or ridiculed against the overflowing sink and sideboard, a relationship being aborted behind the door. And still there would be room for revellers kicking on from the Albion after 10 p.m.

When Jane Clifton and Jan Cornall to the Dark Tower came, they had misgivings about this catch-as-catch-can male household. The Celibacy Club surprised them. A fucking moratorium had been declared.

What's the point of a revolution
Without general copulation?

they wondered with the inmates of Charenton in *Marat-Sade*. Was it because of limp libidos, great unhappiness, sickness, or a desire to sublimate their jism into *kunst*? A ploy to make the men fantastically, unreachably attractive, the women decided. Men displaying headgear of Afghani knits or bright be-pompommed teacosies from Harlem needed all the additional mystique they could get. Cliffo squeezed herself, her wardrobe and her Marcosian collection of shoes into the second largest room overlooking the Police Station and waited for the thaw. Bob Daly came mooching by. He liked the vibe and threw his cap in the ring—Made in the US of A, floppy peak, faded blue, paintsplotched. He liberated an outhouse on the roof garden and started illustrating the kitchen wall late at night. Much later, with the coming of the spraycan, the graffiti-burdened wall that divided the Tower from the Pram Factory was emblazoned with the scarlet legend: Free the Walls!

To the evolving towerhold came Carol Porter under a shock of henna, her eyes smouldering with kohl like Theda Bara. She occupied another windswept outhouse without any modern convenience, the better to get into the zen bones of things. Robin and Bain Laurie, sis and bro of good socialist stock, mucked in and found pozzies for themselves. Robin had come on the scene via the film push at Melbourne Uni. She had joined in the workshops at La Mama, particularly the one run by Sue Neville from Melbourne State College, who had workshopped in Poland with Grotowsky. She never thought of herself as an actor but had been the first Maureen in *Dimboola*. She preferred to commit to real-life projects like going to India with her boyfriend to avoid the draft. Upon her return she entered alternative realities such as making *Dalmas* with Bert Deling and sharing a house with Red Symons and Peter Cummins and defining herself as an anarcho-surrealist insurrectionary feminist with Margo Nash.

Then long tall Ruth Maddison came and bunked in with Bob. She was one of a bunch of women who took up cameras and seized the day from a feminist perspective—Ponch Hawkes, Carol Jerrems, Micky Allen, Jillian Gibb—who were in and out of the kitchen.

Towerchildren and the Fitzcarlton house network were not simply persons sleeping with each other and doing drugs and plays. In a myriad small acts of creative exchange, they took a self-conscious pleasure in communicating with each other. There are relics of the recorded thoughts, handicrafted gifts of laughter kept by Jane Clifton, *chanteuse* and bower bird. She remembers the gentle art of correspondence, as practised in the '70s, the 'Carlton letter'.

> We wrote notes, postcards, collages on brown paper bags to one another almost daily &/or at the drop of a hat. Did you ever get one of those elaborate exercise books from Greig Pickhaver? with the rock quiz and the jigsaw? Treasures! The occasional, fugitive artworks of Carol Porter and Bob Daly, the exquisitely detailed cartoons of Laurel Frank and the ego-stroking photographic essays of Ponch, Micky Allen and Ruth Maddison . . . The thing is . . . we all had this drive not just to communicate verbally but also to create these little haikus. Professions of love, admiration, apology, jealousy, anger and of course, my favourite, requests or grantings of permission to sleep with someone. We had to write things down—beautifully, succinctly, perfectly, self-consciously. When people travelled—interstate, overseas, to another suburb—the postcards were chosen with enormous care and frequently. Perhaps we communicated better on paper (or paper bag).
>
> When Helen Garner was in Paris on one of her earlier forays, she wrote to me practically daily—in the laundromat, at home, at the pool—and I wrote back a lot. Then when she came back we saw each other and had almost nothing to say. No animosity or anything but it was just a vacuum. The writing had had a life of its own.
>
> Why it is now called, derisively, 'getting a Carlton letter' by some of us, is because a lot of the letters and notes were about having it out with someone (quite often someone who lived in the room next door) and were full of 'I mean' and 'I guess' and 'what I'm trying to say is that I really, really feel that'. Another bizarre example of writing it down: there was a plague of crabs at the Tower and surrounding fiefs and someone actually drew up an enormous 'crab tree'—trying to trace the plague back to its source by writing down who was sleeping with whom. And remember the notice boards? In the kitchen of every communal house. Collages of 'thoughts of the day', photos,

Tower patio with Jon Hawkes juggling, Eddie van Rosendael writing, Lindzee Smith musing. (Carol Porter)

newspaper cuttings, handbills and, of course the Roster. The sum total was yet another work of art—structured chaos—you added to and subtracted from the board with great thought. Remember the barter system? The way Greig built everybody those loft beds and Laurel and I gave everybody haircuts (well, the same haircut in fact!) and we all learnt to take photos and develop film in Ponch and Micky's darkrooms—but no money ever changed hands.

Max Gillies in the People's Lounge, mid '70s. (Carol Porter)

The hole in the wall between the Tower and the Pram Factory office. (Bill Garner)

Many Towerchildren are encrypted in *Monkey Grip*, Helen Garner's *roman-à-clef*, bricabracollaged from this ghetto culture. Eddy, the hard-line, 'don't call me a Trotskyist—man!' ass-kicking drummer with *Stiletto*, may or may not be Willy but he certainly dwelt in the Tower longer than anyone else. Trottishly, he took over the People's Lounge. Arguing with Eddy, everyone agreed, could clarify one's position wonderfully. Musicians, acid casualties, escapees and outlaws flitted through the community and joined in the dialectic. Smelly, holy fools, like Hollywood Dave, the walking talking encyclopaedia of Australian film, were in the kitchen. Michael Byrnes, a victim of good works, unhappily released from jail by means of a successful production of his play *The River Jordan*, stayed on after the season. When no one else would take him home anymore he dossed in this open, drug-tolerant zone until even the Tower's patience ran out.

The APG was regarded by the occupants of the Tower, who were its non-paying sub-lessees, as an unhip, bourgeois fogiedom—much in the way that the Group itself looked down upon the MTC. People who lived in the Tower, on the whole, were idealists who wanted to live at work and work at play and avoid the nuclear family. All of them were veterans of communal living in shared houses from North Fitzroy to Nimbin to New Mexico and back to Toorak. Yet the Tower was simply a shared tower, not a thorough-going commune or a collective. This could be ascertained by the mountain of dishes in the sink. 'Home' being a bourgeois concept, it was not quite home either, except in the sense of a place you hang a hat and awake unsurprised in the morning. Jon Hawkes defined it as a work-based social unit and defended its coyness about the rent by pointing out the unit's caretaking function. At Christmas when some of the non-nuclear particles about the parish got to feeling lonely and unaccommodated, the Towerchildren used to organise the Orphans Banquet.

Back in 1973, Tony Bilson was cooking cheap, ravishing food at the Albion Hotel. Here, after sundown, the absence of a band made sexual collusion more conversational and amenable than in decades to come. Bilson revolutionised pub food and the comrades set off on the Long

Lunch. Exotic young women called in from Balwyn, Bentleigh and Glen Waverley at the weekend. At closing, genial Bert and Gino bounced everyone out and a licentious throng would spill onto Faraday Street and try and find out where the party was and race themselves off. More often than not it was declared to be at the Tower, usually by people who did not live there. Any time of the day or night, particularly Saturday night, Towerchildren were used to surprising polymorphous couples perversing in their beds. 323–325 Drummond Street was a nest of Reds in bed, rife with paycheck and teaspoon-thieving junkies, with subversive agents of Community Aid Abroad, the Light Powder & Construction Works and the Australian Surrealist Insurrectionary Feminists, in and out the whole time, in full view of the Carlton Police Station. For all that, the place was never busted. Marcusians complained of repressive tolerance. Former readers of World War II escape novels recalled that the safest place for a French Resistance cell to be was right on top of Gestapo headquarters. Students of Machiavelli thought that if the Police had the 'wood' on the Tower, the Tower had the 'wood' on them. Once during a fund-raiser in the theatre a constable staggered in and tried to lay charges of illegal sale of liquor. He was bumped out for being drunk and returned at the head of a paddywaggonload of inebriate colleagues. Push came to shove

August 1981, drinking outside the Albion on the corner of Lygon and Faraday streets. L–R: Bill Garner the actor, Eric Beach the poet, Danny Kramer the Carlton identity. (Ruth Maddison)

and they were all at the bottom of the wine-dark steps uttering threats of which nothing more was heard, due to the number of learned counsel present willing to defend the charge on a day to be appointed, gratis. The Tower saw Lily the Law legless in the bacchanalia that reigned every Christmas at the Magistrates' Court next door.

After the obscenity bust in '69, a La Mama audience and much of the clientele of the Albion and Stewarts Hotels—many hundreds (thousands, according to Garner)—took to the streets and besieged the Carlton Police Station. Jack Lazarus QC appeared for Rivka Hartman. He got her off—and consequently the rest of the cast. Over the years, it may have been, police sergeants preferred a valorous discretion about the excesses of the children of privilege over the road. These ratbags were a grungy *jeunesse dorée*, well connected, attracting clientele to local business, increasing the cultural and real estate value of the neighbourhood. Such might have been the analysis of fell Sergeant Plod.

The Great Helmsman was prominent among the household gods of the Tower. The bad news about the Cultural Revolution in China went unheard. Simon Leys wasn't there to give a stoned rave in the People's Lounge. If he had, Eddy would have fanged him as a running dog reactionary adventurist just as he had fanged John Lennon for singing

The alley on the north side of the Tower. L–R: Carlton Courthouse, parking/film location, Carlton Police Station. (John Gollings)

> *If you go carrying pictures of Chairman Mao*
> *You aint gonna make it with anyone, anyhow.*

The Red Guards were perceived as a bit over the top but basically OK. The idea of Mao's New Cathay was sustained by the posters on the walls, naif, idyllic scenes of the Commune's Goldfish Pond or the Commune's Ducklings. The play of ideas was the thing in the People's Lounge, the consequent material messes were left unexamined.

Some nympholepts were zealous in the practice of the Chairman's exercises. More were content with lip-service. Jane, the colonel's daughter, had been exposed to physical jerks in military cantonments around the British Empire so did not bother. Bill, the headmaster's son, hungover and stooped with shaggers back, would plead the primacy of menial labour and slink to the kitchen. He could hide behind the impossible heap in the sink where he might find Bain and Bob and Eddy also ducking it but not Carol or Robin who were pretty conchy. Lindzee seldom fronted. He would sing in the shower:

> *'O say I saw Ted Hill last night'*

and go to Tamani's for breakfast with his shades on.

The Tower, April 1980, with plaster horsehead highlit and Eileen Chapman about to cross Drummond Street and ride south towards Faraday Street. (Ruth Maddison)

Towerchildren readying to take the Great Stumble Forward in 1973. L–R: Ted Heald, Ruth Maddison, Jan Cornall, Greig Pickhaver, Jon Hawkes, Bob Daly, Shuv'us, Jane Clifton, Patrick (?), Carol Porter, Alan Robertson, Robin Laurie, Bruce Woodcock, Kelly Hoare. (Seated) Steve Hill, Lindzee Smith. (Ponch Hawkes)

Cooking was a rarity in the Tower kitchen. The staple meal of the day was breakfast and it was always taken at Tamani's (now Tiamo's) on Lygon Street, and prolonged. Piero and Angelo were instructed how to make toast, rather than burning Italian bread as formerly. The art of scrambling eggs in a soft and buttery manner and the importance of marmalade and Vegemite were conveyed in pidgin Italian. The women out the back soon got the hang of it. Latte after latte, deals were sought and done, advice given and received (mostly the former), fantasies expounded. A congenial and coherent way of addressing the business of the day, Towerbreakfasting was more focussed than the shouting ruck of the APG at the pub, a situation where more plots were lost than hatched. The Tower cabal at Tamani's recalled for some members the way the Sunday sessions at La Mama commenced. Enthusiasts with hangovers fired up over continental breakfasts at Graeme and Kerry's, the Carlton Street house (the one before Drummond Street) opposite the green shade of the Exhibition Gardens, where they went to build their first pyramids out of themselves.

5 ★ Cell Formation and Division

BEFORE THE APG became identified with the Pram Factory building, it was centred on the idea of the autonomy of the performer. The performer was idealised as a free agent, whereas a mere actor was a dependent, tied down to a theatre with strings attached to management, directors, writers, a subscription audience and established tastes. Actors had got themselves a bad name. For a rising generation boasting an expanded consciousness of national identity that name was Pom. (Quite unfairly, given what was going on in radical British theatre at the time.) The smooth effete actorine, voice-primed, passive, dead from the neck down, whose body was something that got in the way of the furniture, whose autonomy was nil.

Audiences had likewise got themselves a bad name. They were the monster in the dark, connoisseurs of ennui and the old hat, all dressed up behind the fourth wall, rustling and coughing, pretending not to be there or wishing they were at the Old Vic. For the children of Marx and Sarsaparilla, the APG was a declaration of independence from all that.

These Australian performers were not bound to the boards. At first an audience was dispensable. Improvisation based on the transactional analysis of Erwin Goffman, the theatresports of Viola Spolin and the gurus of *TDR* was sufficient unto the improvisors. A group was being formed. Plays were replaced by a constructed group experience. Improvising was self-justifying:

> An act of discovery is underway which carries with it, not only its own logic, but a need to fulfill itself which has reached the point of obsession.
> (Brian Davies, programme notes for the La Mama season, January–February 1969).

When they started visiting themselves on audiences, the peculiar demands of playing Bourke Street or the Yarra Bank, on the beach and in

Beach Theatre at Elwood (1971), protesting minister Dickie's statements against immigrants with 'dark blood'. Historian Margaret Williams bends over as Tony Taylor, Kerry Dwyer and Bill Garner extract her 'dark blood' with clyster and commedia dell'arte. (Mal Dobbin)

Dr Karl's Kure (John Romeril). Political medicine show at the Footscray Institute of Technology. Blundell and Garner in power struggle over possession of the microphone. (Lloyd Carrick)

Opposite: **Poster for *Brainrot*.**

factories, dictated the elements of their style. Claiming and holding attention in the open air required high energy, broad physical strokes, fearlessness and a contradictory mix of team spirit and self-reliance. Performers sweated, they could cope in all kinds of conditions. Where an actor would dry, a performer could fly. Actors were pawns, shadows; performers had auras.

The idea of performance was no longer restricted to the old texts and contexts of the regularised acting profession. Now it must include all mental and bodily skills, sports of all sorts, the circus, cabaret, music, song and dance, sex, politics and religion. Which is as may be, and may be not, as the reach of performers exceeds their grasp. The thing is to go for it. Bastards of the illegitimate stage, unite! If this was not a new idea, in the '60s it floated back into what period guru Teilhard de Chardin called the noosphere.

However jealous the young performers were of their autonomous preserve, a first cause of their formation as a group was textual—a season of plays. The unmoved mover was Jack Hibberd, Warracknabeal-whelped, Bendigo-bred, a med student with a bit of a reputation as a poet. Lexically extravagant, he was allergic to yankwank and esoteric excess. *Brainrot* was 'an Evening of Pathology and Violence, Love and Friendship', half a dozen microplays, as Hibberd categorised them, presented at the Prince Philip Theatre within the School of Architecture at Melbourne University in April 1968. Eponymous Phil would not have been amused at these sketches for a vernacular theatre of the absurd, nodding and winking at Beckett and Pinter and their own cleverness. They were a palpable and historic hit for their largely student audience. After Hibberd hopped on a boat for Europe there was a cabaret version, a funnier one by some accounts, in which the performers loosened and

★ Cell Formation and Division ★

**BRAINROT:
AN EVENING OF PATHOLOGY AND VIOLENCE AND
LOVE AND FRIENDSHIP   BY JACK HIBBERD**

BRAINROT

**DIRECTED BY DAVID KENDALL : GRAHAM BLUNDELL
ARCHITECTURE THEATRE : 17-28 APRIL !!! MULC
BOOKINGS : ALLANS & UNION : PHONE 34 0484**

PETER BURLEIGH 1968

The comrades on an AEU-sponsored factory tour in 1970. L–R: Yvonne Marini, Graeme Blundell, Kerry Dwyer, John Romeril, Rod Moore, Wilfred Last. (Mal Dobbin)

opened up the text. The performers wanted to stick together and so *Brainrot* begat the informal Sunday workshops of that September. The workshops begat the La Mama Company and, in the latter part of 1969, the La Mama Company begat the APG.

Not long after that seminal season, while the cast was hanging out as a group and swelling, the Monash push arrived and swelled it some more. These were ratbags different from the Melbourne Uni species, red in tooth and claw, the thundering minions of Marx, Mao and Marcuse for whom everything was political. The heaviness was all. In solidarity with the fuckin working class, theatre was a fuckin means not a fuckin end. A fuckin weapon in the fuckin class war. A fuckin waddy to fuckin whack your fuckin *weltschmerz* into the fuckin *weltanschauung* that would lead to the fuckin dictatorship of the fuckin proletariat, mate. Your Melbourne Uni ratbag tended to be more of an aesthete. If one of them upped and kicked against the pricks there, it was more likely to be against Jindyworobaks, or featurist architects. Romeril, Smith and Hawkes and Co. came down like wolves on the fold and did the soft, subjective, Viola-Spolin-loving, hippyish element like a dinner. Up against the wall motherfuckin bourgeois individualism! The political consciousness of dilettantes and careerists had to be raised. We performers are theatre workers who should be engaged in the struggle to liberate the people from the toils of imperialism. We must bugger up its engine, the industrial/military complex, and confound its cultural lackeys in the media. Bourgeois-pleasuring was a not on, bourgeois hierarchy was the enemy, and so was John Sumner, the petty officer of Pommy Rep at the MTC, and so was Stanislavsky, the silver-tailed betrayer of Chekhov. A worker-controlled creative ensemble is an exemplary microcosm of a better society at large, was the Monash line: let us therefore become one, pronto.

It was all a bit of an act. They were also into drugs and sexual indulgence and therefore, even in their own eyes, *petit-bourgeois* deviants. Behind his hornrims, David Kendall, for one, took a dim view of these yahoos for whom politics preceded performance. Here was an end to interior exploration, to the systematic refinement of the instrument, the discovery of the Method that he sought in a driven, drunken rage for order. 'Can you cope, Kendall?', Smith roared at him, pissed. Kendall didn't see the point of merely coping and went off presently to England to seek the discipline of craft and pluck out the mystery of performance from traditional and alternative methodologies over there.

Marvellous Melbourne, a vaudeville revision of history created by a collaborative ensemble, was the work with which the APG first deliberately set about defining itself. Drummed up by the research of historian Margaret Williams, a glow of enlightened nostalgia for the golden days of melodrama and panto, the heydays of Dampier and Coppin, when Australian theatre had been local and popular, was in the air. (Other consultants to the group included Glen Tomasetti, Therese Radic and Ian

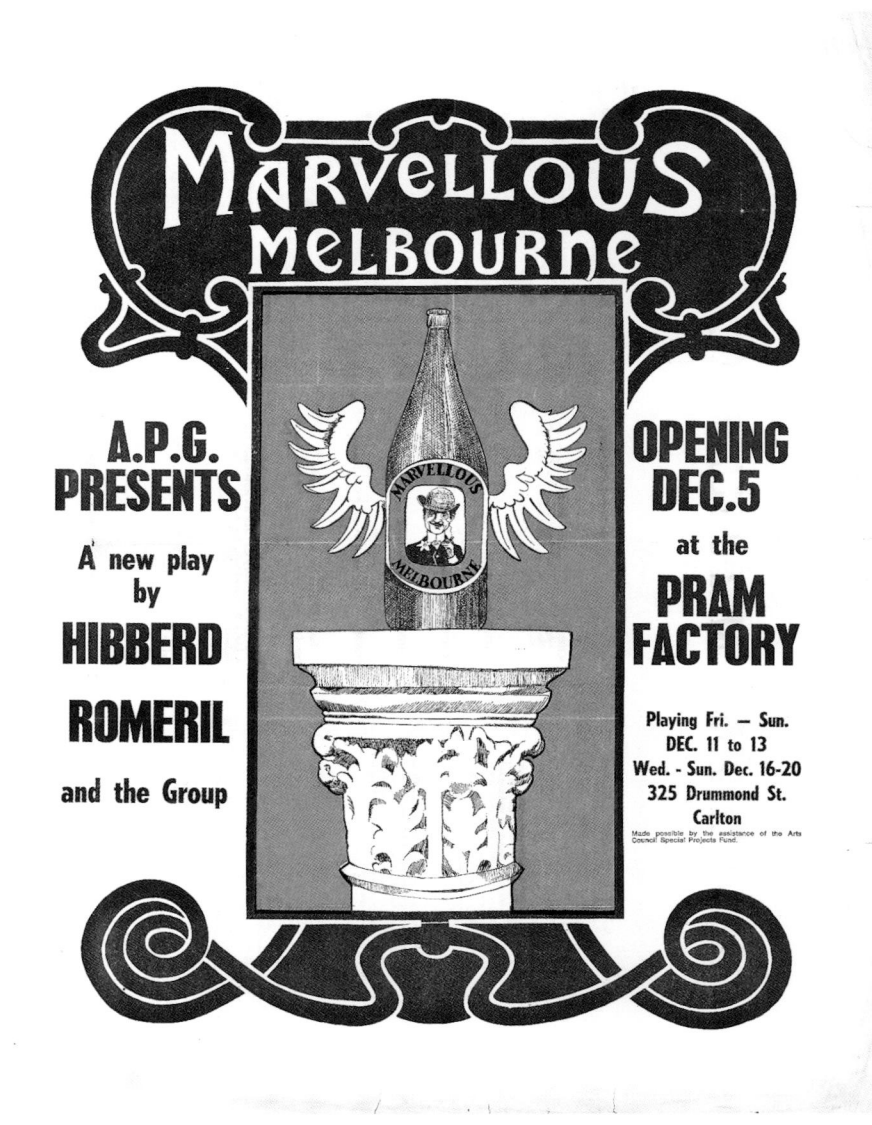

Poster for *Marvellous Melbourne*.

Turner.) Nationalist boosterism was cut with a satirical relish for the exposure of the skullduggery rampant in the period 1888–1901. The revelation of the political and financial depravity of the town as an historical constant aroused the group's delighted indignation. Quixotically, they aimed to make the work by a process to which there was similarly no end, according to an ideal of continuous organic growth. The show was developed through a six-month actor/writer workshop subsidised by the Group's first grant of $2000 from the Drama Board of the Arts Council. Workshopping began in June 1970 in the Ballet Guild's space on the State College campus, made available through connections of Max Gillies and Claire Dobbin, who were working there. The Open Stage at the College was another Carlton theatrical seedbed.

At first the workshop concerned itself with personal histories—Who are we? Where do we come from? Parents were assembled and their

Wheels are turning at The Pram Factory

We think we've unearthed the grooviest new rendezvous for people in theatre. It's The Pram Factory established by actor Graeme Blundell, John Timlin, Australian playwright Jack Hibberd and a committee known as the Community Arts Foundation. The factory was originally a hire-your-own-horse stable. It then became a dance hall, a dye house and, finally, a pram factory. Truly. In its new guise, the factory is an "audience participation" theatre, where the action of a play can be adapted to any section of the floor space the director wants to use. The Community Arts Foundation aims to explore creatively the open areas that exist in the building as part of future productions by local and overseas authors, for children's theatre and for new "experimental" theatre. Members of the foundation also hope to involve people from the high-rise flats, from the local factories and from the Melbourne University. So we wonder whether it was good luck or good management which placed The Pram Factory slap in the middle of Drummond Street, Carlton, one of Melbourne's most cosmopolitan areas where flat dwellers, workers and students are all within stone-throwing distance of one another. The Australian Performing Group also uses the factory. Their recent season began with discussions on early Australia, with illustrated lectures on folk song from Glen Tomasetti. Then there were talks on Australian drama by Margaret Williams, from Monash University, and talks on political and social history, with anecdotes on the side, from Ian Turner, of the history department at Monash.

The result was a theatre piece called . . . "Marvellous Melbourne." Jack Hibberd and John Romeril created the plot and the dialogue and Janet and Jerry Lester composed the music.

"Marvellous Melbourne" recreated the atmosphere and events in the city from the exhibition in 1888 to Federation in 1901. And we were told that this success was only the beginning.

Avant garde Australian films, plays and even folk operas are planned.

Already The Pram Factory is humming with creative activity.

We wish them luck.

The Australian Performing Group doing their horrendous thing at the old Pram Factory in Carlton.

attitudes and reminiscent intercourse over afternoon tea was minuted by Helen Garner. However the treatment of the mass of colourful material uncovered through historical research, thanks to the influence of Brecht, allied with a bodgie radical nationalism, saw a male point of view prevail. Hibberd had established a knack for writing Jonsonian, language-loving, 'humour' characters for university college productions like *Klag* and *Epic J. Remorse*. The prodigal output of Romeril and Hibberd in the workshop, enough for three or four plays, broke away from the intimate and the anecdotal, towards satire and burlesque, pointing up the historical parallels. Their political caricatures of public men like Honest Tom Bent and Theodore Fink caught with their pants down came to dominate proceedings. Bill Garner's memorable creation of Sir Wallace Pork—athletic, ithyphallic, grotesque—would stand as its icon. On 11 December the work in progress opened the newly hollowed-out Pram Factory with daggy éclat. After 10 nights it was reworked and presented again in March 1971 for a season of four weeks. The male monsters had claimed the space.

By defining themselves they divided themselves. In 1972 the women rebutted with *Betty Can Jump*, a register of the crimes of the patriarchy since settlement, improvised from primary sources with a bias toward history as experience, avoiding caricature. Earthy, funny and physical, *Betty* sought a deeper emotional response than the bawdy pantomime of *Marvellous Melbourne*. The boys found it mawkish and sentimental. *Betty* was guilty of self-indulgence and bourgeois individualism, and was a notable box office success.

These two shows marked a bifurcation of approach to performance in the APG from the start. Yang and Yin. The dominant mode was a macho get up and go, jump in and do it attack. It was comic and fuelled

Opposite: **Marvellous Melbourne**, **collage of cast in rehearsal.**
(*Woman's Day*, 25 January 1971)

Above left: **Marvellous Melbourne in performance, Front Theatre, 1971. Wilfred Last kneeling. L–R: Rod Moore, Lindy Davies (obscured), Tony Taylor, Kerry Dwyer, Meg Clancy.** (*Masque*, June 1971)

Above: **Poster for** *Betty Can Jump*.
(Latrobe Collection, State Library of Victoria)

by an aggression precluding intimacy. The Yin lurked hungrily, sniffing after tragedy, hankering after depths and darkness and subtleties, concerned about the processes of creation. The division was signposted even earlier. Part of a season of seven plays over six weekends, put on at La Mama in January–February 1969, was a brace by Megan Terry. While the boys did *Keep Tightly Closed*, the girls did *Calm Down Mother*. The vibe in both rehearsals and performances was as antithetical as the titles.

The APG house style was characterised as rough and broadly physical, rooted in (some would say by) vaudeville. Yet in such intimate spaces the voice, gesture and makeup used to reach distanced audiences in larger theatres were theatrically ludicrous, false. Peter Cummins says of working at La Mama:

> An actor who relaxes with the audience drinking coffee, who serves the coffee, sells tickets, talks to latecomers prior to an external entrance, discusses the play and sees the audience out and who does this, not as a phony patronising gesture to break the actor/audience barrier, but to get the show on and provide for his own comforts, must in time develop a natural relaxed familiarity with his audience.

Beware of Imitations (Barry Oakley), Front Theatre, 1973. Max Gillies as McLucky directing his faithful batman Roy (Bruce Spence) to fumigate one of his Cinque Portes. (Ian McKenzie)

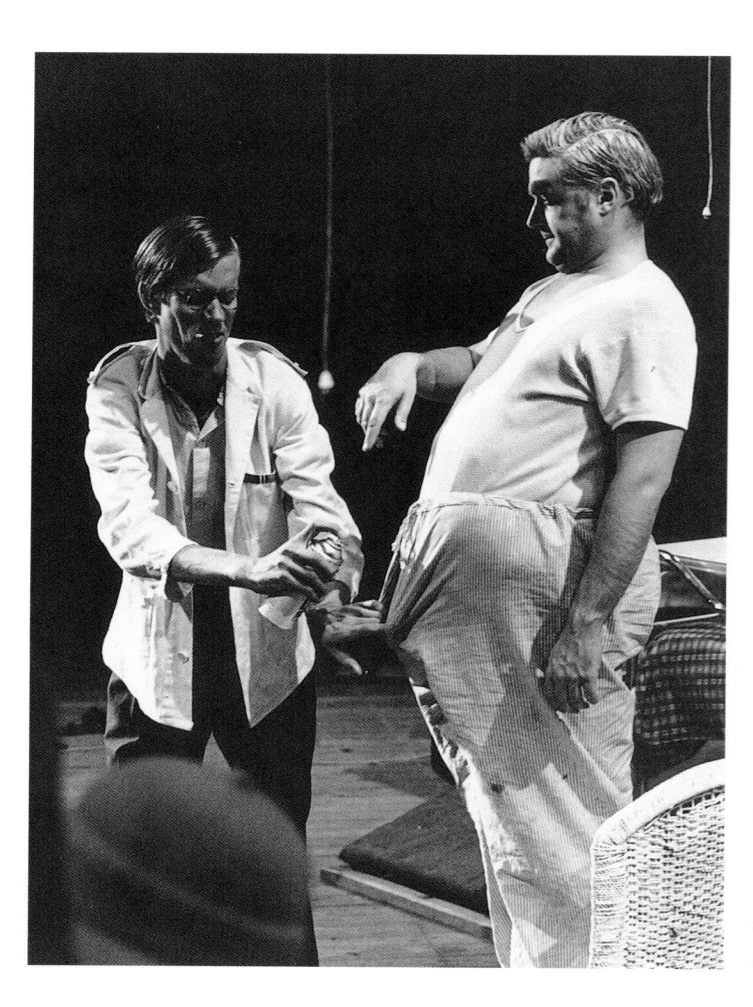

The effect on the audience could be far from laconic. Watching Cummins and Spence beating up on Paul Hampton in *The Removalists*, mixing farce and violence as natural as you like, was a truly visceral experience. 'Supernaturalism' they liked to call their acting style at the time.

However the style of shows like *Marvellous Melbourne*, *Dimboola*, *Sonia's Knee and Thigh Show*, *Don's Party*, *Beware of Imitations* etc. was stereotypic, caricatural, part of the performance baggage people brought in from university theatre, architecture revue and playing in the streets. Performers actively sought an increased command of traditional, popular, empirical tricks, and this was universally approved. In 1975 *The Hills Family Show* went off bellringing, tapdancing, mindreading down the middle of the theatrical road. In 1976, the mock Maoists of *The Great Stumble Forward* trained themselves in feats of the circus that were politically correct and beloved of the people.

When heroin arrived at the Pram, around 1974, it brought in another acting style, among a few who chose to work that dark Nightshift of the soul. Heavily into terrorism, suicide,

Ladies Revolutionary Bras (sic). Robin Laurie (L) and Ursula Harrison from the Women's Theatre Group at a Beat Your Breasts concert. (Ruth Maddison)

fascism, nihilism and foreign samizdat, this was bare, raw and jagged, a vector of a nocturnal lifestyle and minimum rehearsal. It was pretty much being yourself in whatever heightened state you were in. There was a frisson of danger, of riskiness, there was shooting up in the dressing room, nearly karking it and not getting on at all. In that case a band might play. Or not. Spodeeodee.

Over the decade 1968–78 two radically opposed attitudes to performing in character were to be discerned. In one camp were the comedians, neurotic, citified and demonstrative, like Max Gillies, Graeme

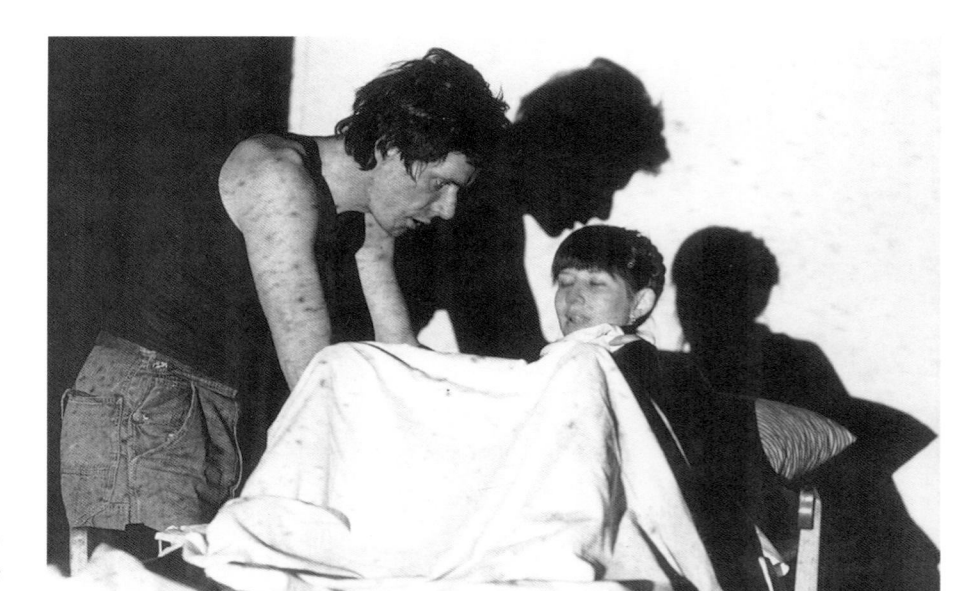

Nightshifters Shuv'us and Carol Porter looking into the dark side in *Michi's Blood* (F. X. Kroetz), Pram Factory, 1977.

The Architect and the Emperor of Assyria (Fernando Arrabal), Front Theatre, 1974. Max Gillies, acting; Jon Hawkes, being. (Ponch Hawkes)

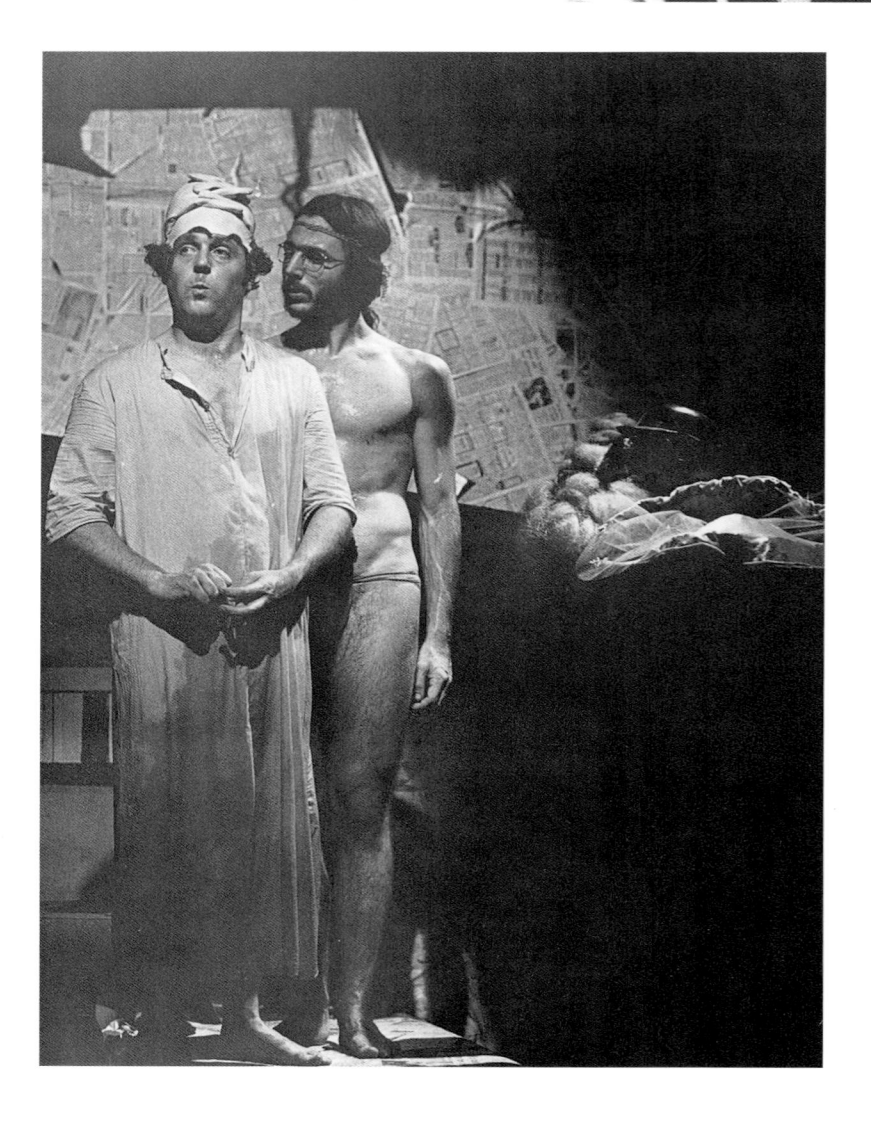

Blundell, Tony Taylor, Evelyn Krape, Bruce Spence and Peter Cummins, who shared an impulse toward pretending behind a plausible comic mask and a thirst for getting laughs. The opposite camp largely eschewed make-believe, seldom put on accents and were into being themselves in solidarity with the working class and smudging the line between Art and Life. The division was as clear as the wall between the Tower and the Front Theatre. A bit before Lindzee Smith's production of *The Architect and the Emperor of Assyria* in 1974, a passage was knocked through the wall and the Arrabal play was the medium for a cultural clash between Gillies and Hawkes. Gillies, the Emperor, pop-eyed in Bombay bloomers, was clearly in character and not Max. Hawkes, the Architect, a bespectacled Adonis in a jockstrap, refused to be anybody else but Jonno.

Max's side of this ideological division, the Rump of the APG for the first half of the '70s, was linked to the old Melbourne intellectual tradition of lefty nationalist dissent—Brian Fitzpatrick, Ian Turner and the pub radicals—and playwrights such as Jack Hibberd and Barry Oakley. They voted Labor, they drank liberally, not a few were Celts, catholics and teachers. They enjoyed the satirical stick, high energy comedy with clever words and physical action, and they prided themselves on a policy of no surrender to gurus. Jonno's side, the radical Mountain of the Tower, was internationalist, fond of American trips. They didn't see the point of party politics or voting. In performance their *locus classicus* was the famous production of Jack Gelber's *The Connection* or the living theater doing Jonas Mekas's film *The Brig*. On one side le Club Hot, playing on from popular comic traditions; on the other, le club Cool, who may have liked Danny Kaye and George Wallace but also seriously imagined themselves in a revolutionary scenario. Both clubs shared the belief that you learnt about performance by doing it. Praxis was the go. Classes in institutes and academies were discredited. Performance skill was picked up as you went along and more so before an audience than in rehearsals.

The Rump of the Pram was less of a performing group, more of a Writer's Bloc, a red meat and wine brigade, who were in the habit, oddly private-school, of calling each other by their surnames. They displayed their true colours at table. Foregathering at Hibberd's, or Oakley's or Williamson's or Timlin's, but most often at Timlin's, they would become inflamed and engorged. They would fang each other, hector and humiliate each other and, postprandially, cuckold each other. Dinner provided prodigious amounts of raw material for works of art. There are grounds for a retrospective royalty for the diners and party animals of the period, whose sociopathic behaviour at table or parties authors appropriated for conversion into intellectual property. Dining in an atmosphere he has compared to the Bitter Criticism sessions under Mao drove David Williamson out of town to Diamond Valley. There the rankling memory of all those destructive dinners was exorcised by writing plays about them. Lunch by comparison was mere escapism, the vehicle for cheap and passing shots. Dinner, especially when coterminous with Lunch, was where the fang was bared and the boot sunk.

I was Mr Inbetween. I felt a sympathy with both embattled writers and liberated performers A double agent, I drank in the pub and smoked in the Tower kitchen. Talking up shows, canvassing opinion, drumming support, raving, sharing illuminations. Australian red with Timlin, Acapulco gold with Hawkes. And shout after shout of pots. This was unwise. Under the whip of pleasure I was bloating in a fog. I spent a lot of time walking the streets of Carlton and Fitzroy at night, in between cliques, in between beds, a byword for bottomlessness.

In the year that would see the Labor Party withdraw our boys from Vietnam, the Clag of common cause was coming unstuck at the Pram. The big, bad, red rads were overseas seeking sources of inspiration, because Melbourne, after all, was only Melbourne. Intrigue and internecine conflict over shares of a limited budget grew inward-looking and acrimonious. The plural politics of the APG had always got personal. It was often not a nice place to be, if you knew what was going on. Brian Davies, a founder frozen out, had long ago left to lead a revival of Fauldings Chemicals in Adelaide, and many another early workshopper had fallen away towards parenthood and proper jobs. Since the end of 1971 the Blundell/Dwyer sphere of influence had been flattened by a phalanx of erstwhile teachers.

In that year two furry specimens of Fabian Irishry, Bill and Lorna Hannan, were at Moreland High School conspiring in the total reform of the education system. Moreland was a rough, unlucky dump and idealists in the Age of Whitlam were there to support the disadvantaged. It was the source of a number of APG recruits. Kerry Dwyer was teaching Drama there—Lorna said it couldn't be done and Bill was letting her try to prove that it could. Kerry was friends with Anne Timlin, the English teacher, and Kerry and Graeme soon met Anne's husband John. Tony Taylor and Paul Hampton were student teachers, and with Bill and Lorna they all followed Kerry to the Pram.

The Hannans were an institution within the collective. Bespectacled, untheatrical, Lorna birdlike and knitting, Bill a wombat with a perpetual frog in his throat. Absolutely unmuddleheaded, both were armed with minds like steel traps though of different gauge and mechanism: Lorna darting and picking at self-interest and inconsistency, Bill shouldering his burly way through the chickenwire of tory or revolutionary unreason. Of Irish catholic stock with a ceilidh of piping, fluting, fiddling, fairhaired girls all with fine Celtic names, at the Pram the Hannans seemed as untypically steadfast in marriage as in argument. Bill had served an apprenticeship as a playwright with Wal Cherry. In fact his first play, a comedy with songs called *Not With Yours Truly* opened the Emerald Hill Theatre. Wal had wanted a local script. Bill came up with one about a call-girl racket run by foreigners in Kombi vans and it was

Hannans. Non-nuclear, cosmopolitan, extending, 1991. Back L–R: Siobhan Hannan, George Xylouris, Elizabeth Hannan, Bill Hannan, Tony Tiganis. Front L–R: Lorna Hannan, Shelagh Hannan, Deirdre Hannan, Mairead Hannan with Ceallachan Hannan, Carlo Carli, Kanji. (Ponch Hawkes)

workshopped into production. As a partnership, the Hannans' first offering at the Pram was *Hackett Gets Ahead* or *The Compulsory Century*, a bit of improving, audience-participating, knockabout on the failings of the State School system, to mark its centenary (1872–1972). Performers disliked it, but it proclaimed the radical democratic socialism that led them to co-found a salary-sharing economic union and push theatre out into the community. The Hannans were stuck on the idea that information should be universally circulated and decisions made within the APG collective meeting, not in beds and pubs and kitchens. They were idealists.

They found an ally in Max Gillies, an escaped drama lecturer like myself. He had broken the bounds of formal courses to try experiments with trainee teachers along similar lines as the group at La Mama but with more emphasis on texts—Brecht, Beckett and Arden. Max was not as much into improvisation, and when directing he is remembered by Kerry Dwyer, admittedly a hostile witness, as plotting and blocking every move, in rehearsal and out of it.

The conflict between the group and the individual talent, the democrat and the performance daemon were embodied in Max. One of the few Pram Factory collaborators who made good in the commercial sense, his success provoked jealousy and dislike. His talent for mimicry and physical comedy could not be denied or held back. He tried to harness it to the common good. When Richard Franklin snapped him up for his early lacklustre comedy *Eskimo Nell*, Max ploughed the lucre into the Economic Union, keeping only a modest tithe for himself.

A sturdy, chunky clown, he hefts a head for politics on a neck like a bison. This chunkiness is deceptive, for Max is a light fantastic tripper in

A Stretch of the Imagination (Jack Hibberd), Front Theatre, 1976. Max Gillies as Monk O'Neill. (Brendan Hennessy)

performance. His comic creations aspire to dance. In life a worrier, as the bison also in his wariness, he often seems ill at ease. A die-hard smoker until the bypass, he often seems to be keeping up appearances, somewhat maladroitly, as if preoccupied by something inadmissable eating at him. A hoverer, a swiveller, a darter, coughing up a heartiness, he looks guarded, in search of an out. In performance all the tensions within him are resolved; they somehow come good in fleet, powerful comic forces, precision drawn. Loath to reveal himself, he is eager to use himself to demonstrate other selves, and relaxes on stage.

In his cubby without a title at the bottom of the Hannans' garden (whose leafshed had created a feud with next door), to my children he was like a nocturnal marsupial, one who let them play *The Wizard Of Oz* on his (then) exotic VCR while he tried to sleep in the daytime. Max was and is a media freak, an information junkie, a sound and image state-of-the-artist, massively into storage and retrieval. The kids could have had any classic movie of the 20th century, footage of the famous clowns, comics, politicians, any journal of current affairs and opinion, reputable and disreputable. All they ever wanted was *The Wizard of Oz*, to which they were unfailingly helped by the amiable, dressing-gowned insomniac. All I ever wanted was W. C. Fields playing pool. Max could show me the moves without putting on the video. He had studied them all in the watches of the night.

The Melbourne State College mob had given up on learning how to teach drama in order to do it, and like the bolsheviks, the maoists and the anarcho-surrealists they were not about to join someone else's group. They were becoming the Australian Performing Group, making it their own thing. One and all were committed to the Spirit of '68 and that meant Meetings. These were as much a part of the arsenal of our revolting youth as sex, drugs and rock 'n' roll. The authority of the college that wanted to develop its cultural estate by raising a glassy tower on the Open Stage site, the authority of politically incorrect monsters on the staff, any authority at all could be challenged by the energy and resolve with which motions were argued, put and acted upon. This revival of the political power of the good old time meeting made it a performance arena at the Pram. Fortnightly in the Front Theatre, at the Collective Meeting.

A *cause célèbre* was Yvonne Marini's Salary, or the fact that she didn't have one and Kerry Dwyer did. Yvonne was the only member with the *nous* to perform effectively in the office (which doubled as a dressing room). Those who were uneasy about Blundell's charismatic style of leadership were muttering about old guard cronyism, even financial syphoning—and they were muttering about tens of dollars. Cummins and Spence, succumbing to historical inevitability, had given up their Mexican stand-off at La Mama and re-joined up. They didn't mutter, they bayed—two more votes against Mousie in the minuted meetings, duly conducted, that his new and fiercely articulate peers insisted upon. Max Gillies was manoeuvred into the Chair. Debate became rancorous. Expletives multiplied in the cause of a democratic fair go.

The argument that won the day was that the Arts Council was not going to fork out the taxpayer's dollar to an outfit run on ad hoc, unbusinesslike lines. The upshot was a spill of all salaried positions and a decision to advertise for a full-time Administrator. An Employment Committee was elected with Bill Hannan, Ian McKenzie and Micky Allen on it. Timlin applied for and won the position over Hutchinson (the minimalist poet, cyclopaedist and old guard crony) at a salary of $100 per week. Yvonne Marini was retained as an assistant on $70. Of course she was only working in the office because there was nothing much for her to do live on stage. Yvonne grew disenchanted with her performance opportunities within the APG. When the Grotowski group passed by she skipped out to run through the woods with them, off on a meta-theatrical holiday.

In 1973 the group came to be owned by its members as a cooperative society under the Companies Act, limited by guarantee, the only practicable interface with the Law for the anomaly of a Collective in Victorian society. Such was the advice of a charitable circumlocution of attendant lawyers, friends of the Pram like Lloyd O'Neil, Dick Dufty and Phil Molan, who formed a buffer zone between Mammon and the Pram. Speedy John Bryson, a lapsed ornament of the Australian Bar, bought a property over the road wherein to cultivate his prose in a shared house among *le tout* Carlton. He became the APG Secretary, which put him on the theatre cleaning roster.

If the APG had had an Artistic Directorate all of it would have been on the cleaning roster. We didn't have one because we didn't have an Artistic Policy to direct. Decisions were made by Planning, Programming and Executive Committees and ratified by the vote of the Collective Meeting. The principle of self-management and the quest for a grassroots connection with the community were always more important than questions of artistic taste, style or excellence. Aesthetics were fought over on a show-by-show basis and were settled by gut feeling and the force of the personalities in the various Project Groups.

Backstabbing (Bob Daly)

Opposite: **The Feet of Daniel Mannix** (Barry Oakley), Front Theatre, 1971. Bruce Spence plays His Grace, Max Gillies lurks in the background with cloak and dagger as Greensleeves, aka B. A. Santamaria. (Ian McKenzie)

That the Pram Factory was a closed shop is a myth. Until 1973 membership was a matter of being the right person at the right time or by invitation. Thereafter it was open to anyone with the gumption to get through the shit and derision you had to negotiate to become first an associate and then a full member. There was from a distance some vicious circularity in the business: to perform you had to belong; to belong you had to have performed. On both sides of the divide, hanging out and hooking on was the meat and potatoes of it. It tended to attract people to whom the fact of its being a Collective was more important than its being a Theatre. Some rigorous materialists criticised performance talent as a bourgeois concept.

When the internationalist brigade re-grouped after recharge abroad, they approved the smashing of the power clique by the people but they were put off by these people's style and their nationalist high horse. They were aesthetically dismayed by what they as an ockercult of frumpish, middleclass pedagogues and clerks. Agog with what they had seen on their travels, they judged *A Stretch of the Imagination* a bit of a literary jerk-off, too verbal, too long, too local. The travellers, seconded by remnants of Tribe taking up residence in the Tower, were not that impressed by the proud new Australian drama rocking in what Hibberd fondly called the cradle of dingo theatre. They overlayed the *scheissenkrieg* of everyday business with the counter-cultural *scheissenkrieg* between the Chauvinists and the would-be Cosmopolitans. It was *Captain Midnight V.C.* and *The Feet of Daniel Mannix* versus Handke, Arrabal and Heathcote Williams.

What they loved and what the other, mainly childless, members who could manage it, loved—Greig Pickhaver, Michael Price, Richard Murphett, Graeme Isaac, Hellen Sky, Jane Mullet—was an overlapping crossover of projects. Some would be off rehearsing the Circus Oz show at

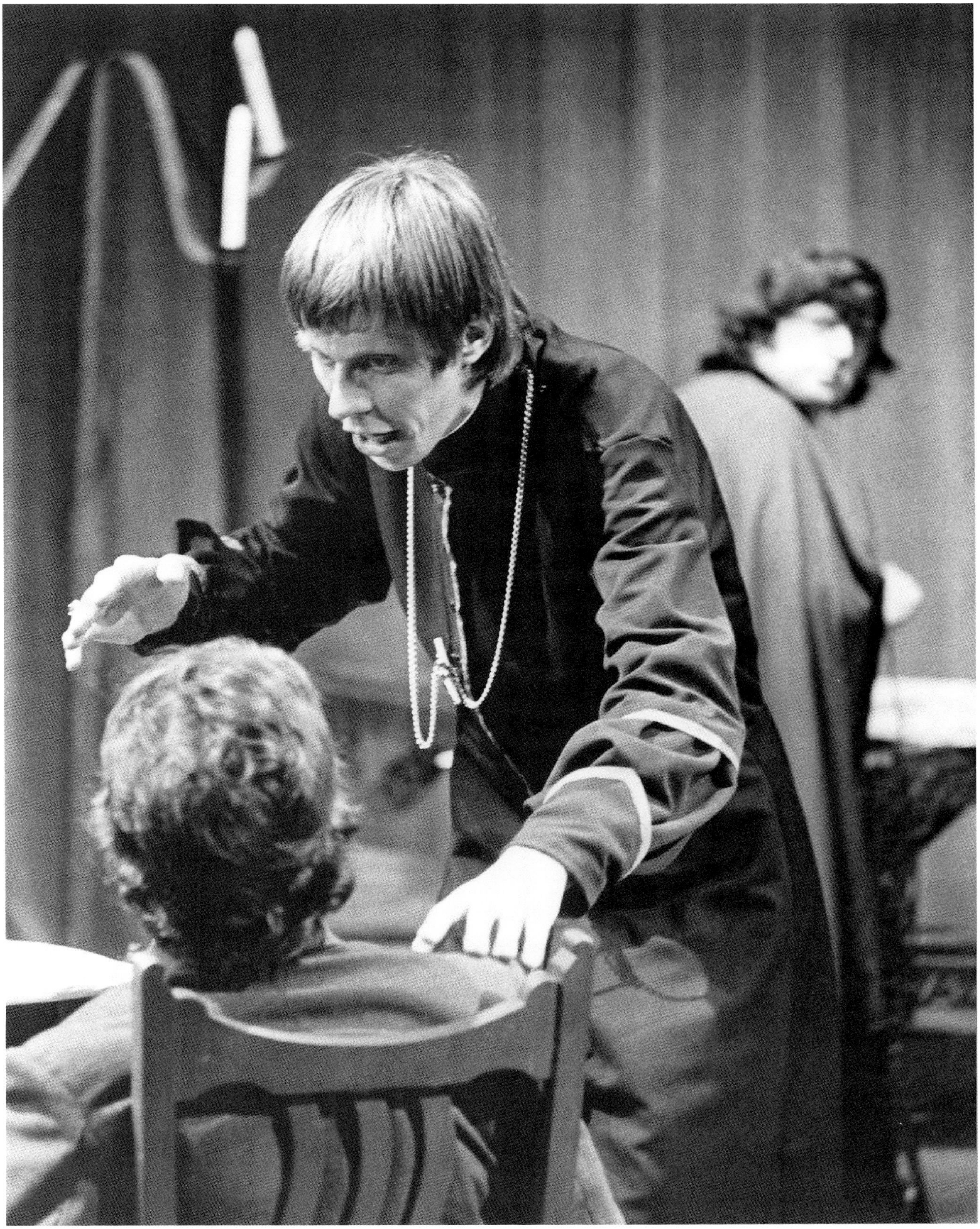

My Foot, My Tutor (Peter Handke) with Bob Thorneycroft and Joe Bolza, Front Theatre, 1976. (Carol Porter)

the National Gallery during the day and performing *Dreamers of the Absolute* in the Front Theatre at night. Others would be doing *The Hills Family Show* at the APG while workshopping their days away as Stasis, freeing the natural voice on principles they had learnt from Rowena Balos (a voice teacher from NYC) and applying it to Ibsen's *Peer Gynt*.

There was not a collective 'us' at the APG, we were an abrasion of 'thems'. Barry Oakley confesses:

> I never felt comfortable at meetings. Partly because, at least in those days, I was shy about getting to my feet. Partly because though (if one can make this separation) while I was all for their kind of theatre, I hated their politics—hated the idea of a Collective, hated Mao and his doctrines, couldn't abide Romeril's and the others unfairness about capitalism (for me faulty yes, evil no) and their myopia about socialism. Like most of the group I was middle-class but unlike many of them, not ashamed of it— yes, the Oakleys had a tidy (how sad! how bourgeois!) and perhaps even stylish house (worse!) with (you enemies of the third world! you overpopulators! you consumers!) a sixth child on the way. So I loved getting plays on but hated the views of many who allowed them to go on. I believed in quality, that some were more skilled in acting and writing than others and that Mao was not only wrong about the intellectuals but a mass murderer. I'd have needed the courage of Danton to get up and say these things but I did sometimes say them in Stewarts when I could stand Smith's stupidities (he defended the terrorist bombing of innocent civilians at an airport) no longer.

The unpleasantness over *Bedfellows* brought things to a head. At the end of '74, Oakley submitted the well-made, wry, three-hander of that name to the group. It had its partisans, it read well, but its subject matter

The Mother (Bertolt Brecht). (Peter Corrigan)

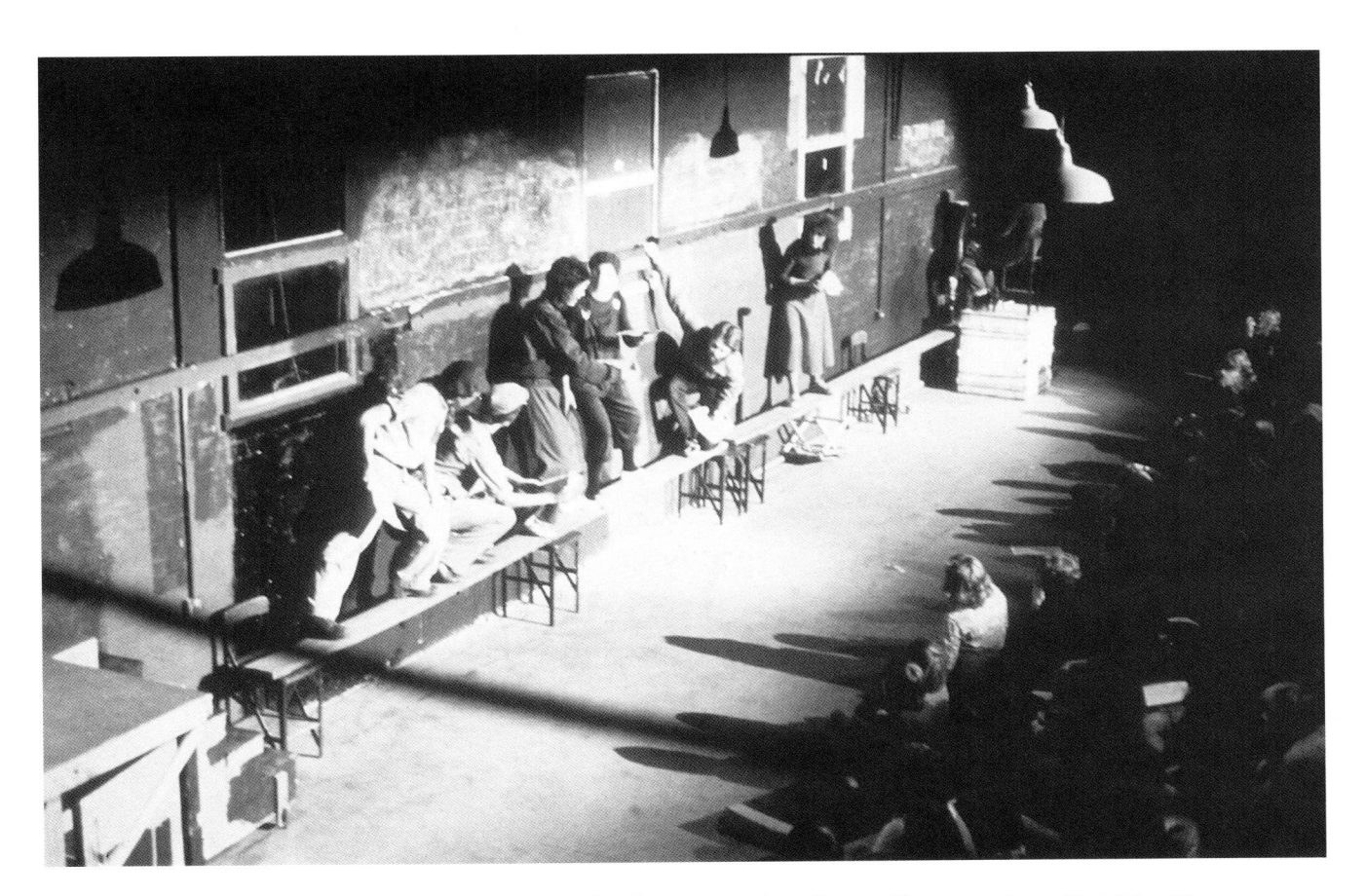

stuck in the craw of the stern ideologues on the Programming Committee. The playwright was summoned to make out a case for his play and, years later, it still rankles:

> I was treated to an hour's patronising interrogation about why I thought an institution as obsolete as marriage (and its quaint concomitant, adultery) was worth writing about. I told them that the justification, if there was one, lay in the script. They had found it diverting in an antiquated, middle-class way. I said I was surprised by their elitism—an awful lot of people were middle-class, including, it was pretty obvious, myself. They let it through reluctantly, as if I had offered them something ague-ridden, rather than a script that resulted in sell-out houses, good returns for the group, tours to Adelaide and Brisbane to rave reviews.

Proof positive, Smith would have snorted, had he still been around to snort. That this sort of play got up on the programme at all was an indictment of the Pram for him. So he and Jon Hawkes with Carol Porter and Robin Laurie took off for the States for another cultural fix. They got there in time to witness the historic split of the living theater in Pittsburgh. They penetrated the charmed circles of Joe Chaikin and Richard Schechner. They saw the legendary Mabu Mines. Snowed in at Antioch College, Ohio, they watched the San Francisco Mime Troupe on video doing Brecht's *The Mother*. Lindzee determined to get it on back home. They applauded the work of the amphibious Otrabanda. In winter Otrabanda was an experimental theatre group; in summer it subsidised itself by rafting down the Mississippi as a Dixieland jazz band.

Back in the Tower they were ready for anything that was not old hat, safe bet, crafted formula; they were eager to apply their fresh inspirations. Carol and Robin immersed themselves in the Women's Theatre Group developed show about women and madness, *Add a Grated Laugh or Two*. Carol was buzzing with design ideas. Robin was itching to get into Super 8. Lindzee directed *The Mother* as one part of a double bill. (The Popeye Puppets did *The Elephant Calf*, as the other half.) While *The Hills Family Show*, *The Les Darcy Show*, *One of Nature's Gentlemen* and *Bedfellows* ran and reran, Smith was in there batting for the Other, to see that the Shadow got a run at the Pram, directing *My Foot My Tutor* (Handke) and *Act Without Words I & II* (Beckett) with Bob Thorneycroft and Joe Bolza, *AC/DC* (Williams) and *Dreamers of the Absolute* (Motherwell) in the Front Theatre, working at the same time as a principal agent in the emergence of the Nightshift cell. As much as it was formed by the attraction of the writing of exotics such as F. X. Kroetz and R. W. Fassbinder, Nightshift found its local habitation in the work of the prolific Phil Motherwell. Jonno and Carol and Robin had lost interest in the Front Theatre as the domain of the Writers' Bloc. Jonno had begun juggling three balls to music while moving around. They were off on The Great Stumble Forward.

6 A Group Mugshot with a Partial Anatomy of the Group Head

DAVID BOWIE was stuttering, androgynous in space, and

Ch-ch-ch-ch-ch-changes!

was the anthem of the early '70s. Lindzee and Jonno were sporting tea cosies on their heads like black dudes from Harlem. The hair of the male comrades was worn Che, Christ and the apostles' length, or else very short like Lou Reed, who was pretending to be a coloured girl in a bar in Berlin. All around marriages were showing signs of wear and tear as, for ideologically sound reasons, partners hopped into the lineaments of gratified desire. They ripened, opened and split almost organically. We heeded the insistence of guid Dr Laing that madness be allowed its vision and ecstasy its due. 'The family, the family's to blame!' We went along with that.

    RISE ANGRY
    MAN WOMAN

exhorted the writing on the wall at the corner of the highrise on Station and Elgin streets.

Despite nearly losing the text roistering through Ireland in 1969, in *Dimboola*, the Wedding Reception Play, Jack Hibberd had contrived a sentimental burlesque of repudiated rituals, an ultimately reassuring send-up of what had become a disaster area. Dramaturgically it provided a simple solution to the performer/audience relationship that had also become problematic. He slashed the gordian knot of how to get the audience to participate in the action by casting them as wedding guests and ensuring they all got a drink. Everyone knew the decorums, how to join in and how to misbehave. Hibberd deserved a guernsey in the *Tulane Drama Review*. What he received was the disparagement of hip,

Mary Shelley And The Monsters By Tim Robertson
Memories of Stewarts
Barry Dickins 31-8-95
Marvellous Melbourne
The Floating World By John Romeril
A Stretch of The Imagination
Goodbye Ted by John Timlin

Dimboola (Jack Hibberd), Front Theatre, 1973. A rising concern about the decline of manners at the wedding table. L–R: Maureen (Fay Mokotow), Morrie (Bruce Spence), Shirl (Kerry Dwyer), Knocka (Tim Robertson), Dangles (Bill Garner). In the background, Lionel Driftwood and the Piledrivers' Dick Duffy, unknown, Lorraine Milne. (Ian McKenzie)

born-again Americans in the Tower for whom the boozy bucolic romp was an embarrassment. Not that Jack needed reassurance. No one did in those dead set, cocky days. He thought *TDR* the bible of cringeing faddists, and had the last laugh when *Dimboola* went commercial with a long run at the Chevron Hotel. Even the hip jumped at the chance of their first pro. season. Even Carol Porter, who played the bride when Denise Drysdale had to go off and spin the wheel with Moonface, and Jane Clifton, who took on Shirl the burling bridesmaid and put up with Steve Spears as Dangles, the best man. Both avant-gardistes fattened their accounts along with their *derrières*. During the extensive mute intervals that fell to their characters in the second half, they would unhook each other's gowns and wade into the pav.

Lindzee Smith was built like a brick shithouse, as if designed to be the bouncer of the Mudd Club NYC he at one stage would become. He and Jon Hawkes were old mates, an XOX, psychedelic/bolshevist David and Jonathan. They had surfed together at 13th Beach, past Torquay, when Lindzee was an Eltham *ingénue*. After getting into yoga and the APG, they would still go down with other Towerchildren and, after blowing a few numbers, do headstands in the sand. Among their naked, inverted compeers, they would focus through the third eye, feet rooted in the sky, scrota aflop. In younger, roaring days, after a big Geelong victory, they would lair back to Lindzee's original home turf on the wrong side of the highway, with Hawkes taking up a dare to ride clinging to the rim of the windscreen. These brothers were out to out-rad the most rad. Had he come of age in the '50s, ponytailed Jonno, clydesdale of a lad, son of an Anglican minister, might have become a catholic. In the '60s he was bound to become a Maoist. Lindzee and Jonno discovered

Opposite: **'Memories of Stewarts'**, Barry Dickins compound cartoon. Top: author (in jug). Second row: Bill Garner, Wilfrid Last, John Timlin, John Romeril, John Bryson. Third row: Max Gillies, Peter Cummins, Jack Hibberd, dope-smoking Muse. Bottom: Evelyn Krape, Barry Dickins. (*Overland*)

America together, on and off. 'Dentist' Smith, with that frenzied grin that said yes to the weirdest shit possible, was ineluctably drawn to California, Ultima Thule of the Weird.

Doc Hibberd looked a little pale and scrawny up against these renegade apaches but they were wary of his proverbial fang when deriding his euro-celtic cultural bag. They could all laugh, boys together, somewhat forcefully, and Hibberd would bogart the joint in a sub-textual culture clash between peers of rural backgrounds. The earring meaning 'I don't belong in Geelong', the tattoo signifying 'AUM' on the fist of El Smith, these raised Jack's hackles. Suffering a Hypostasis of the Vernacular himself, he would wince at the nasal newyorkasing of the vowels, the rolling of the final r's:

'Hey, man, this here is Hunterr. He used to be an action painterr. Now he's gotten minimal. Orr minimallerr.'

Favoured forms of greeting between Pram Factory persons were an ironic 'chief', 'captain', 'squire' or 'boss' ('Godda joint, Captain?' was a catchcry of the house). This was part of the levelling urge in a ruck of egos out to equalise, yet we all remained dandies of different kinds: yankee-doodle, Baudelairean, third world, all of us were out trying to cut a figure. A prominent element of display was only to be expected from a performing group in a perpetual season of rut. Very few of the males wore the bag of fruit. 'Suits' were becoming the contemptuous synecdoche now used in reference to members of the executive/managerial elite. John Timlin, socialist/capitalist adventurer of Irish convict stemming, whose managerial sang-froid helped balance the group on the brink of financial dissolution for ten years, wore a suit. The group bought it for him. He claimed it as a costume, respectable beggar's weeds in which to petition funding bodies.

Strangely there are no Timlins to be found in the Melbourne phone book. They hail exclusively from Ballinar near Sligo, and are genetically disposed to keep their heads down and stick to their home patch. They found ways and means to eat their way through the potato famine. If the name is not in the book there are no doubt dark and sufficient reasons; non-existence should not be inferred. Timlins are biologically driven to do their hailing by phone. John Stephen has phone numbers encoded in his DNA and certainly exists in Melbourne because someone is always there asking where he is and someone else always knows he has moved into St Vincent's (Private) to have his kidney sliced (for no good reason it turns out) and then you run into him at Percy's, on the wagon, denouncing his surgeon as a brain-dead loser and being called to the phone. Only the blocking of access to the phone seems life-threatening to Timlin, so surnamed by intimate and alienate alike. He will not come at mobiles, sneers at them that do as he clings to the old style of doing things. The inventor of a new, improved weighbridge, he prides himself on his judgment and balance as he operates in the virtual reality of the arts of finance and the finance of the arts, trying, in this bad world, to live a

John Timlin and Max Gillies on the White House set of *The Gillies Report*, **ABC studios, Ripponlea, 1985. (Ponch Hawkes)**

decent life. From the time the group acquired its Pram Factory venue, until the honourable wind-up of the new Ensemble, Timlin was always there, in person or as the subject of conversation about his health, his rat acts, his bodgie demeanor—administrator, facilitator, fixer, fulcrum. He did duck out in '77 for nine months or so to go, disastrously, into pictures. While he was out he also teamed up with Hibberd and slipped a Footy Testimonial show into the Chevron Theatre Restaurant in the wake of my production of *Dimboola*. Entitled *Goodbye Ted* (after Ted Whitten, the Footscray legend, who stands next to Ludwig Wittgenstein in the Timlin pantheon), it proved a tidy little earner and he invested the royalties in a house in Falconer Street. This purchase demonstrated the tension in the balance mechanism between our Collective and our Capitalist Steward. The house had been a Tribe house, a group household for years. It was Nora's house in *Monkey Grip* and now here comes Timlin, like bloody Lopakhin in *The Cherry Orchard* buying it up, hollowing it out with slate and glass, uprooting the happy, hippy ethos. Timlin, regarding Karl Marx as a comic novelist, never buying the half-baked critique of capital attributed to Karl round the Pram, remained defiantly unrepentant. The renovated house was not to be a happy one, becoming the site of yet another nuclear implosion. Timlin pretended a hide too thick to feel the satirical barbs of the evicted; whipping-boy was ever part of his job description.

Hibberd was prone to wear jackets and waistcoats after the manner of a wine bar exquisite, the leftover persona of the *poète maudit* he had paraded as a student. He favoured dark, morbid colours and would have blended into the jungles of Le Douanier Rousseau—trousers tangerine, mauve or maroon, socks that flashed like parakeets. Timlin's suits came more from the palette of Brack's *Collins Street,* in financial fawns and

Sadhu with panacea. Lindzee Smith in *White Nigger*, Phil Motherwell's adaptation of Brecht's *Jungle of the Cities*. Back Theatre, winter 1974. (Carol Porter)

Tony Taylor sewing for psychological hygiene in 1977. (Ruth Maddison)

gubernatorial grey, contrasting the plumredness of his cheek and jowl. Jon Hawkes sometimes appeared in tropical creams and a panama, with shades and no socks, a look that smacked of Colombian drug baronetcy. Lindzee never wore suits, or not as himself, the brigandish character of the *demi-monde* he was building up anyway, only in performance as ugly and/or derelict Australians. His look was loose, crumpled and unbuttoned, a boxing trainer with a touch of the sadhu and the opium eater. Subfusc with afro-american exclamations about the head and neck, red and black and traces of silver and gold. Over the top and edgy.

There was, after a fashion, a Pram Factory look: op shop radical chic, proletarian plain or fancy. Both sexes were committed to boilersuits and overalls. Patches were flaunted like badges of honour, rainbow covenants with more handiwork to them than the garments to which they were sewn. A deal of patching and knitting went on during collective meetings and rehearsal. The skills were much admired in those men who could publicly exhibit them. Possibly for reasons of psychological hygiene, Tony Taylor knitted fairisle complexes, a vibrant glow at the tips of his needles, lightning rods channelling rage and energies repressed into warm, socially acceptable abstract expressionism.

Woollen fabric issued from Evelyn Krape, organically it seemed. One of the original great balls of fire, Ms Krape converted huge quantities of high anxiety and frustration into many woollen golems for the legs, the feet, the necks and backs of friends and relations and their babies, for herself and sometimes even for the backs of the patriarchy. The Mme Defarge of the company, crowned with a brazen head of fleecy curls, a henna'd periwig ('O toison!', groaned Hibberd), she knitted, *presto*, golden spex aglint, spiky and cuddly. Scorning, scoffing, scimitar-schnozzled sweater girl, turning out a 10-metre rainbow serpent of a scarf and embodying in her pint-sized person the trinity of gamine, siren and clown. In attack, like the skua, diving into the jokers, the cronies, the conniving misogynists of the pub push, she would take them on and take them off. She gave the definitive female Mousey in a touring production of *One of Nature's Gentlemen*, a crazy mirror image of Blundell's which shared the same sort of buzzing energy, Evvy and the little goy from Reservoir both rampant manifestations of the short person in showbusiness syndrome.

Female parts were hard to come by. Talent alone could not shine through the bushel of group and sexual politics. A touch of Philby in the night was required. To score, persons of whatever sex needed to be either clear-eyed, networking machiavels, or desperate enough to do anything,

One of Nature's Gentlemen (Jack Hibberd), Back Theatre, 1973. Peter Cummins as Bull, Jude Kuring as Dolly, Evelyn Krape as Mousie. (Ian McKenzie)

Waltzing Matilda (Tim Robertson and John Romeril), Front Theatre, 1973. The Nativity of the Virgin Jumbuck (Evelyn Krape) attended by maggies (Wilfred Last, Fay Mokotow, Jan Friedl).

Sisters (Robin Thurston), Front Theatre, 1976. L–R: Ponch Hawkes, Jane Clifton, Suarupo, Jenny Jones, Claire Dobbin, Richard Murphett. Seated: Robin Laurie, Kerry Dwyer, Ursula Harrison, Margo Nash. (Ponch Hawkes)

and preferably both. Women had to shift for themselves and by 1973 they had done so, setting up the Women's Theatre Group on the loan of a smell of an oil rag in what Sue Ingleton regarded as her old room in the Tower. To get in the Front Theatre shows, female talent was obliged to be versatile and forbearing. In *Waltzing Matilda*, a polymorphous, nationalist pantomime, Evelyn played a jumbuck born of the Virgin Mary. The same show gave Jane Clifton a chance to go straight in a funded situation: the role of Cupid, a koala. She was also the Stage Manager, something most shows previously had not had and which most performers did not wish to be. Ingleton, back from England and ready for anything smacking of bent gender, played the Swagman who loved the bosomy jumbuck.

Women looked swell in tails and smokings. Sometimes they looked like armed mimes. Female appearance, offstage, often had a paramilitary edge to it, like the warriors or campfollowers of irregular armies. Snappy, feral androgynes stepped out and about the traps. The beret was back. And sandals and sensible shoes, although dressing up high fantastically with Lucy in the Sky with Diamonds was still popular. There was abundant silk, velvet, cheesecloth and patchwork. Curtains, tablecloths, coverlets from ransacked trousseaux were worn by mar-auding muskrat ramblers cruising the Reefer Cabaret or Much More Ballroom. Part of the look was the touch, and a touch of the orient predominated.

The blokes on the other hand, tended not to touch. In the pub, where they kept abreast of events, embracing, fondling and caressing were frowned upon. Thumping was possible, jabbing and kicking, the odd cuff, OK. Women only entered the pubs with cheques to sign, inamorata to meet, or ultimata to deliver. Few actually sat down. Fay Mokotow did, with her legs tucked neatly beneath her in a pub asana, as befitted a Tribe survivor, to work over the Grant Strategy, say, with Timlin. Fay's liquid brown eyes surveyed the smokehazed shambles of many a long and liquid lunch. She could maintain the focus on the crisis of the hour at Stewarts when the afternoon sun strained through the apricot curtain to fall in a heap on the unspeakable carpet next to Dickins, and Timlin's aimless whistle filled the pauses around four, or when the bar was roaring and ribald after six, sometimes even when it got venomous, forgetful and irrevocable in the fatal hour before closing.

Let us close in on Dickins as he lies there, next to bald legal eagle Ed Flannery, who having approached the bar has now fallen from his stool. Barry had stretches of Christopher Brennan by heart and had been overcome by bardic bends deep in the first stanza of *The Wanderer*. Nobody could tell if he was making it up. Dickins made himself up, although by no means self-composed, for when not comatose, he was always in a state of agitation, or whipping himself towards one. I mean he invented personae to play in Carltonia, a Bohemia he botched up for himself. Barry arrived from Reservoir the way glory-struck heroes of French romance came to Paris from their provinces. Having invested the dump with mystique and allure, he came to conquer it. A small pen and wash drawing he sold my mother, in the persona of the derelict genius, illustrates a scene from this daggy *vie bohème*. (It was done after he had been shaken up, well we all were, by the raw brutality of Ray Mooney's *Every Night, Every Night*.) A self-portrait with Jacks in Little Gore Street: Dickins centre, holding false teeth and manuscript, is caught in the torchlight of one of two sergeants of police, the one with the warty penile nose and tacks for false teeth. Dickins bows as if reflexively, a gummy, hunchbacked pierrot. There is something of Guernica in the play of light,

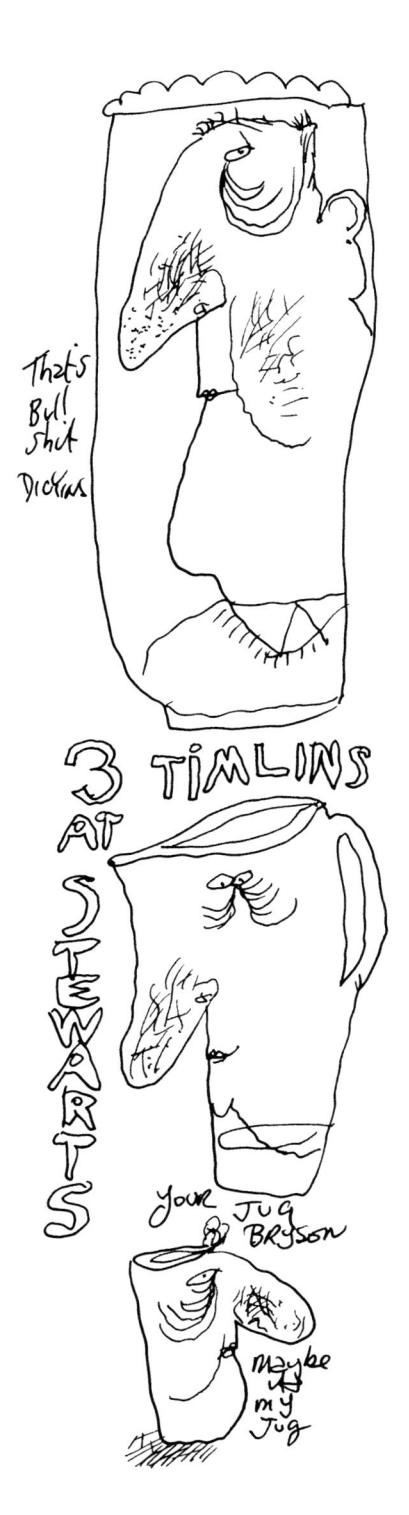

3 at Stewarts. (Barry Dickins)

though the lovers caught embracing in the garbage can are French and the graffitti on the dirty brick wall:

> *the fountain*
> *leaps and flowers*
> *in many roses*
> *the crystal petals*
> *breaking, breaking*
> *forever*
> *are changed to*
> *falling tears*

is signed Charles Baudelaire. He first haunted the streets as Benny Lettuce. Perhaps Italian, some orphic orphan, starveling poet, who dropped his battered little spirex in my letterbox, a supplicant. Benny enlarged into K. G. Fish, who was more your rag and bone man of letters on the mean streets of Brunswick, his tremendous tin ear cocked to the music of the spheres, the people's tribune and surrealistic confidante. K. G. Fish blurred into Dickins. He attempted to pass himself off as a descendant of the great Charles, despite being a vowel astray. Few but the dyslexic continue to believe him. There are some resemblances it may be argued: the persistent prodigality of output, a wild veering between sentiment and grotesquerie in the work, a performance compulsion, the need for attention, the taste for actresses. Dickins swears there was a clerical error at a register's office. A sensitive soul, he will offer violence if gainsaid too far. He has the stocky, all-of-a-piece physique of the stockfish. The head/neck alignment is quite fused, the neck astonishingly pulled in.

Truth is Barry Dickins made up all the denizens of Carltonia, the boys in the pub, like a dinkum Damon Runyon. Danny Kramer soliciting at the door of the Albion, Magog and his grog; Danny's protégé Steve Mastare, potpoetaster, obsessively spiralling his hair; Harry Horsetrough, dead dapper in a titfer; Ed, out to it on the floor beside him; the lot of us. Gab is his gift and he has the voice of a butcher at the Vic Markets to pass it on; the bars, restaurants and parties of Carltonia were his stage for spiels extemporised on his favorite themes—Yass, neckchops, teeth, David Mitchell, the ghosts of showbusiness past and their relationship to the Old Postal Exchange, whatever—the raves of Dickins, performance-playwright, are among the funniest at which I ever pissed myself laughing. On a good night. In conventional spaces he was less accomplished and cavalier with cues, loath to repeat himself. Word that Dickins was in the house was dreaded by actors. He seemed unable to

A sensitive soul. (Barry Dickins)

Barry Dickins lights up a clown. (Peter Hosking)

CRACKED ACTORS LEAD TO SMILES WITH A CROCODILE

Arthur Horner cartoon of *Fool's Shoe Hotel*. (*The Age*)

maintain the passive posture expected of an audience. Between dozes, invention would rise in him, reddening his neck, engorging his head, to burst out of him, slumped or crouched there aggressively, in honks. Fay, arbiter of propriety, poured a jug of cold water over him and he came to his senses, to hop into their systematic derangement once more.

For various reasons there were those who kept clear of the pub or maintained a position superior to it. The group was divided along drug lines: depressant v narcotic, Alcohol v Dope. Timlin and Smith were terms in this polarity. The Celtic, catholic, wobbily married rump parked itself in the pub, as it had since time immemorial. The single, separated, or fluctuating cohabitants of the Tower had a low tolerance for alcohol but would condone, indeed abuse, everything else. Of course there were many like myself, who enjoyed a catholicity of ingestion, an oecumenical abuse. Lindzee was to be seen in the pub but usually to work out as

Freaks. L–R: Greig Pickhaver, Bain Laurie, Jon Hawkes, Max Gillies at Christmas party 1976. (Ruth Maddison)

an antibody, bearding the lion lushes; he wasn't quite at home there. He came to pick up on the latest with an entourage of likely lags—Shuv'us, Gallagher, Billy Tisdall, say, mahogany-faced, like harpooneers off the *Pequod*, out on a dismal spree, looking to score.

Smoking was unconfined. Timlin avoided narcotic admixture. Prudentially concentrating his mind on the demon drink, he counselled wrestling with a maximum of two drugs at a time. The weak kif of Carlton was especially rife in kitchens. A joint and a bit of a rave had succeeded the Bex and a nice lie down as accompaniment to a cup of tea. The nice lie down was now more frequently enjoyed *à deux*. The tea was fashionably a tisane of camomile, rosehip, jasmine—another sign of an oriental drift to incense, unguents, tantrics, macrobiotics, to Eastern aesthetics and mysticism.

Naturally the catholic literary ascendancy poopooed these foreign influences and paraphernalia. Oakley, for ex-ample, would have no truck with that scene. With the air of a prelate unfrocked but still buttoned up, he surveyed it, straight as a ramrod, pent, occasionally releasing high stacatto guffaws, sucking on anally constrictive, low-tar cigarettes. Oakley joined the group

> because one Saturday morning (in 1971) Graeme Blundell and Timlin arrived and asked me to write a play about the Catholic Church. I had written three plays for La Mama, one of which Graeme had directed (*A Lesson in English*). So we had some approximate value of each other's talents. They saw the piece as a revue-style treatment, a satirical/critical treatment. Then they went away for me to think about it. I did and thought I'd base the play on Mannix. I suggested this to them (not to any committee at that stage, thank heaven) and they gave me the go-ahead.

So I wrote the script, Romeril and Williamson wrote some lyrics and Lorraine Milne wrote the music. There were fortuitous aspects. Spence was perfect for Mannix, and Gillies' genius for mimicry hadn't been fully realised till he did Santamaria.

The success of *The Feet of Daniel Mannix* kept the place going at a crucial time and it built up a good working relationship between Bruce and Max, which was exploited a year later in *Beware of Imitations*. Of the genesis of that show Oakley remembers somewhat shrewishly:

There were some group or sub-group discussions about what should go in a Menzies play. It was here I learned the art of the group-developed show. What you do, if you're the writer—a title not always acknowledged by some in the group, this being regarded as worthy but no more than a journeyman, a tradesman, don't get too many big ideas about yourself, thanks, just because you work with your head and not with your hands, thankyou Chairman Mao. The art consists of nodding your head at almost every collective suggestion except the most asinine, then quietly going away and dropping what you didn't like. Out of this overtness (the play-group) and covertness (me writing it after) came a basic script from me, which, in rehearsals, combusted into highly creative scenes. In this Max and Bruce got on as if in a dream, as if they were having an affair, as if they could do no wrong—and their little improvisational romance was creatively directed and assisted by Bill Hannan. It was the most creative and exciting improvising I've ever been involved in, and made all the Pram Factory's tenets seem to be right—but the reason was not so much the tenets as the talent.

Barry never went a-dope-hunting, in Tigerland or any other land. Around the shared households of North Fitzroy there was always somebody on a dope run, or waiting to score, a dealer neverendingly imminent. Prodigious amounts of time and money (proportional to income) were outlayed in securing drug recreation. A vain pursuit of pleasure in defective vehicles for some buddha on a stick out at Templestowe, or in quest of microdots in Sunshine, would fetch up in Johnnies Green Room, snookered by Motherwell, speedrabbiting on about Burroughs and Céline, our discourse slowly strangled by dawn's greasy fingers.

7 Head fer the Hills (and Stasis)

With damn near 100 members on the cleaning roster, to the undistracted eye the Pram was always grungily ill-kept. This was because everybody had more pressing roles to play. Everybody wanted to perform. Everybody had the right to perform. Nobody was just an actor in a play. You were an actor/writer/director, or a designer/wardrobe/puppeteer/stage-manager, or perhaps a strong man/juggler/entrepreneur. We cast ourselves as renaissance persons often from necessity, simply because some bastard hybridisation was what nobody else wanted to do. Greig Pickhaver for example was well regarded as a stagehand/setmaker/would-be actor/proven babysitter. His comic talent went unrecognised until he branched out to 3CR, Triple J and TV, becoming a language-generating clown, 'one of two boofheads talking in a darkened room', and going on to win international renown by taking the piss out of the Olympic dream. H. G. Nelson remembers:

> I carved meself a niche in the good ol' Aussie avant-garbo, Fitzroy/Carlton days. Hellcyonicidal days of horseplay and hullaballoo at the Pram! As if it was yesterday, natch. What a meet of minds! I rubbed shoulders there with some of the friskiest feminist fillies of me generation. Bloody near lost a couple of digits to a flashpot in a special effect. The unstoppable Cosmo Topper nearly blew his face off, I recall. Me mate Johnny Harrigan, the well-known racing identity from Sydney, was on the scene there in the early stages. Trying to buy the world rights for *Dimboola*, and he reckons there'd be a crate in it, see, if he got the right deal. Never saw it. Not a taste! Funny the little things you remember, isn't it? Like that fully operational service revolver that went moonlighting from *The Dudders* jittabugger show one night . . . Saw some service in a chemist I believe. Heh. And speaking of darkened rooms, who was that A-rab from Tassie,

★ Head fer the Hills (and Stasis) ★   77

The Timor Show, 1976, factory tour. Front L–R: Larry Meltzer, Richard Murphett, Greig Pickhaver, Michael Price. Second: Lorna Hannan, Robin Laurie, Caz Howard. Rear: uncommitted, lunching workers. (Ponch Hawkes)

the bloke who spelt himself with an apostrophe—Shuv'us! I'm stuck with an image of him, his face all pink spots from his impetigo ointment, a bare foot from the screen, staring at the Teev, in a darkened room. Flickering. I dunno, wacky ol' days, eh?

Competition for comic spots in the group was as fierce as between the old-time bananas of vaudeville. Best parts were usually spoken for in an unspoken sort of a way. Max Gillies, Bruce Spence, Peter Cummins, Graeme Blundell pecked first. Evelyn Krape, albeit peckerless, got a look in. Spence and Williamson gave each other an early symbiotic boost. Gillies began to hit the straps in Oakley's plays with Spence. *The Feet of Daniel Mannix* and *Beware of Imitations* set him off on a career of satirical mimicry, a parabola of politicians rising (or descending) from R. G. Menzies to R. J. Hawke.

In 1975 Max, hankering after the performer autonomy ideal of the early days, felt an urge to liberate himself from the written word. He proposed a comedy workshop in which performers would develop their own comic personae. Performer parthenogenesis! Get it out of our own heads! Cut out the middleperson! He'd always wanted to appear in a chicken suit. Napoleon in a chicken suit perhaps: 'I am ze 19th-century boomer, bong soir. Voulez-vous ze pullet in every po? Avec un whiff de

The Hills Family Show, Front Theatre, 1975. Fanny (Evelyn Krape), Clifton (Rob Meldrum), Sandringham (Bill Garner), Adelaide (Sue Ingleton), Antigone (Fay Mokotow), Winston (Tony Taylor), Fitzroy (Max Gillies) in curtain tableau of the play (*The Accidental Poke*, by John Romeril) within the play. (Ponch Hawkes)

grapeshot?' Or whatever. But no more feeding us the lines! No more Writer-Diktat, however bloody good the lines are. How after all had Keaton and Laurel and Hardy and Chaplin created their characters? Almost everybody in the collective rolled up to the Project Meeting. Max was forced to declare for his instincts against the orthodoxy. He insisted that not everybody was suitable. Cutting out a cast with the optimum mix of skills and types was a process of exercises, argy-bargy and steely manoeuvring. Protestation, desperate appeals, the gnashing of teeth and the quack of lame ducktrinaire democrats was heard long after dark. Eventually Tony Taylor, Evelyn Krape, Fay Mokotow, Sue Ingleton, Rob Meldrum, Bill Garner, Bob Thorneycroft, Buzz Leeson and Max Gillies had the floor to themselves.

Max had a vague notion that whatever they were on about, they were going to play performers of some kind. Tony Taylor knew exactly. He was rapt. A pierrot in a Beano comic, he would have been drawn with a lightbulb over his nut:

> Let us drink from the very fountainhead of a discredited tradition. We are a theatrical family—touring variety acts—our time is past, we're on our uppers—TV, no talent, going down the come-back trail. All of us rivals . . .

Something like that. A wizard wheeze. It just so happened that the collective had been persuaded to acquire a magnificent set of brass handbells (along with pictures and posters) that had belonged to the legendary Lynch Family, renowned glassophonists and campanologists. Questions had been raised at the time as to the utility of the purchase. Cloth-

Reverse ventriloquy: Tootle disempowers Winston and Fitzroy. (Ponch Hawkes)

covered, they crowded out dressing-room–cum–office space and were at risk of being converted into low-grade heroin. Right there, in the Lynches, was a model from which to make themselves up. Buzz Leeson began to tinker with the bells. Someone thought it a good bad joke to call themselves the Hills Family and name the members topographically. Buzz would have no truck with funny names. Evelyn sang:

> The Hills are alive!

Tony became Winston, Australia's own Mel Torme, heart and soul of the Hills workshop. He had grown up in England with a love for the kind of low–middlebrow entertainment that dared not speak its name around the Pram, or not without irony, not just for fun. Here was the opportunity to sing 'Moonlight on Velvet' and 'What are you Doing the Rest of your

Life' with impunity. He began composing songs in the genre and letting out a voice that did more than justice to their execution. He workshopped a Vegas lounge act croon with an epileptic vibrato, his brows furrowed to the point of blackout. He insisted that everyone elaborate a character biography. Bill Garner, a veteran of public biography sessions in the Tower, could do this with ease. Tony sorted the complex, ever-expanding, lurid Family history into a Tree, pretending the truth of it all in a way that bugged the Brechtian in Gillies. Windy's relationship with his family was cankered. The care of accident-prone but indestructible Granny Fanny Hills to whom he was bound by love and hate, over form guide and potty, wound him up closer to grandmatricide as seasons wore on.

Evelyn was Granny. She spent a deal of time knitting woollen varicose veins into lisle stockings and took an acrobatic approach to her character. In her wheelchair, she became a randy, geriatric liberty horse, forever bolting back to the past out of control. As workshop transformed into rehearsal, Evelyn's commitments with the Women's Theatre Group often left the wheelchair empty and liberties were taken. She would however fearlessly seize on the excesses fantasised during her absence. Evelyn never ceased to be amazed by audiences taking her for real, despite these extravagances.

Romeril provided them all with bits in *The Accidental Poke*, a flash, C. J. Dennis pastiche, a play within a play for the Hills to cock up in a low-Pirandellian fashion. Its authorship was fittingly appropriated by the character Max played, the sodden Fitzroy Hills, failed playwright, wit and sage, now dominated by Tootle, a ventriloquist doll, with injured innocence congealed in eyes round as fried eggs.

Fay Mokotow and Rob Meldrum went terpsichorean. Their characters sought to raise the tone of the family by flapping toward the Empyrean of Art. Fay was Antigone, a *danseuse-exotique-manquée*, with a panting heart and a thing about Chekhov's *Seagull*. Rob, looking like a neat, pint-sized Abbie Hoffman, was Clifton, tap-dancing fury with serious ambitions as a choreographer. From Roy Jones, a ballroom trouper, they learnt the Art of Simultaneous Dancing and presented *Midnight Encounters In Canberra*. As their billing claimed: 'You have never seen feats like these'.

Bill Garner, after Conan Doyle, picking up on a continuing sceptical fascination with the paranormal, created a manic-depressive, boring old fart, Sandringham Hills, working professionally as Magneto Master Mind. From the underworld of occult Bill recovered certain hoary mysteries. The secret of 'mental transmission' he refuses to divulge to this day. Magneto was assisted by his servant Tarza—Tony very surly and daggy in turban, dhoti and socks.

Sue Ingleton was Adelaide Hills, the Irish vocaliste/comedienne. Of a certain age, teeth and smiles radiating at a dangerously high voltage and afflicted with an accent inherited from her Granny Fanny (née

Kelly). Buzz Leeson directed the music, unsmilingly grinding his teeth as David Hills. He left before the Hills's subsequent Victorian country tour to become a Millionaire, one of an electrified quartet of them. He was succeeded at the piano by Jack Weiner, who gave the world his superannuated infant phenomenon with duck fixation. In this Jack followed to some degree in the nimble footsteps of Bob Thorneycroft, the choreographer of their collapsible ballet. He contributed Bobby Bojangles, his idiot-savant hoofer to the in-house production. Bill Hannan, a pigeon among cats, was there to vouchsafe the odd line and an 'outside eye'. A thankless function. Progressively alienated, the eye fell out. Laurel Frank and the Basement Manifold (Bob Daly, Kelvin Gedye, Graeme Isaac . . .) handled the technical side. The BM had by now exfoliated into the Popeye Puppets and the infrastructure of Circus Oz. Laurel was Stage Management, appearing occasionally as the depressed Mona Vale, since one of the charms of the Hills was their uncertainty about whether they were on or off stage, or where the audience was. Jon Hawkes went on tour as Albert Alp, the manager who claimed a kinship with the family as the third cousin, twice removed of Seymour Klutz, the second husband of Adelaide's sister, the late Ginger. He would appear and juggle this and that and go off to Mount Adelaide.

The Hills do choreography (by Bob Thorneycroft). Mona Vale (Laurel Frank), stage-manager, is uncertainly supported by Winston at left. Antigone by Sandringham in the foreground. (Ponch Hawkes)

Hills emplaning for interstate tour. Jack Weiner joins Magneto Mastermind and company as a pianistic infant phenomenon. Fitzroy is now controlled by a sinister usurper lusting after Antigone. (Ponch Hawkes)

A typescript of the show, roughly transcribed and filed away some time after it had gone on the road, bears the following disclaimer: 'A bare outline of the happening . . . merely a guideline. Improvisational skills are needed . . . certain acts may need to be changed depending on the talents of the cast available'. There is a nice period ring to 'happening'. A bill of acts from a lost tradition provided the structure to improvise around. Every night began with improvisation. Before the audience arrived, they were there, grumbling and jibing each other into character, and usually Tony before anyone else. Through the life of the show his *lazzi* with granny became more extended and extreme. In deepest Gippsland the audience was led out of a community hall towards a level crossing where he threatened to abandon her. At the Bondi Pavilion he trundled her over the sands towards surf and shark attack. On the bus to St Arnaud all of them got dressed, alighted in character and stayed in character all day around the town. Granny and Windy went off shoplifting. Fitzroy spent a pleasant afternoon in a beer garden with a crippled wedge-tailed eagle.

There was no interval for the performers. Windy cooked up popcorn venomously. Clifton asked people to hear his lines. Family squabbling continued. The action was all making up, breaking down, its comedy classically predicated on failure, dysfunction and entropy. From their initial non-appearance The Hills become progressively unstuck and they collapse in a burlesque ballet and brawl. With a Hibberdesque cadenza of showbiz bromides—'Ferment and effervesce!'—feigning angina, Fanny, the matriarch sticks them back together again:

'Give. Give to each other. Give to your public.'

The Lynch Family Bells are wheeled in and they all chime in. The audience is enchanted.

The Hills Family Show was the summa of group creation for the APG, a comic triumph. Unburdened, funnily enough, by social or political conscience, unashamedly dedicated to the bluebird of happiness, they were an ensemble of characters as memorable as any that the group's writers came up with. It could still be touring the South Island of New Zealand, the performers as decrepit as their creations.

If it was an exclamatory point at the end of a line, for some of the performers it was not enough. Rob Meldrum had seen a notice beneath MTC letterhead on the board at the Pram about a six-month course in Voice. Carrillo Gantner had arranged (with funds from the Whitlam-boosted Arts Council and the Myer Foundation) for Rowena Balos to come over from New York. Meldrum went along. He copped a bit of friendly flak in enemy territory but he knew he was onto something. He had joined the group in '73 with *Dimboola*. Before all of us Pram Factory 'heavies', arrayed in a post-Stewarts somnolence along the wedding breakfast table, none of us with our lines down, he delivered all of Leonardo Radish, pat. We all sat up and applauded this deft, dapperly afro'd virtuoso, quaintly dressed up in sports jacket and tie (as himself, we discovered, not as Leonardo), with a rather actorly, faintly pommified resonance to his voice. This odd man out fitted into the group nicely as a utility player, but like that first ready-made character, he found a lot of the work unchallenging and was hungry for Experiment. Enlargement. Development. Depth. Like a lot of the membership, his training was limited to drama at university before drama schools existed. Bodies had been exercised by everything from tapdancing to tai chi, but acting as a craft, a mystery, went unexamined. It was fine for Joe Bolza to have his mime skills and Bob Thorneycroft his dance and acrobatics. Voice Production was reactionary, Elocution dispensed by broken down divas. The powers Evelyn Krape and Jan Friedl had developed were only used in parody until Hibberd supplied them with a vehicle in *A Toast to Melba* and *The Overcoat*.

By the time Rowena Balos came to town, many of us were running out of breath. Native wit and animal spirits were feeling the strain. Rowena's mission was to continue 'freeing the natural voice', the project her own teacher Kristin Linklater had begun and outlined in her book of that title. Its provenance went back to Elsie Fogarty in England, to Iris Warren at LAMDA, and included in its ambit the exercises of Moshe Feldenkrais and the technique of Australia's own Frederick Alexander. Meldrum felt he was being fed what he needed. Days, weeks, were spent in slow meditative work on the floor, in circles, 'contacting the breath', 'integrating it with feeling', 'reprogramming the body', surprising it into doing things it can't. Gently, slowly, avoiding 'end-gaining', they learned to release the jaw and all the tensions of gullet, guts and groin, to connect breath to image and image to sound. He found it stimulating to be doing this among new, interesting, non-Pram-Factory people—John Gaden, Gerda Nicholson, Nancy Black, Wendy Robertson—and it was in this circle he met Jenny Kemp. Jenny looked doubtfully at the seemingly preppy enthusiast to whom she was obliged to give a lift in her bright trippy van just back from commune country.

Full of the good oil, snotty-nosed Clifton Hills approached his Aunt Adelaide one night before the Hills went up, and told her: 'Look, there's another way you could be working. It's your mannerisms, if only you . . .'. 'Well fuck you Clifton', said Adelaide and went off in a huff. Sue was rather pleased with herself and her first bit of writing for performance. She was getting laughs, she thought she'd done good. She was rattled by Rob watching her work and doubting it but she was also jealous of this new Knowledge he laid claim to. She was jealous too of his freedom from children that allowed him to go out after it. There was a part of her that knew that it had to be harder than what had become the Pram Factory style of 'just getting up and doing it, open-ended bucketing out'. She was sick of the baggage she was bringing on stage with her. She was ready for something more stringent, ascetic even.

Response was minimal to Meldrum's notice on the Pram Factory notice board proposing a show about women writers of the 20th century, starting off with workshops à la Balos. Jane Clifton and Carol Porter came to the first meeting, but they decided this breathing, lying on the floor, rolling through their spines stuff was not for them. Too uneventful, too inward. Yvonne Marini (brimful of Grotowski) and Kerry Dwyer (seeking another power base in the group) came and stayed a while. They both wanted to direct according their own lights and soon found this was not their opportunity. Susi Potter diffidently hung in the potent little ring that became *Stasis*: Sue, Susi, Rob, Roz de Winter and later Jenny Kemp.

'Darkness and stasis', a line from a Sylvia Plath poem, gave them the name for their first show in the Back Theatre, 'made up of our own dreams and some of Sylvia's poems which we seized on as having images that were tough and humorous and seemed to reach our centres'. They liked the sound of the word. Checking the sense of it in the OED: 'a stoppage of the circulation of the fluids in the body', they panicked briefly, then abundant rationalisations welled up. 'The still point that dances neither from nor towards' in Eliot's *Burnt Norton*, that was where they were heading. The name stuck. As Ecstasis was Greek for being out of your self, Stasis was rooting yourself like a tree in the present and tapping the primitive energies usually the reserve of lovers, children and the insane. They rejected the idea of a performance ever being established or a matter of repetition. 'Our work is to make ourselves available to the moment and whether that moment is in Sylvia's life, or Peer Gynt's life, what matters is the text and the openness of ourselves to each other and to our audience.'

None of this was part of the APG style, and their series of modest proposals to the collective was not well received. Hibberd, attacking for the Vernaculars, told them they had no business messing about with Poetry and the foreign Classical Repertoire: '. . . we should go on building our own . . . Peer Gynt is a closet play, a school play . . .'. They might have rebutted by pointing out Jack's own forays into Baudelaire and Gogol, but the Stases weren't any good at debating and just felt guilty, alienated. Part of their angst was that the Vernaculars had not supplied the deep potent language with which they wanted to engage. They withdrew to non-Pram-Factory rehearsal and performance space. They organised school tours using material from their work in progress, applied for (and were refused) a grant, in a game attempt at self-sufficiency. Susi Potter opted out. Jenny Kemp opted in as an 'outside eye'. Like it or not, she was obliged to perform in *Antony and Cleopatra*. Stasis clung fiercely to the premise that if you weren't a performer, up there, in the moment, you

Stasis does *Peer Gynt* (Henrik Ibsen), St Mark's Hall, Fitzroy, 1976. L–R: Sue Ingleton, Suarupo, Rob Meldrum. (John Gollings)

weren't part of it. The bonding in the group grew deep and strong and so did the quality of the work.

The texts were not sacred. Ibsen and Shakespeare were edited, stripped down, intimately possessed. As they let the language work on them and recovered a structure and meaning for themselves, they communicated it with the simplest of means. They all knew all of the roles of the recreated text and delighted in playing them across gender, picking them out of a hat before a performance of *Antony and Cleopatra*. In the *Young Peer Gynt*, Peer was whoever wore the waistcoat, a shifting incarnation, the more vivid for being split. Huge old PMG cable drums (fallen off a truck) rumbled awesomely about the wooden-floored, whitewashed St Marks Hall. These, with basic lighting and Neil Giles on percussion, were the elements of the *mise-en-scène*. The rest was language, quickened by breath, coloured by sound, poetry made sexy, of the body as they had learnt to transform it.

The group broke up when Rob and Sue went back to vaudeville in *Back to Bourke St*. Roz, her nose a little out of joint, and Jenny Kemp, her eyebrows slightly raised, soldiered on to collaborate with the Brothers Grimm on the schools circuit. Jenny went blazing off as director/dramatist. Her version of D. M. Thomas's *The White Hotel* remains seared in my memory. Sue went off on the road in Europe and returned a fully fledged *femme de théâtre*, to create a rout of astonishing characters.

Early in the Stasis solstice the phone rang hot with calls for Roz de Winter from Hector Crawford. He was casting the mother in his new series *The Sullivans*, and when Roz politely declined the offer he, as producers will, became obsessive. Bouquets of flowers arrived and the Stases said, 'Well, go on, take it!' 'No,' said she, continuing to listen to her inner voice, 'this is more important.' Roz, ironically no longer much enjoying performance, weighed down by the severity of her judgment of herself, became the frustrating, maddening, inspiring mentor of Stasis.

Roz de Winter had been in the performance game longer than anybody else at the APG. Professional flights into make-believe had begun on the wireless as a child, newly arrived from England. She played on the telly when it started. She was in the Union Theatre Company with Wal Cherry before Emerald Hill. She was drawn away by the magnet of Lecoq and had served six years in English weekly rep. She went to Japan, to the Kyogen theatre, and returned to work with George Ogilvie and Rodney Fisher in Melbourne and Sydney. When I asked her about the past she went all of a-tremble. She didn't want to talk about all that stuff. I remembered her performing in Adelaide, trippingly elegant in a Marivaux comedy with the South Australian Theatre Company. She was utterly incurious about when or what play. 'I was what Jan Friedl wanted to become—a leading lady in the establishment theatre', she said and sniggered like a naughty gnome.

She had got the boot from the Comedy Theatre for being out of her tree. Escaping with some relief the persona of an establishment actress, she first came to the Pram as an audience member with some friends, to be greeted by Bill Garner in performance, practising his alienation effect. All grin like the Cheshire cat, Bill cried, 'The bourgeoisie has arrived!' and gestured to Roz and her companions. They turned and left. She was at the time producing things for the CAE and had approached Jack Hibberd about doing *Dimboola* with the Eltham Little Theatre. As it turned out they decided they would rather do *Sailor Beware*, but Jack remembered that somewhat distraught little woman in a mac when he and Williamson were casting about for someone to play the mother of the bride with the APG in '73.

Thus Roz came back to the Pram. What impressed her about the rehearsals in the Back Theatre was the way people at the end of the day just walked away from each other, simply left. This absence of a code of feigned politeness suited her fine. Having come unstuck in darlingdom, she was happy to discover that being in the alternative theatre meant not having to say goodbye. So amazed was she by the crackling egos around her, by the assumption that actors had a say, by their 'empowerment', that it was some time before she said anything. She stayed around and was in lots of shows. Most dramatically, she gave up being Roz de Winter, turned orange, went to India and took up the role of Suarupo. There were precedents for people lighting off to the Orient in the Collective but they were never seen again. Suarupo came back.

Suarupo's eyes stare at you, questioningly, is it? Seeker's eyes, deep green ones, that seem to be looking for more. Her gaze makes you grumble inwardly: Why does she moon so, beam mystic-wise upon me, why did she have to change her name . . . ? Then you discover it's an error of parallax, that you're way off-beam. Suarupo is shortsighted, she has lost her contact lenses and cannot afford new ones. You are a perplexing blur.

★ ★ ★

The former Stasis ensemble (minus Jenny Kemp) visited me for a rave for this record. They were barely through the Interviewer's fly-door before they were divulging last night's dreams. Sue had dreamt of laying a turd on Richard Murphett and Jenny Kemp's floor. Suarupo of Bill Garner. Rob wasn't telling. An afternoon of recollection (during which Bill Garner kept popping up like a running gag in the oddest way) was followed by a monstrous pot of Boho gumbo. Mid-gumbo came a moment when Suarupo stopped being daffy and discontinuous and her eyes caught me. 'When you look at me,' she said, 'you look at yourself. What's worrying you about me is what is worrying you about you. What you like about me, you like about you. You are looking in a mirror.' The tables were turned on the Interviewer.

'Are you interviewing yourself?', the ex-Stases wanted to know. 'Where are you in the picture? Claim the work', they urged. 'I'm trying', I said.

8 Group Creation: Some Little Known Facts

THE IMPORTANCE OF THE PRAM FACTORY as a playhouse and the primacy of its associated playwrights have been laboured by one Melbourne critic. The players are neglected in *The State of Play*, a headmasterly register, grounded on the assumption that 'the playwright is the life blood of the theatre'. Len Radic has ever bugled thus and his account of all the Pram plays is strictly reliable. Len with Vladimir and Estragon kept his appointment. However the magic of wordsmiths was the chief magic of neither the Pram nor La Mama. This proceeded from the reckless, indefatigable creativity of performers unbound. The genius of these places resided in their ephemera and was to be found in tremendous trifles Radic does not consider, in the Suppershows for example.

Beginning at La Mama early in the '70s, Suppershows were an outlet for the wild ambition of performers seldom cast in plays and an occupation for idle musicians. At the Pram the tradition was continued, but when no one made supper any more, they became the Late Shows—*The Love Show, The Antimacassar Show, The Women's Weeklies*. On 27 November 1973, the day the Maharishi predicted the end of the world, the Great Stumble Forward with Skyhooks provided *The Suddenly Last Supper Show*. It was at these events you felt the freewheeling, ad hoc spirit of the place. You caught it bopping to the Gents ('the band with integrity'—Tim Coldwell, Bob Daly and Buzz Leeson) or, minimally, on one occasion when George Dreyfus and Paul Grabowsky played for a single couple because no one else turned up. It was to be found in anarchic balls-ups and fugitive comic epiphanies like *The Sennet Icecream Show* with Rod Quantock, Mary Kenneally, Geoff Brookes and Steve Blackburn in the Back Theatre. It was present with Peter 'After-Dinner Moose' Lilley, the truck-lovin' Eltham hillbilly, Johnny 'Cosmo' Topper and friends doing never-to-be-published originals like *Mechanics in a Relaxed Manner* or *Gone To See A Man About A Dog*—off-the-wall, *naif* performance, got up in fits and starts from smudgy, gestetnered samizdat.

The talents and contribution of the playwrights are not in question. They have been much analysed and justly applauded. At the time it was they who felt abused and marginalised, the devalued, disregarded objects of condescension, angst which Williamson has feelingly recollected on numerous occasions. Their writings were like so many jungle gyms in a playground. They were swarmed over and taken for granted. Writers were given a low profile, a physical impossibility in the case of Wmson. Nevertheless a good part of the continuity and success of Australian plays in the '70s was due to a series of performers whose larrikinous and theatrical intelligence had a profound influence on the style and direction of those plays. Such informing performers were by no means restricted to the Pram Factory. Writers of the Nimrod stable such as Blair, Boddy or Ellis would also acknowledge the difference made by these actor/editor/provocateurs at large on their scripts. Infuriating, silly and savvy by turn, it was their intuitions, excessiveness and commonsense that brought a dramaturgical dimension to rehearsal.

Trouble was, once included in the traditionally privileged dialogue between director and playwright, the performers insisted on talking amongst themselves. The bastards wanted a part to play in the primary stuff, in the choice of the material, the setting of basic intentions. They began to work out the dynamics, discover the dialectics, revel in the jouissance of Group Creation.

For after a generous collaborative genesis, Pram Factory playwrights had tended to go back to writing plays in time-honoured solitude. By 1972 they were largely men intent on getting their texts performed just as they had conceived them. Although in the upsurges of group creation—the revues, *The Migrant Show*, *The Timor Show*, *Back to Bourke St*, *The Hills Family Show*—the writers made themselves available, once having established their voice and audience, Authors became impatient with rash untutored Players. The literary authority of *Stretch of the Imagination* behind him, Hibberd's hackles were increasingly hairtriggered. Oakley, now a comic novelist in hardback, would bristle over control of the jokes. Authors assume Authority. To this end Hibberd began to direct himself. His loose-leaf prentice scripts were replaced by final drafts, sturdily bound in plastic, with a professional, finished look.

In the heart of the APG there persisted a desire to create as a group. Scripts that were developed collaboratively were hard to distinguish from

Mechanics in a Relaxed Manner. Garage theatre with Peter Lilley, Sally McNae, unknown, Cosmo D. Topper. (Jane Clifton)

litter. Romeril, Robertson and Dickins remained more or less willing to keep drafting until the last moment. Before a preview Romeril might walk in, greatcoated and beanied against the cold, cradling a Remington in the crook of his left arm, and gingerly proffer a nerve-stoked cast member a rewrite. A group-developed script only became anything like an integral text when a prompt copy was required to line up technical cues. No performer ever wholly possessed the entire script of *Betty Can Jump* or *The Hills Family Show*. This was in keeping with what Hibberd declared in the programme notes for *Marvellous Melbourne* (given away with a free coffee):

> a theatrical event [should be] the expression of a creative ensemble and not that of one or two despotic figures . . . our aim is to prevent the ossification of finality . . . to encourage development as long as [*Marvellous Melbourne*] is performed.

In the early days, of all the writers who subscribed to Group Creation, Williamson was the most conscientious. His overnight write-ups of the ideas and impros for *The Sonia Knee and Thigh Show* were a crafted development of workshop proceedings. Romeril on the other hand was often stimulated to take off into the unknown. In the case of *Dimboola*, successive productions marked a progressive adherence to a text. At the Melburnian Reception Rooms and La Mama there was a lot of improvising before and during the show. By 1973 at the Pram and directed by Williamson, the text was delivered almost as clean as a radio play. Out in the theatre restaurant circuit the performers, Maurie Fields for a shining example, took charge of the jokes again.

Authors were seldom thanked for their pains and their success did not breed respect. Williamson was abused: Voyeur! Sellout! Naturalist! More straightforward production houses like the MTC or even Nimrod, in which an Author was a client, not a pariah with administrative and janitorial responsibilities, beckoned invitingly.

Dorothy Hewett asked me somewhere in the mid '70s when I was going to write a play by myself. Seemed like the Earth Mother thought I was gutless, wanting, wayward. Group Creation looked to her like kindergarten, therapy, or another way to madness. Early attempts to collectivise the writing process at the Pram proved null or chaotic. It was soon agreed that in this field a division of creative labour according to skill is a Good Idea. However, Group Creation, where performers were part of generating the themes, intentions, the style, the action, characters and language of a work, in collaboration with a writer, produced a sequence of shows that typified a Pram Factory show more than the work of any one playwright. *Marvellous Melbourne* and *Betty Can Jump* were the seminal works. *Mary Shelley and the Monsters* was a bloom and *The Hills Family Show* an autumnal fruiting; so was the work of Stasis. Many another has slipped down the gutter of time. In a critique of Arts Council funding priorities, John Timlin observed that by 1975 the programming orientation of the Collective had

> noticeably shifted from the scripted play to works which may be writer-inspired but through lengthy rehearsal, workshopping and discussion, achieve their final form as much through performer injection [sic] as they do from writer inspiration. The APG began working this way and increased subsidy has enabled it to return to the concerns of stylistic exploration rather than slavish reliance on 'the Word'. It is no longer experimental to do Australian plays; even the establishment theatres have found there is a market for the local product.

My induction to the workshop of filthy creation was in September '72. I chipped in to *He Can Swagger Sitting Down*, Romeril's number on the rise of George Wallace, the populist, racist governor of Alabama. Gillies was in it showing what he had learnt from our own George Wallace, the High Prat of Falls, the Prince of Precision Swivelled Drunk Acts.

He Can Swagger Sitting Down (John Romeril), Front Theatre, 1972. The author as spittoon-carrying Chester in Ms Pussy's saloon waiting for Max Gillies as Governor Wallace to spit. (Ian McKenzie)

I encouraged gritty agitprop into flights of fantasy with a finale taking Wallace into a far-right Hillbilly Heaven. *Swagger* was also a workshop of over-acting and upstaging, the competition for comic dominance reaching its height in Miss Pussy's Saloon. Jude Kuring could top anything with a fast draw of her zealously tanned breasts, which Max didn't think was very funny.

At the end of 1972 myself, Martin Armiger, Dave Stocker, Buzz Leeson, Greig Pickhaver, Susi Potter, Neil Giles, Linda Achren (all from Flinders University) with Graeme Blundell, John Romeril, Kerry Dwyer, Jude Kuring, Yvonne Marini, Bill Garner, Soosi Adshead, Chris Berkman and many others too many to mention, all avid for carnival, produced the sport that was *A Night in Rio with a Few Stupid Mexicans and Other Bummers*. An ample terrace on Canning Street was turned into a mare's nest of creation which became known as the Men's House. Mere anarchy was the methodology here—gymnastics and typewriter composition for

A Night in Rio with a Few Stupid Mexicans and Other Bummers programme, illustrating the show's components, structure and organising principle, by Peter Lillie. (Latrobe Library)

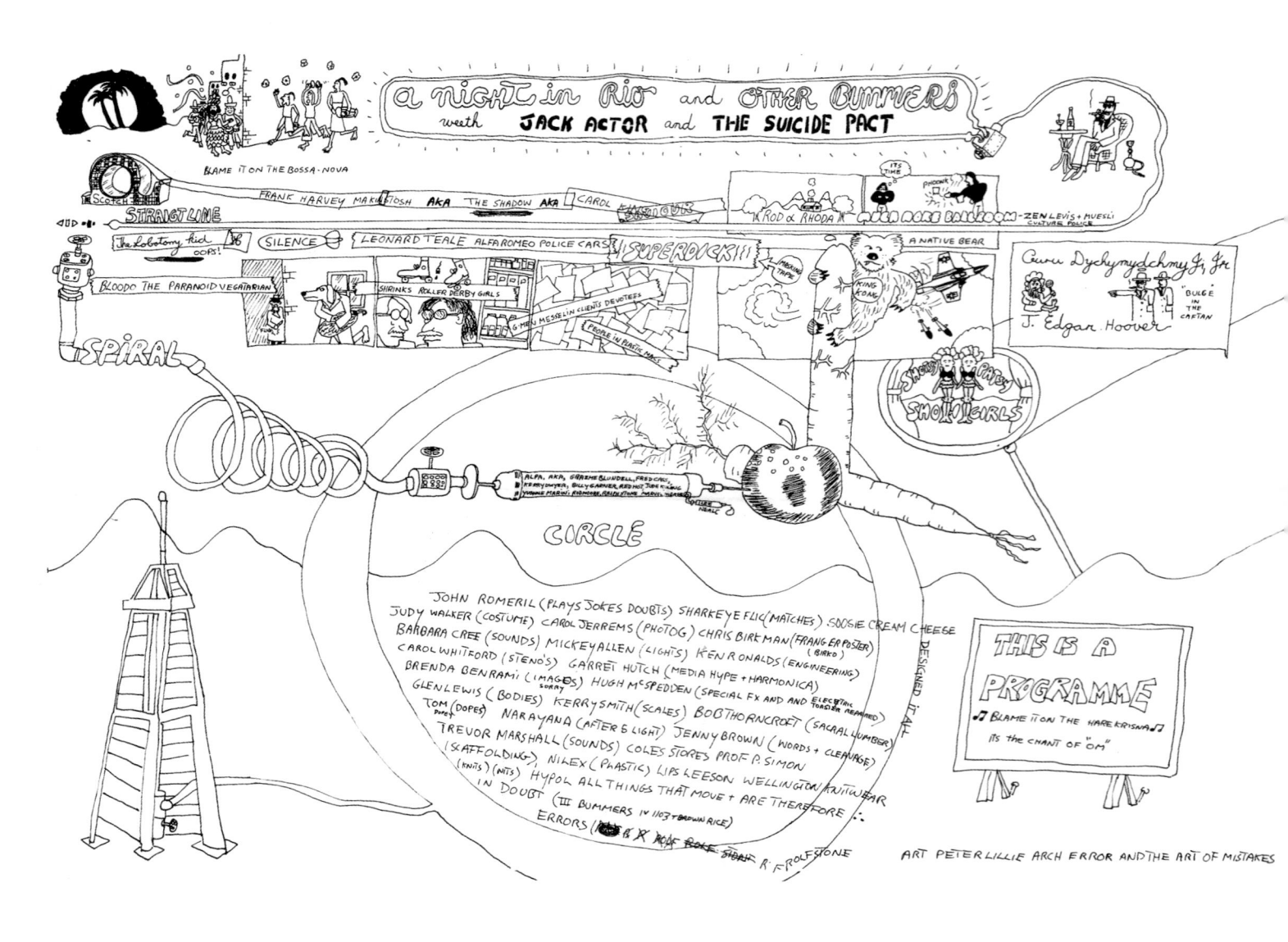

eight hands, joints at all hours, munchies at midnight, stints and stunts in a midden of overflowing ashtrays. Armiger, a Harpo Marx/Keith Richards hybrid, hustled up the Band: himself guitar and vocals, the inscrutable Lee Simon (ex-Spectrum) piano and vocals, Red Symons (ante-Skyhooks) rhythm guitar and vocals, Fred Cass (minus the Cassettes) drums and vocals. Everyone wanted to pull off a popular synthesis of rock 'n' roll and theatre. *Tommy*, the Who's magnum opus about the deaf, dumb, blind pinball wizard, was a much-admired model. That season the Rock Opera was the moon to shoot at and the ground was littered with the wreckage of failed rockets. The commercial success of *Hair* had made the genre a bit suss, a bit kitsch. Hipper models were to hand—Frank Zappa's *200 Motels*, the Grand Magic Circus doing *Moses to Mao*, or the New York Theatre of the Ridiculous doing *Turds in Hell*.

While the creative performers are preparing the body electric, working out on mats, tapdancing and sketching skits, out there in a parallel universe amid the mullock heaps of Castlemaine, John Romeril is writing his own surreal lampoon of the counter-culture. He plots the adventures of Rod and Rhoda Much-More-Ballroom and Frank Harvey Mackintosh, a fundamentalist gumshoe with a ferret for a sidekick, the latter ensuring Blundell a major role. Comic universes expand at tangents, intersecting only occasionally. Simultaneously Garrie Hutchinson is busy promoting a show (that remained purely conceptual) called *Jack Actor and the Suicide Pact*. The essential contemporary production elements of Scaffolding and Smoke obtain, plus special f.x. and flashpots from Leaping Hugh McSpeddon. When Brenda, a single mother living with Fred the drummer, is discovered to have a happy knack for doodling baroque and gothick cocks, this folk art is incorporated as images to be projected on Frank's plastic mac in his mad scene. Thus the scene around the show scene contributes to a production, which ends up as scenes around the Band. Anarchy is syndicalised but those with the amps predominate.

Bummers drew a cult audience. It was as much a band with a show as vice versa, after the manner of Tribe's antics in rock 'n' roll venues gone by. Tribe members, checking it out, could not credit the time and money splurged on these incompetent fuckwits from Adelaide to produce such utter shit, but they hung around to dig the band. Some of the show's phantasmagoria entered counter-cultural folk memory, for a short term. One scene, set in the Martin Esslin Clinic for Sexual Perfection, had the male performers flashing around the arena naked on roller skates, except myself wearing rude snow shoes made out of sawn-off tennis rackets. The female critic from the *Digger* belittled our endowments. Cartwheels performed without knickers by Mss Dwyer, Marini and Kuring provoked unqualified astonishment and applause. The Vice Squad attended and was unmoved by any of this or by the spectacle, in the White Goddess Cabaret, of the porridge of the mythic Cerrydwen being lustily stirred by her husband Tegid. In the heat of the summer of

'73 it became fashionable among the more *outré* of the *Bummers* patrons to attend in a state of nature. It was hip to pretend not to notice.

Mid-season, my wife Robin gave birth somewhat before term to our daughter. There was no demurral from the cast over my immediate upsticking for Adelaide. Greig Pickhaver obligingly took on the unrewarding roles of the Lobotomy Kid (played with a plastic bucket over head) and Dylan Thomas (played with a plastic Welsh accent). There was time for one last orgiastic turn at Kerry and Graeme's to celebrate the birth, and the morning after the critic from the *Digger* gave me a lift to Sunshine. I hitchhiked home to meet the tiny darlin' summer puddin' and Robin got on with the rearing while I laboured, Walter-Shandy-wise, over the problem of the right name, an auspicious name, a name of sweetness and power for our creation. Only the requirement of a birth certificate, by Infant Welfare in Melbourne, brought forth Anna Pome, reJoycing. Anna for Livia the river, Pome because she was the apple of our eye and Anna Pome elides with a fluid gravitas. It has proved wonderfully efficacious.

We three got to Carlton to find that the fresh air and green shade we had become accustomed to at Devil's Elbow could be found in Warrandyte, so we settled ourselves out there. This proved a mistake I was to reflect upon at 2 am in Heidelberg or Doncaster Shoppingtown, hitchhiking home from aftermaths of *Dimboola*.

We moved back to the inner city, Shakespeare Street, Carlton. I liked the name. In a dinkily renovated, two-up two-down dolls' house, a little cramped for an open marriage *à la mode*, I set about scribbling lyrics and sketches for a nationalist pantomime of the ridiculous. Tonto from Adelaide would drop by with little pellets of hashish and the odd ode—*To a Floater*, for example—to add to the mix. Freebooting young women with a yen to perform would come round and I would encourage them with soufflé omelettes. And this was cool, according to the *zeitgeist*, so long as all such concocting was above board.

Romeril had come up with a great Dame, Nellie Smelter, for *Waltzing Matilda*. The title delighted Timlin as a dream to promote. I was dickering over the name for the Demon King, an economically dry hypnotist, whose social platform was to add value to the population by converting them into pies. I was dickering with Zneddon Zneeze Zeitgeist, after the liberal pollie who was to achieve as climactic a consummation as could be wished. Timlin was dead against this slur on a good bloke favourably disposed towards the APG, and took me aside with a pipe of port to put me in the politico-cultural picture.

> During the passage of the Arts Council Bill (1973) there was bitter controversy over Whitlam's insistence that the Chairs of the various Boards be elected by the Arts minister, namely himself, rather than by the Boards themselves. This, of course was anathema to the comrades of the Pram. Two APG members had slipped into the corridors of power by this stage.

★ Group Creation: Some Little Known Facts ★   95

A certain distance: the ALP and the APG. A campaigning Gough Whitlam circumspects his footsoldiers. L–R: Jane Clifton, Bruce Spence, Claire Dobbin. (Mal Dobbin)

Garrie Hutchinson, who had found favour with Dr Coombes (Chair, Australian Council for the Arts), was the radical rep. on the Theatre Board, Jack Hibberd was on the Drama Panel, but to little avail, and our purchase on the funding faucet had not much improved.

The State Government was no help. From the office of Eric Westbrook the director of the Victorian Ministry of the Arts came underlings with an effusion of compliments backed up with a bare pittance. While something of a radical in the Visual Arts, Eric like Gough was an egregious First Nighter and a fan of the MTC.

The Prime Minister had no love for the Pram Factory. As Leader of the Opposition he had come to *The Sonia Knee and Thigh Show* where Margaret and he were subjected to the trauma of enforced audience participation. There was a sketch (by Williamson) on working-class displacement into high-rise flats. The audience members were required to leave their seats and take up some other, allegorical, uncomfortable confinement. The democrat (or fascist, from the Whitlam POV) in Evelyn Krape could not see why the Whitlams should be left out of these proceedings. There was a classic confrontation of the irresistible and the unmovable and thus the vexed issue of audience participation came to have an effect on patronage and the Group's income in the years to come. When the Oz Council Bill was going through Caucus, John Button begged to differ about the appointment of Chairpersons. 'You've been talking to those radicals from Melbourne!', boomed Gough (the ingrate, as the APG had campaigned for the ALP in '72 and '74). Button let Hibberd know he was wasting his time on the matter and he might as well go and see the Libs.

Now Hibberd had a friend from medical school days, one Jack Best, who was the private secretary of the leader of the opposition, Bill Snedden,

Waltzing Matilda. **Pie-scape by Bob Daly, pie machine by Andy Anderson. Traverse stage traversed by unfocussed personnel from the Basement. (Ponch Hawkes)**

and from Best he had learnt that there was a push in the Liberal office to try and establish a left-of-centre Arts Policy as an outflanking manoeuvre.

The son of a Perth butcher, fond of his footy and a drink, a bit of a player, Snedden was not your stereotypical liberal. He didn't have the blue ribbon ticket, he had no relish for putting on the dog and he was a fellow Victorian. I found that warmer, more liquid relations were possible with him. When Romeril and Robertson were writing their panto I found myself in Snedden's office writing his speech on the Australia Council. The pay-off came in 1974. The APG again receiving but a few measly grand from Westbrook, I decided to call up the debt. I rang Snedden to tell him the group was being starved out. Snedden rang Hamer to tell him that a debt was owed. Hamer rang Westbrook to tell him to give the APG $50,000, without going into any details. I went in and waited on Westbrook for the cheque. The bureaucrat was flabbergasted. The politicians had removed his patronage from him. How had this happened? Why were the conservatives siding with these uncouth, ratbag lefties?

Directing at the Pram went by indirections. A director was a kind of pontoon upon which performers expressed their doubts and dissatisfaction before leaping off into the sea of autonomy again. As the role was seen as elitist it was not much sought after. Some of the best things at the Pram, like *The Bob and Joe Shows,* flew by themselves without a director. Others were the result of a non-hierarchical, collaborative process, like *Beware of Imitations* and *Waltzing Matilda*, where the director was an eye and a buffer, a booster, a gofer. The essence of the job was joining things together and keeping them going. The tasks of the director of *Waltzing Matilda* will illustrate the role.

A good deal of the charm of this National Pantomime with Tomato Sauce derived from its innocent Austral Spectacle and Primitive Machinery, principally a Kinetic Pie Machine. Characters—the Australian XI, HM Queen etc.—were pushed into it and after mincing, stirring and crusting, it elaborated them, as economists say, into pies. The conception of this allegorical contraption was joint, its realisation manifold, but its genius was an unsocialised sculptor named Andy Anderson. From Scandinavia via Perth, in full flight from domesticity, an habitué of the Albion, Andy was of a morose, Kierkegaardian cast of mind. He was drawn to our fable of the horrors of consumption. He began to harness the power of discarded electric motors to gears that revolved bits of this and that and delivered people wearing sponge rubber pie crusts down a slide into the performance space (a traverse on this occasion).

John Timlin, who had earlier passed on the rudiments of the Art of Welding to some of the members, produced a strong, practical slide in short order. The contra deal struck with the kineticist—six bottles of beer for every four hours and a flagon for every four hours thereafter—made the creative process haphazard and extensive. Working alone, he was prey to black doubts and anomie. He required dialogue to continue. Some was supplied by Bob Daly, who would duck in to paint his monumental Piescape along the north wall. After midnight Andy was an angst-ridden berserker. He might turn on his own creation at one moment, sink into lassitude the next, or unloose a stream of horny misogyny. Bob would duck out back to the Tower. Then it fell to the director to bring the focus of the kineticist back to the washing machine rotation apparatus that would shake the plywood pot when the Demon Pieman hopped on a bicycle saddle and pedalled.

Early in 1974 John Wood had lobbied his double bill *On Yer Marx* onto the programme, Hibberd's *Stud* (renamed *Peggy Sue*) had a slot and so did Romeril's *Floating World* (in a draft that would have run four hours). A Women's Theatre Festival was scheduled for May and Theatre Projects were bringing in *The Oresteian Trilogy* in September. After that was a blank. Not that there was a scarcity of potential material. On the contrary, there was an embarrassment of it. Authors unconnected to the Pram, mute inglorious Wmsons, submitted a constant trickle of unsolicited scripts. There was an unplumbed pool, feet deep in a cupboard.

On Yer Marx (John Wood). Front Theatre, 1974. The Brothers take on Capitalism: Chico (Lex Marinos), Groucho (Max Gillies), drag act (Terry Norris), Harpo (Evelyn Krape), ingénue (Fay Mokotow), Wilfred Last. (Ponch Hawkes)

Before the Programming Committee (aka the Gang of Three) was formed, scripts went missing unskimmed in the office or in the ever-changing domiciles of the members. As one of the Gang, I began a fairly random and unrewarding review. Most of the stuff I judged dull and unplayable, the lucubrations of writers isolated from performers. There were whacking great three-acters set in rooms, slender imitations of absurdists set nowhere, scads of logorrhoea and pretension, and amongst it *The River Jordan*, by Michael Byrnes.

Written on stationery from the office of Wacol Prison, Queensland, it was overwritten in gaolese, a language away from language. It treated 'life in the raw in symbolism', according to the playwright. It was clumsy, self-indulgent, religiose, archaic even, but it grabbed me. I recognised the true voice of alcoholic unreality, expressing rage, desperation, horror, but with the sort of waggish humour Melville said 'lurks in all your horribles'. Michael was in for armed robbery, doing six to eight for bailing up a bottle department in the Sunshine State with a toy pistol. He was the son of a brickie and had started drinking at 15 when a quart of brown muscat was 2s 6d. A way with words had won him stints on the *North Shore Times* and *Stockade*. He had gained a lot of form in the gaps of an institutionalised life, for shoplifting mainly, with a partiality for scotch and hi-fi records. Beside the Redfern railway line he had been turned on to the White Lady (aka Mistress Sugar and Musical Milk) by associates like Geordie Moses, a black shunter, and his brother Ikie Nick, a forger of Namatjiras. He wrote about them in another play, *White Mother*. He wrote all his plays, five in five years, in gaol.

I had found a suitable case for treatment—a project to spring a playwright by developing his embryonic play into a successful production.

★ Group Creation: Some Little Known Facts ★ 99

A Methylated Miracle Play for the Theatre of Social Surrealism! I circulated a synopsis:

> Daniel James Cameron, Margaret Dorothy Parker and Arthur George Ryan are alcoholic derelicts approaching their end in a council tip. They are visited by a charismatic messiah-figure with a wheelbarrow containing a drum of meths and gardening tools. One by one they surrender to this influence and make a garden of the tip. They are reported in the media, denounced by the council and charged on a dozen counts by the police. Cameron successfully defends them and starts a new life afloat on the harbour in a luxury cruiser. Parker is packraped and Ryan is burnt by teenage boys as he sleeps. Cameron returns with Beet, one of several eccentrics who visit to the tip. He immolates himself, buddhist-monk-style, with the meths. Beet plays the last movement of the Choral Symphony on his old wind-up phonograph as Dan cries: 'And now I gladly give up my status as grain of sand and say without anger "Muck you Beach. And muck each one of you".'

The River Jordan (Michael Byrnes), Front Theatre, 1974. 'Beets' (Robert Meldrum) conducts the seventh, sublunary symphony. Mask by Susy Potter. (Ponch Hawkes)

Michael Byrnes. (Barry Dickins)

The Collective got enthused by this conjunction of social action and nihilism to the nth. Timlin wangled a grant for me and Lindzee to make a flying visit to the prisoner. Inside we spoke to him in a shiny room the colour of cold tea. It was as full as Groucho's cabin in *A Night at the Opera* with a painter, two screws, tea trolley in and out, blue with smoke and sirens punctuating the constant drumroll of tropical rain on a tin roof. I quickly developed a migraine. Michael shone, despite the fact he was in disgrace, temporarily suspended from his duties in the library for imbibing the fluid from its ancient duplicator (100% proof, he cooed). He was sharper than the screws, gaunt, his body wasted but with a glow in the hollow of his wellshaven cheeks. His haughty, well-maintained head of brown hair was lustrously brylcreemed and he smelt of soap. I never saw him this way again. His eyes were milky, avoiding contact and when caught they locked into a harsh, challenging stare. Mystified to learn he was now an associate member of the APG, prisoner Byrnes was delighted with the symbolism of the Pram taking his baby and gave us carte blanche on the text. The unincarcerated Author would have found the edit hard to tolerate.

The project group that formed around it resolved to reduce words to a minimum and create transformational images to the max with a lot of musical accompaniment. The performers were to work the illusions and transformations, especially the primal one of Wasteland into Garden. All characters except the three principals were to be masked. Susi Potter put her talent to work on heterogenous pop images in crepe rubber—Beethoven, Henry Bolte, Michelangelo's Moses, Ginger Meggs. In Tech Week Lindzee had a radical flash: 'It's not working on the floor,' cried he, his eyes like coals, 'what we need is a fuckin monster ramp'. He was right, and it got built partly because the cast included Wilfred Last, a socialist/masochist with a strong line in nasty old cockney codgers, very handy with a hammer. Under the shadow of 'Dodger' Ryan's flatcap, Wilfred's full-lipped, *premier-danseur*–like features were translated into those of a voluptuous Steptoe (*père*). Eileen Chapman came in as Mag and with Eileen came Wayne Stewart. She was perfect as the crone/love goddess; he was not really the right stuff for the charismatic guru. However, it was unspokenly plain that this was a package deal. He was an ardent practitioner of *tai chi* yet awkward as a performer. There was something of the Nimbin Elect about him. 'Hey wait up,' spoke an interior voice within the Director, 'we've got an allegorical figure to be played here, not a character!' Wayne was keen—he and Eileen were out there with the Community Theatre group delivering *The Sport Show* (group-created with Jack Hibberd) to hospitals, workplaces and prisons. His hair was right and he played the clarinet a bit. Wrap him in aluminium foil and get Ken Oliver in to teach him to produce a dove, insisted the interior voice, he'll be fine as a smug messiah. And so he was.

From the office, via the principle of democratic casting, came Peter Dyke, who had done sufficient sterling service to claim the reward of a role in a Front Theatre show. He assumed the masks of Godman, Detective Grabsem and Eddy, the teenage rapist. Rob Meldrum and Greig Pickhaver also tripled roles and Max Gillies was videotaped in as a TV reporter. The Tower was represented by Lindzee giving a raw, Donald Wolfit kind of a performance as Dan, raving with a staff and shoulder-length hair. Robin Laurie shot rolls of fire and flame on Super 8 to project on him for the immolation. Carol Porter did the poster (with Baudelaire coupaged as a derelict). Michelle Johnson taught herself expressionist lighting, seeking correlatives for an alcoholic reality, the Blue World of the Bells.

We went as a group to an AA meeting, we met with people from the Gill Memorial, the Salvos and the Alcoholic Foundation, even met with an actual Mr Jordan. Ideas came from everywhere, sometimes simultaneously to the group mind. I remember Lindzee and I both arriving at rehearsal with pictures of Sepik River tribesmen. 'If we start like this,' we raved, faces covered with kaolin, 'we can ring in another transformation!' Susi had visions of carrots springing up like jack-in-the-boxes, of sunflowers jogging along a clothes line. We had the blood, sweat, tears and friends enough to help her realise them, indeed to choreograph them to Beethoven's 7th. The carrots drove us to drink but Dickins recalls the enchantment of walking into a scene of little human brains, florets of cauliflower attached to tiny parachutes, floating down from the rafters to the strains of 'Clair de Lune'.

We worked the magic. 'Razor' Jillett of the *Herald* applauded Byrnes's 'strangely naturalistic nightmare' as the best Melbourne production of the year and the playwright was sprung on the strength of its success. The APG commissioned him to write another. Ill-advisedly, someone donated a case of Grange to toast his success and Michael was back on the grog. I don't think he ever got to see the show but he fell in love with Mag/Eileen. The character was based on the woman he was living with at the time of the 'armed' robbery, who deserted him before he was sentenced. He stayed with Robin and Anna and I for a week until we couldn't stand the smell and the complaints. He moved into the Tower. I lost track of him, but for years afterwards he would pop up out from behind a bush or a bus shelter, still miraculously alive, and greet me with a mocking smile.

The Pram Factory playwright in residence for 1974 did not expect to be allowed to choose a subject and write a play about it. Nor did I desire so uncool a genesis. The creation of the show, subsequently called *Mary Shelley and the Monsters*, began with a project meeting on the decomposing sea-grass matting in the cramped back room of a former shop in a terrace on Rathdowne Street. The function of a project meeting was to firm vague interest in a notion for performance to commitment. The project with an estimated budget was then put to a Collective meeting for approval. The atmosphere was hot and sweaty, Indian summer torpid.

We went as a group to an AA meeting. (Barry Dickins)

Bruce Spence had already sown a seed; after a rave with Lindzee he had avowed: 'Frankenstein is the go!' Fate, happenstance or Jenny, his wife, having passed him a copy of Mary Shelley's book, Spider could see a part for himself, possibly a killer double, playing both Doctor and Monster. Lindzee had seen the Morrissey camp/schlock/horror film, *Flesh for Frankenstein*. My thoughts turned to the original, to Mary Shelley and her mother Mary Wollstonecraft, icons clanging in the feminist wind. In the US, poet Robin Morgan had recently published *Monster*, a slim volume drawing attention to Freud's *On the Uncanny* and his perception of the female genitalia as the monster Vagina Dentata. All of us were susceptible to the perennial sway of the shadows within Dr Caligari's cabinet, the movies of Karloff, Chaney, Price and Jean Cocteau. Minutes for the project meeting read:

> Sat afternoon. At Home.
> Desiderata: Conceptual jumps or camp scenario.
> Whole space, the weather of horror, the House. Spook the performance.
>
> Play horror offstage.
>
> Pirandelloze
> Dellasandro's head. Morrizeze.
> Plot historical situs making up a horror show.
> Ask Collective.
> Tell Sigrid.

So the first thing the writer did was read and précis Mary's novel in order to exhume the original from under the encrustations of popular imagination. The writing credit on the 1931 movie reads like a group creation: 'Based on the novel by Mary Shelley. Adapted by John L. Balderston from the play by Pebby Webling. Screenplay by Garret Fort and Francis Edward Faragoh'. The next jump was discovering Mary's Letters and Journal. Under the dome of the Reading Room I lost myself in what seemed the primal hippie world of the Shelley ménage, roaming in penniless, scandalous exile from odious, perfidious Albion, getting high with Byron. I revelled in correspondences between the decade of the 18 teens and our own—politically radical, socially disordered, sexually experimental. Then I read Thomas Peacock's satires of the ur-hippies as a tonic against romantic identification and borrowed something of his attitude and tone. I began writing discontinuous scenes beginning with an Induction of a couple of stoned creatures breaking in from the roof of the haunted Shelley museum in Rome with the fixed intention of fucking on Shelley's bed. So they do, setting Shelley's heart, that reposes in the bedside cabinet, a-ticking and a gaga concatenation of events unwinding.

While the musical consort—Buzz Leeson, Graeme Isaac, Eric Gradman—got itself together with koto, harmonium and violin, Alan

Robertson tried to referee the clash of casting in a workshop situation. The democratic principle came unstuck causing shams and shambles. In circumstances of egalitarian political correctness the possession of performance talent could be a liability, seen as a threat. The naturals and those of proven track record had to exercise much tact and diplomacy for fear of being thought to be getting above their station. In the jostle and slather, push-cum-shove of the workshop, people with non-performance skills in networking and research, the confident and the articulate, the tough ones with political savvy, prevailed. These skills and qualities were not always enjoyed by the best performers and the director was denied, or refused to exercise, that personal prejudice which goes by the name of artistic choice. Positive Discrimination and Endless Delay won Claire Dobbin the title role from a field of favourites. Claire Clairmont, played by Evelyn Krape, became the dominant female presence on the stage. 'A mouse-like Mary', the arch-critic of *The Age* would opine. Claire Dobbin was a founder member, an excellent convenor of workshops, an energetic teacher and committee person. She had paid her dues and it was her turn. Too preoccupied with other business arising from the APG to become as engrossed and obsessed as creative development of character requires, she remained on the level of the matter of fact.

The disaffected, under-parted, under-cast Tony Taylor, Roz de Winter and Michael Price went off and turned themselves into a sort of chorus calling itself the Harpies. They played Servants and Peasants, muses and figments. The other actors with characters with names would have to go down to the Basement and workshop with the Harpies. Through improvisations they developed psycho-sexual fantasies around the real-life events of the period: a trip across the lake to the Castle of Chillon,

Mary Shelley and the Monsters (Tim Robertson), Front Theatre, 1975. P. B. Shelley (Bruce Spence) faces up to a birching from Sir Timothy Shelley MP (Evelyn Krape, with whip hand on Wilfred Last), as Mary Shelley (Claire Dobbin) looks on. (Ponch Hawkes)

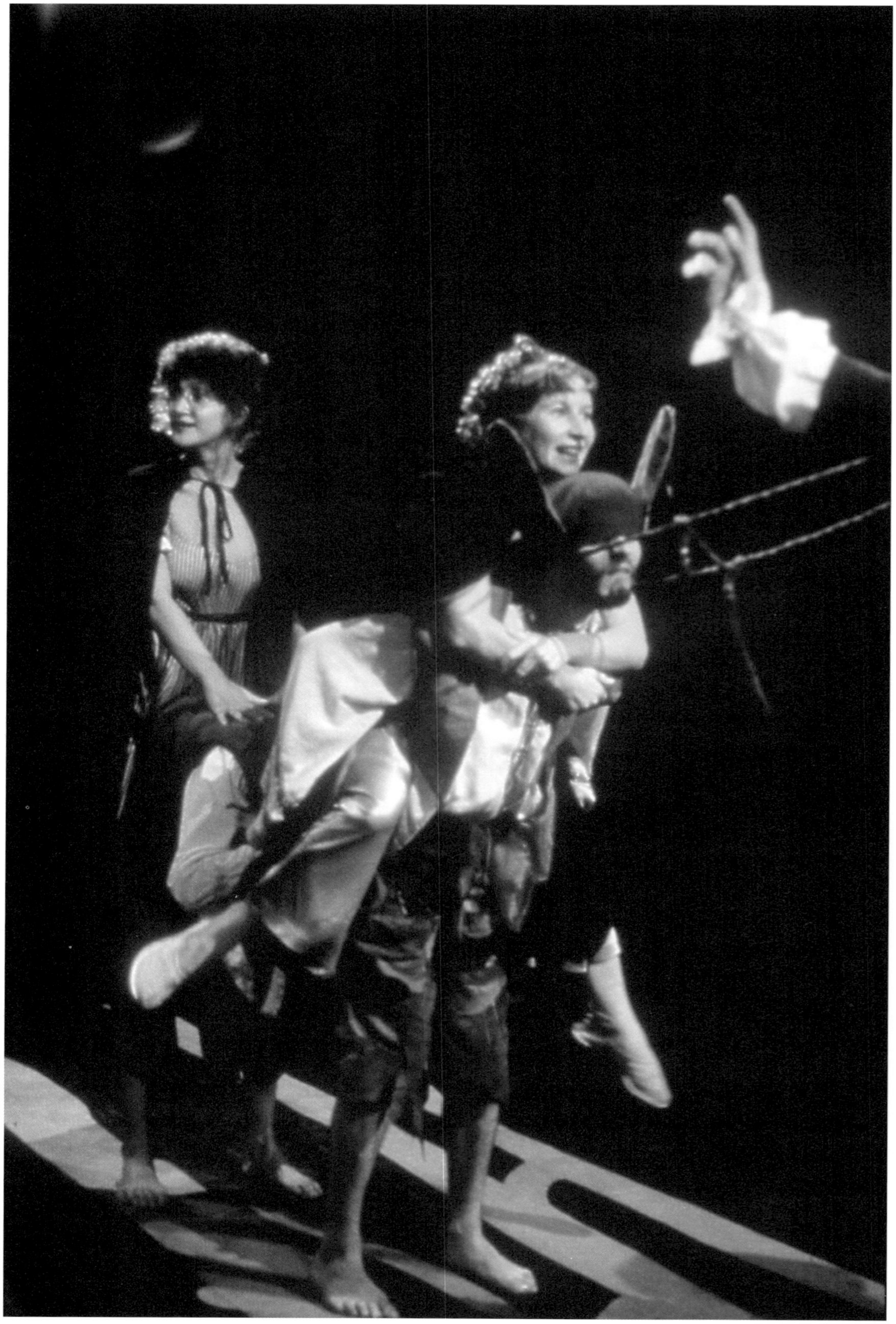

Opposite: **Backpacking in the 1820s. Claire Clairemont (Evelyn Krape) and Mary Shelley (Claire Dobbin) mount Tony Taylor and, it may be, Michael Price. The hand of Percy Bysshe Shelley (Bruce Spence) beckons them on.** *Mary Shelley and the Monsters***, Front Theatre, 1975. (Peter Corrigan)**

Round midnight in the Pram Factory office, a production meeting for *Mary Shelley***. L–R: Alan Robertson, Tim Robertson, Kelvin Gedye, Buzz Leeson. (Bill Garner)**

the horror story contest suggested by Lord Byron, the horrors of infant mortality, of procreation and sexual obsession. They were like an autonomous Id rising to plague the Ego of the playwright, ushering in death and madness. They took over. I felt driven to shave off my hair as a symbolic act to grab some focus. Recording, editing, linking the slippery variants of improvisation into the steady state of a script, concording that with what was already written, complying with demands like 'Polidori must die—a musical demise, please', all this was not good for mental hygiene.

Four days before we opened, the sequence of the second half written on the blackboard read:

>L.B.'s Entrance
>The Museum
>Claire and on to Waterloo
>Travels with a Donkey—Destination Hell
>Dream
>Clubfoot to the Lake
>The Lake
>Meat for Mary
>Claire's Baby
>Polidori's Story
>Cocoa scene + Moon
>Come Monster—Writing scene with Harpies
>Musical Demise
>Percy Unbound to the Blues
>The End?

Dr Polidari (Rob Meldrum) takes the pulse of the philosopher William Godwin (Tony Taylor) in a thickening fog of muffin-induced afflatus. *Mary Shelley and the Monsters*, Front Theatre, 1975. (Micky Allen)

Rob Meldrum remembers a late-night agony, trying to work out the end, crawling on the scungy floor in various attitudes and configurations and crying out to Alan Robertson and myself, 'Like this? Like this? O God, will this night ever . . . ?' We were never looking, distracted with other, weightier matters. A run-through of these scenes in search of a play had never been attempted. People were late in and out of rehearsal because of the duties of self-management, and Claire's lot seemed particularly onerous. Bruce, having finished making a fist of designing a poster and without a newspaper to read, complained of idleness. He was sternly rebuked: 'Shut up Bruce, you're giving me the shits'. Spence had received an education at La Mama, the Pram and environs but now he began to think it was time to graduate. The main game for a performance group, he thought, was doing it, doing it well and bringing in an audience. That the process became more important than the product seemed self-defeating and he began to leave again.

Oblivious to all the angst and *Sturm und Drang* Peter Corrigan the designer sleeps, dreaming of laying a stage cloth and circling it like the belly of Ubu with a mystic omphalos, lichen green.

Corro, one of several *monstres sacrés* at the Pram, spoke in the whining drawl of a peevish Jimmy Stewart and, having committed an offence, would walk away with his shoulders pulled up into a righteous hunch. He was the only person to whom my expansively tolerant wife had been obliged to show the door of her kitchen. He had been around the APG, notionally at least, before he'd hunched around Harvard yard as the brilliant young visiting professor in architecture. He was Blundell's guide to the livewires and fleshpots of New York in '71, who lovingly preserves a memento from this time: a drawing of a giant necktie, emblazoned with "A.P.G." where the naked lady would be, were it to be worn by a giant badtaste mobster. This Corro envisioned, all vibed up at a distance by the leasing of the Pram Factory as he was, as the Logo of the house, fluttering like a Japanese kite in Drummond Street. It did not matter to him that no one in the place, apart from himself and Timlin, wore neckties. *Qua* designer, he tended to operate transcendentally, over and above the performer and the text, with the best and worst of results. On the dreary night of the *Mary Shelley* rehearsal in question, he was about to excel himself. He obtained, or caused to be obtained by female stepinfetchit, a quantity of stevedoring hawser and suspended it from the trusses in the roof at one end of the space in a massy, hempen fall. In this Spence, as the drowned P. B. Shelley, hung swaying, and from it he was drawn by the Harpies onto the beach at La Spezzia to be burnt by his friends. A killer *coup* and one that Corro did not forget. When in 1979 Edmond/Corrigan, vernacular architects, developed the model of a visionary plan for the development of a cultural enclave from Drummond through to Lygon Street, there appeared, near the front entrance of the theatre, a rope waterfall.

★   ★   ★

Like Bruce, I was starting to leave as well. *Mary Shelley* was the last new thing on which I collaborated with the group. The process had become self-destructive and so had I. Unlike Bruce, who made a clean break to live and work freelance in Sydney, my departure was protracted and disorientated. I was a ghost in a fog machine. Mine was a five-year span, creatively, at the Pram, and by 1977 I had spun out. I remember seeing a French movie, *Le Feufollet*, around this time and identifying intensely with the barfly anti-hero, left behind when the rest of the crowd moved on in their lives. There were a few of us like that round Carlton. The boys who stayed too long at the pub, for whom the hangover was part of the universal human condition. When Bob Ellis observed to inebriate farewell diners at a Playwright's Conference that I had alchemised mine into an acting style, I thought this good and proper.

The flicks of my memory of this period are jump-cut fragments, scratches on black alternating with painful over-exposure. There is however one sequence in clear focus: the memorialist is seen crossing Grattan Street, bitumen shining wet on a rainy Saturday morning, up the steps into the Royal Women's Hospital he goes. His POV, steadicam through the maternity ward as if drawn by the gravity of, close-up: starchild, dark eyes burning bright, tangle of black hair. Title: Matilda Bree. (Robin named the names this time, seconding that of Jane Fonda's character in *Klute* to one that waltzes, etymologically, 'shining in battle'.)

After Shakespeare Street, we had removed to Rathdowne Street, into a shared house and group living. A damp, dim, turn-of-the-century shop in a terrace of them, renovated by un-rendering the brick, spreading seagrass on the floor and woodchip in the yard. Next door was still a shop, a deli, revived in cerulean blue and aquamarine, and an ancient Greek lurked in the cobbled back lane. In a dark brown kitchen there were quantities of brown rice and a kitty, always the subject of controversy among a succession of fellow occupants, mostly connected to the Pram Factory. Susi Potter, vainly flapping towards constant coupledom with the feckless Neil Giles who suffered from a chronic Jim Morrison complex. Buzz Leeson, avoiding eye contact, making up song after song in the upstairs front room. The downstairs back room was at one stage taken by a severe, braided Polish beauty, the mastermind of the Magic Mushroom (school-touring) players. She would take Robin's part as our strife increased and roundly denounce my enormities. Her consort was a performance artiste, who wrapped himself like a mummy, donned a digger's hat and took to the streets, sometimes with identical multiples.

The exotic of the household was Lyle the Lodger. Lyle was a Liberal, a nocturnal student, who kept bar somewhere and slept in his suit. He did this in what once had been the shop proper, in a clutter of boxes and other people's lumber. He had nothing but contempt for socialist shibboleths like kitties and rosters and grants. I was shocked by his whole-hearted admiration of Doug Anthony. Perhaps I protested too much, sensing the old Adam, the anarcho-tory, stirring beneath my impersonation of *gruppenmensch*.

In 1975 a young couple Robin and I had known in idyllic Adelaide days, now married and returned from Europe, fatefully moved into Rathdowne Street. Andy Miles was a budding ginger academic and Charmayne Lane a budding actress, the eldest, blonde offspring of the union between a lady lion tamer and a clown. In the butch, dungareed world of '70s feminism Charmayne was frowned upon for being unreconstructedly feminine. She would not desist from shaving her armpits and the application of lipstick—the poor little dupe of the phallocrats. When Alison Richards was on to direct Arrabal's *Garden of Delights*, there was no question who should play the shepherdess. Desire trapped us all by the tails. Orgasmotropic crossover occurred during that long hot summer in the empire of the senses. There was also much pain and bad free verse.

Author with hair, barber and daughter, Elgin (?) Street, 1976. (Ponch Hawkes)

I immersed myself, between drinks and smokes, in the theory and practice of tantric yoga, seeking to conserve the *bindi* within the flow of the *chi,* but failing, and dreamt incorrectly of living in a forest glade with Robin and Charmayne as my *yogini,* one dark, one fair, as per the Indian paintings.

We put out feelers through the APG network for more suitable quarters in which to quartet. The Hannans responded. Having pioneered a new real estate frontier beyond the inner-city ghetto, in Ascot Vale, they were pleased to rent their vacant grey terrace in Shiel Street, North Melbourne. It had a spacious, ecologically sound native garden with Gillies living in an architect-designed raintank at the bottom of it. Things did not work out. It was a crying time of swingeing rages, desperate reconciliations and broken-hearted, exhausted withdrawals. Matilda howling; Anna fearful; Charmayne constantly strung a-quaver; Andy wretchedly lurking; Robin trying to mother through the mess of it; me incapable of making the decision it seemed to be mine to make: sticky, stagnant stasis at Sheil Street.

In the end Charmayne broke away. After haphazardly directing *The Overcoat* (adapted from Gogol by Hibberd and composer Martin Friedl), after a bad case of chickenpox and ongoing agenbite of inwit, I followed her. Bad times, we thought, were over. Andy and Robin went off on a holiday with the kids to mark the beginning of a new life together. Andy swam out too far at Bateman's Bay and drowned.

★ ★ ★

I was dysfunctional at the Pram Factory. My head still bubbled with projections but I was not following through. I was reputedly doing *The Cole's Funny Picture Book Show* with George Dreyfus, following up our successful collaboration on the republican pantopera *The Lamentable Reign of Charles the Last.* Cole Turnley, Cole's grandson wanted to join in the fun. It was reported in the *Perambulator* newsletter that: '*Madder Goo* is the current title for the musical theatre piece once known as *Cole's Funny Picture Book Show.* George is confident Tim has the script well under way although we have not seen it yet, so we have allotted it a space as a SAP show'. SAP, as I probably didn't know, stood for Semi-Autonomous Project, part of a strategy to give a much increased membership access to the spaces for a diversity of shows on a paucity of funds. (Stephen Sewell's *Traitors* was a SAP—director, light and sound person and six actors each took a ninth share of the gate, a sum of $90 per week, each. Doing *Galileo* at the Nimrod at the same time, John Gaden was taking home $220.)

Steve Vizard had stolen a march on me and gone ahead and done a dandy little *Coles Funny Picture Book Show* with Norman Kaye, so I had turned to *The Golden Ass* of Apuleius and was intermittently working on a woggish adaptation. I failed to get up *One of Nature's Gentlemen* with Libby Clark and Peter Cummins in a North Melbourne nightclub. I had

The Dudders. L–R: Susi Potter, Tim Robertson, Bob Thorneycroft, Peter Green, Alison Richards. Squatting: Bill Garner, Bob Daly. At the Shrine, 1976. (Ponch Hawkes)

left Peter Cummins and Sue Jones improvising in bed for 20 minutes at La Mama, delaying my second entrance in John Wood's *Head Over Heels* having a pot or three at the Albion Hotel. I remember little of *The Dudders*, Romeril and Timlin's theatre restaurant treatment of Austral-American relations in wartime Brisbane, except for Phil Molan from Legal Aid nursing me through my lines in the Basement. Nothing remains of David Hare's *Knuckle* except echoes of Evelyn Krape's Scots accent from Caulfield.

I started off a promising career at the MTC when Bruce Miles directed a season of a double bill by Fassbinder and Bauer in the recently taken-over upstairs space at the Athenaeum. Something had to be done to justify the bits in its charter about experiment and development. The Bauer piece, *Shakespeare the Sadist*, intercuts scenes of desultory, pseudo-intellectual conversation about Film with burlesque scenes from a

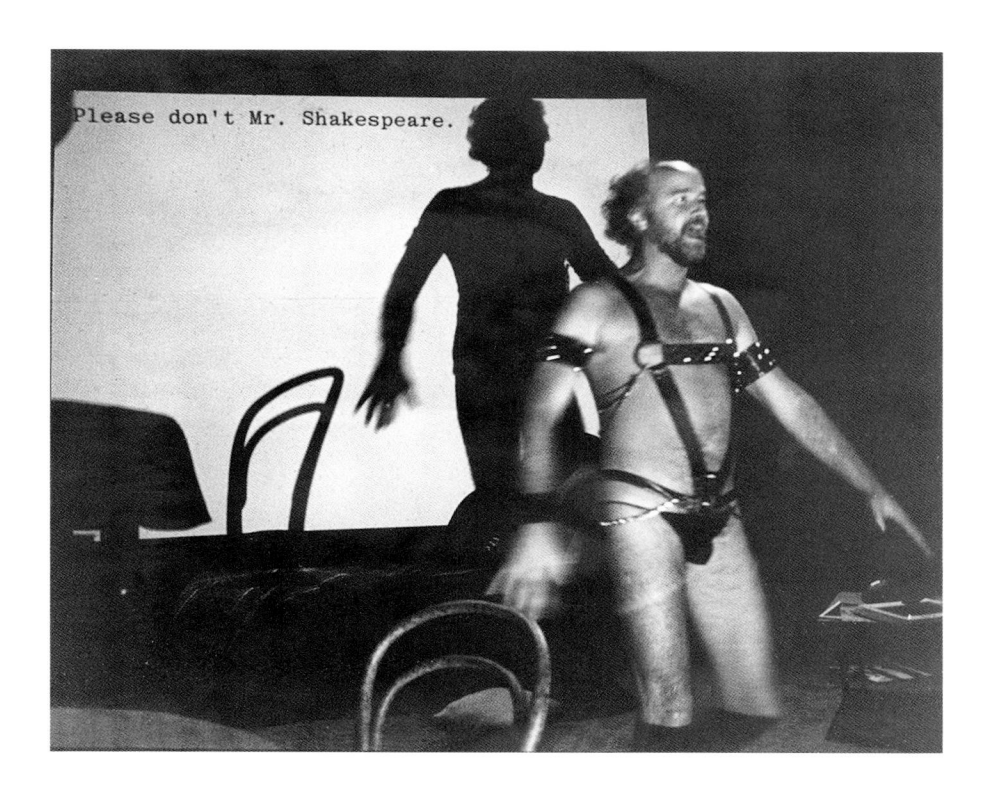

Author as Shakespeare, speaking Swedish. *Shakespeare the Sadist* (Bauer), upstairs at the Athenaeum, Melbourne Theatre Company, 1977.

Swedish porn movie about the Bard carrying on in leather and chains. Someone was required to disport themselves thus while raving in pig-Swedish of his own devising and I got the part. My victim in this bold essay in iconoclasm was the redoubtable Catherine Wilkin.

> *'Halaw leeta krumpert, leeta squoshet moose, ya Sharkespeerer fokkevit, Sharkespeerer Sadista . . . !'*

I would foam at Ms Wilkin, bulging in my chains, flecking the front rows with saliva and sweat, brandishing chairs and whips. Some nights the audience would come to the party. Some nights it sat aghast in frozen dismay, or shaking its head in disbelief, groped its way towards the unfamiliar exit or, as was the inveterate habit of many MTC subscribers, and to my confoundment, slept. One night after an excessive afternoon, in the course of *Bremen Coffee*, the neo-Strindbergian first half, I had to be assisted from the stage by the sumptuous and golden-hearted Amanda Muggleton. Stage-management ruled I was unfit to play *Shakespeare the Sadist*. Behind a nimbus of marihuana smoke I bellowed that I'd never been fitter. The offer of the part of a transvestite English army officer lapsed.

   A bit of group creation that kept me going in 1979 was cobbling jokes and people together for the New Circus show at the Last Laugh. John Pinder and Roger Evans's renovation of the high-ceilinged, 19th-century Forester's Lodge had made it the most splendid room in Melbourne for comic performers. It could fit a family of them, as it did *The Whittle Family* wrangled by Evelyn Krape, but it also suited the making of magic, illusion and spectacle, the imaginative working of the whole space most consummately demonstrated by the *mises-en-scène* of Nigel Triffit.

At the Last Laugh the concept of a Collingwood Surf Lifesaving Club set beside and under the sea was floated. Sue Broadway, Tim Coldwell, Jim and Pixie Robertson, Jack Daniel, Neil Giles and I developed the Manontroppo family, musical crazies in the Italian tradition, who could do everything, anywhere, if not too much was expected. They were picking up musical instruments, learning and exchanging tricks. Pixie taught Sue how to be a mermaid while spinning on the Web (an aerial rope). Tim kept on making, balancing on and calling for 'Another chair!' Jim applied a great swag of circus *shtick*, know-how and lore. Jack battled with the plates act and depression, and Neil Giles, aka Barry Ball, former Toads Nitely drummer, bongoed on. Barracked on manic-depressively by myself, fitfully advised and abused by fellow clowns who dropped in on rehearsals off Gertrude Street, they became the moneyspinning hit Pinder insisted on calling *'Waiter, There's A Circus In My Soup!'*

My last appearance at the Pram Factory was in Barrie Keefe's *A Mad World, My Masters*, a pommy play harking back to the Jacobean City Comedy by Thomas Middleton and written to mark the Silver Jubilee of the second Elizabeth. I played the City Gent with a thing about the Queen who becomes engorged whenever the royal anthem is played. An ingenious, retractable prop, constructed from meccano girders, rubber bands and the spring from an old fly door, allowed me to simulate this phenomenon. The glans, as I remember, was a rubber door stop. A yank on a length of fishing line running to the trouser pocket could effect the erection, all other things being equal. Often they were not and I was forced to improvise. I reflected, waiting for an entrance in a gorgeous goose costume styled by Laurel Frank, on the poetic justice of this my swansong. After an elaborately plotted saga of Lingam and Yoni, from Adelaide to Melbourne, here I was the phallus-bearer, Iacchos himself in a low burlesque. Buoyed up by the laughter of the crowd and flushed with pleasure at the right-ness of things, I would drag an equally flushed, snaggle-toothed Motherwell on for the denouement.

Almost the last group-created show at the Pram Factory was its Auction. (The last was the new Ensemble's *Rezistor Routines*.) *8 Minutes on Thursday* was scumbled up by the new guard, Romeril and myself. I was a minister of the Church of the Unreal Estate in a sacerdotal rig. Barry Dickins appeared as Leonard Teale, Evelyn Krape resurrected Grandma Hills and her wheelchair, Romeril rose out of a coffin as the Ancient

Author goose-stepping out with cross-dressed detective (Peter Green) in *A Mad World, My Masters* (Barry Keefe), Front Theatre, 1978. (Ponch Hawkes)

★ Group Creation: Some Little Known Facts ★   113

Above: **Outside the Pram Factory the author as blind pope armed with a mallet, attended by madhatted, blind blonde (Charmayne Lane), Death (John Romeril), and author's mother (Janet Robertson), who converses with a rakish Barry Dickins to the amusement of Denis Moore and an unknown man eating his lunch. Auction day, May 1980. (Ruth Maddison)**

Left: **Straights. Auction day, May 1980. (Ruth Maddison)**

Max indignans.

Curse of the premises for sale. We were all on offer, spirits of the Pram in a clearance sale. As a Concerned Female Jewish Theatregoer planted in the crowd expostulated to the auctioneers: 'Have some respect for the living dead, already. Leave these zombies a haunt!' Romeril zapped them with the magic word from Waltzing Matilda:

>'Adlitamgnitzlaw!'

Old routines threatened to jump from the windows but all was to no avail. The doomed Ensemble was de-venued but kicked on for a year. It had been created by a committee from some 150 applicants across the country in what Bill Garner impressively described at the time as an 'unprecedented display of critical self-management through which the APG has purged itself by a total heart, mind and body transplant to become a new ensemble marked by strength, intelligence and oddness'. The odds were against them and the transplant did not take.

At the end of that grey Thursday afternoon in May 1980 members of the police closed in on me, threatening to press charges of Papal Impersonation. As defending lawyers appeared from nowhere so did the Bent Brass Band from the Last Laugh. Around the corner from Faraday into Drummond Street they came playing 'Yankee Doodle':

> ***Mind the music and the step***
> ***And with the girls be handy.***

I was out of there.

9 ★ The 'Pataphysics of Peter Cummins

ADUMBRATED BY ALFRED JARRY, 'pataphysics are the laws governing exceptions, and Peter Cummins is one unto himself. A plumber from the age of lead who turned performer at the dawning of the age of Aquarius and PVC, he went on to lead an active retirement between triumphant engagements, inchingly restoring a small Fitzroy cottage with a cracked facade of mediterranean blue. An unfinishable endgame of a place, it is indented one pace forward, two paces back from the line of the other houses in the street. Through the shutter of the letter shoot in the galvanised iron reinforced front door, the guardian light of a naked bulb reveals to the enquiring gaze (in 1993) a bare parlour, in the throes of plastering. Upon gaining admission 20 years earlier, night visitors would have found themselves on the boards, cement grey across the joists, which led to the cosy fastness of Cummins's stand-up kitchen and a heated discussion of the sexing of the Trinity, according to Norman O. Brown. A body seldom sat down. It would lean, Cummins typically at a laconic 45 degrees, athwart the sparse fixtures of the kitchen. On the floor of the front parlour an extirpated fireplace freestands like a sculpture. A weighty deconstructed chunk of the past in the flux of becoming, a plumber's joke, cast irony, the post-modernist hearth, uprooted and at home with an hermit about town.

The Householder was the original Monk O'Neill in Hibberd's *A Stretch of the Imagination*. Jack had Max Gillies in mind, Max had doubts, Cummins stepped in. Not that he himself is not profoundly doubtful about most outcomes, one excepted, which is why the dimensions of the companion way to his bed in a dainty attic are compatible with the dimensions of the St John's ambulance stretcher, a thoughtful design feature to aid in the retrieval of his remains.

The Australian dream of home ownership, practically realised by pretending to be someone else, is no mean feat. Cummins's real estate

Cummins as Monk in *A Stretch of the Imagination*, directed by Jack Hibberd, Front Theatre, 1972. (Ian McKenzie)

was hard won. For starters he was always older. He was 30-something when he saw this group of barely 20s behaving in the La Mama carpark. He was out on a little five-mile run, a constitutional to someone inured to the regimen of Percy Cerutty. He lingered to mock the young wankers, then joined them. If this was acting, he could do it.

There survives a photo of a group at a Sunday workshop: Peter's head cranes into the shot, his right arm akimbo, the rest of him cropped by accident or design. It is the head of a fit young man in the summer of his 30s, dark receding hair revealing intellectual bumps and the attentions of barbers from the days of Brylcreem when barbers in Malvern had poles. None of the heads of the other, younger blokes in the photo have parts. Cummins's left eye is clear and bright, preternaturally so for a Sunday, with a sceptical beam in it. All the male eyes betray a certain scepticism, *vis-à-vis* the unknown object of their gaze. Lindy Davies is wide-eyed and open-mouthed, whether from disbelief or desire is ambiguous. Anna Carmody is quizzical but sympathetic, Meg Clancy blankly incredulous. Who are they reacting to? Perhaps it is Brian Davies theoretically applying Irving Goffman's transactional analysis to performance technique while Graeme Blundell is provoking others into bouts of improvisation downstairs. Here are people standing in the

Workshoppers upstairs at La Mama with body language revealing varying attitudes to Authority (unseen). L–R: Alan Finney, David Kendall, Lindy Davies, Geoffrey Gardiner, Bill Garner, Meg Clancy, Anna Carmody, Peter Cummins. (Lloyd Carrick)

restrained attitudes of those not in the habit of keeping quiet, giving a man a go and it's London to a brick, in 1969, the focus of attention is a man.

Cummins, who first found inklings of performance dynamics teaching plumbing at the Colac Institute, is back in class in Carlton. His stance is a deal more relaxed than Al Finney's—Al is standing in the first position, dressed for combat, a thespic warrior in boxing pumps, one fist clenched on the hip, the other over a fashionably shrouded ear, elbow against a wall. The effect is of a reclining swastika. Dead set. The Tybalt of Faraday Street. Ginger Mick is mizzled to the workshop. Cummins is barefoot, feeling like an outsider. The atmosphere in these sessions was typically aggro, competitive, confrontational. Lindzee Smith would invade his personal space to lock brows and growl in ersatz American:

'You're a bad actor Cummins. This dentist you're playing, he's out of Heidelberg Rep, man. Can you cope with that?'

Having trained with Cerutty on sand, Cummins could cope, to some extent agreed with him about the dentist, but thought what was left of Lindzee's mind had been colonised by the septics and told him so.

'They all hated me', he can recollect in tranquillity with a paranoia mellowed into partial truth. Caring and sharing had not yet been invented and members were cruel to each other. (During one performance, playing from a text, Finney blew his lines. Undismayed, he began to slap another actor about the face to cover his own lapse.)

Balding and over 30, Cummins was a natural scapegoat. Also he was several degrees closer to being working class than various would-be proles, which got up their proto-collective noses.

Concerning noses, Cummins's goes a fair distance towards verifying the Shandean theory of the fatal influence of *der Nasum*. The man has a

Cummins as Kak in *The Overcoat* adapted by Jack Hibberd from Nikolai Gogol, pondered by author in 1976.

hooter from the heydays of vaudeville. He was bound to follow it, to burst from the chrysalis of the artisan into the imago of the artiste. Such a nose belongs among the leathern masks of the *commedia dell'arte*. Lewdness lurks there but also sorrow and nobility. This is no Cyranoic nose, no match for the heroic Medici snout of John Gaden for instance, but it is said when Cummins sleeps his nose slips down the little St John-compatible stairway out into Moor Street and away to St Petersburg, where it roisters, blown out of all proportion with *The Nose* by Gogol and its heirs. Be that as it may, on it perched the half-moon specs of Monk O'Neill; it has borne the horn rims of hardbitten police sergeants from *The Removalists* at La Mama in 1971 to *Phoenix* on the ABC in 1992; on either side of it lay the kopeks on Kak's dead eyes in *The Overcoat* in 1976. When all's said and done, it is a nose of parts.

Cummins was born to play Papageno. He taught himself to play the flute and his voice has a similar coloratura range at moments of indignation or when intoxicated with debate. His complaint is musical, whether playing a derelict under St Kilda pier or Dame Nelly Smelter in a panto, expounding on the perfidiousness of friends or the fascist leanings of Heidegger. His delivery, in spate, has the puff behind it of a runner who pressed on the heels of Herb Elliot. Peter patters presto, Cummins cascandos. He enjoys improvising in social situations in both congenial and hostile company. He will come on as a wheedling loon from the end of a bar, paying out on slights or ancient wrongs, real or imagined, seeking out a comic sparring partner for the fun and anarchy of it. The character is an antipodean Pete in search of a Dud, a salacious and sardonic witness to scandal and misfortune and hungry for more, expert at telling a joke against himself to his own advantage. Periodically he will wear a beret and this can accentuate his gallic vivacity of gesture, a certain slithery swivelling and shrugging of the body. The head is inclined to a certain nodding and rocking, quaint and sub-continental. Cummins could do the masks of Comedy and Tragedy as a stand-up routine, such is the stretch between his glum and his glee. His mouth is generous but held tight-lipped and he will bear a grudge. He is not disposed to wear incoming flak on a chin that is pugnacious as Punch. He can be toey.

He was a stickler for democratic process once a duly constituted collective was formed and uncompromisingly of the left in the world outside it. When he got wind of clandestine dealing and jobbery with the liberal party as a ploy to acquire funding leverage it got right up his nose. He would have no truck with such unprincipled *realpolitik* and resigned.

At the beginning of the '70s Cummins and any number of other APG members would not have got jobs at the MTC because they did not look or sound like the actors required for the plays offered. Homegrown playmaking however demanded the rough heads and vowels and rhythms of the street. As Horrie and Monk, Peter relished finding the music in the dialect of the tribe, indeed taking it to levels of baroque extremes. He risked polyps using a refined falsetto as Dame Nelly Smelter wringing comedy from self abuse, reaching for and failing to find the notes of:

'Ah, sweet mystery of life at last I've found you!'

As performers got into the soft palate, the open throat, the available body, the loose jaw, raising the old Kundalini through their chakras, ventilating their *jaghanas* and sexual cauldrons with circular breathing,

'Pataphysics in action. Dame Nelly Smelter empies Chinese walloper. (Jan Friedl)

Cummins would cast a critical eye over these alien enthusiasms, but he'd give them a burl. He also gave Betty Pounder's dance class a burl. Seeing himself in the studio mirrors he would smile ironically at the rude mechanical capering among the supple chorines in lycra and legwarmers. To a middle distance runner, warm-up and work-out were second nature. While some fellow members did elbow/throat exercises at the pub, he could be discovered limbering up, establishing the vital performance connection between the groin and the throat. He developed for himself a method of learning his lines by singing them into his memory.

Despite an ardent perusal of the works of Wilhelm Reich, rehearsal was always something of an armed struggle for Cummins. He needed to be uptight to get it on. He would rather rehearse at the zoo than the ashram. He actually entertained the notion of celebrating his 60th birthday there, breaking in on the night with kindred spirits, at the orangutang enclosure. In rehearsal he can exhibit anxiety behaviour similar to that of the upper primates. He paces, sulks apart, threatens from a distance and rejects any grooming advances. Then, inclining towards relaxation, his eyes are graced with all the solemnity, the reflective sagacity of our brother the chimpanzee. Apeman angel Cummo, the philosopher scrag, the fussy anarchist, spreading joy through gloom. Always about to give the game away, forever finishing his house, his career. *Homo facilis. Homo faber* . . .

'No junk mail, no latin. Piss orf!'

The voice of Cummins sings out of the shutter of the letter shoot.

'I'll fit my copy of *Homo Ludens* up your Huizinga!'

He opens the door as to a speakeasy.

'It's dogeared, you'll enjoy it, you know. Come in.'

10 ★ Romeril's Art of Work

COGNIZANT OF THE DIFFERENCE between a hawk and a handsaw, with a profile partaking of both, Romeril is mad for his work, the sustaining high of his life. A Casey Jones among playwrights, he likes to get up to speed and push through when the rest of the company lies inert and terminally confused. He hacks at his craft like a new Elizabethan with as violently contrary results. Which only proves how much a playwright's genius is sheer Indefatigability. The rest is Angst, which is one of his favourite words. Still ringing in my ears, a cry from a smokefilled room during the making of *History of Australia*:

'What is Manning's fuckin' angst?!'

We never really nailed that one down. To take a punt at Romeril's own angst, it is like that of Brecht, a poet who would be rational.

I first made this remarkable man's acquaintance rolled in a Turkish carpet. Legless in Perth. It was perhaps 1968. But definitely in Perth. At the University Drama Festival where I was representing the Drama Department recently established at Flinders by Wal Cherry. It was a meeting of boundless enthusiasms and unlimited hangovers. The times were dionysiac and we were of them. We drank and raved through the night and into the morrow's seminar. Ecstatic utterance was the order of the day. I was agog. Here was I roistering with the author of *I Don't Know Who To Feel Sorry For*, the real thing, an Australian playwright. I had seen his stuff in Melbourne and man, like the Future, it worked. At Flinders we had only *talked* about smashing the State and the fourth wall convention. Romeril was out there doing it in the theatre, and in the streets and carpark also. His example was liberating and magnetic. Professing sucks; practice nay, praxis, is all.

Romeril in heroic Eisenstein mode, as Death unsuccessfully opposing the forces of international capital. *Auction Day*, May 1980. (Ruth Maddison)

In 1969 I awoke in fright in the Back Theatre of the Pram Factory with the role of Rod in *Bastardy*. In circumstances as filthy, dank and intimate as the characters', the audience was as close as touch and Jude Kuring, Jack Charles and Peter Cummins all spilt their guts in great jags of language, hideous, hilarious and homemade. Romeril was not about much during rehearsal, which was a fairly chaotic, *sauve qui peut* kind of a process with Bruce Spence negotiating between towering, cantankerous egos. Romeril was living in Castlemaine, building, rearing and writing. He weighed in for the Bump-Out and the construction of a full-on

Fitzroy loft. For this saturnine bolshevist the Bump-Out had a sacramental quality and rarely did he miss one. It was after all the celebration of the people's will that this show, of all possible shows, go on. People who got too pissed or stoned to function were treated with laggish belts of shit and derision:

'What are yer?!'

Meetings were another of his passions. Meetings were the component atoms of the APG mass and Romeril excelled at splitting them. The APG general meeting was a unique dramatic form. To kick off there were various inductions held outside the forum that was usually the set of the current show in the Front Theatre. An executive cabal puts the finishing touches to a *fait accompli* in the office; the New York rump in the Tower kitchen (El Smith, Carol Porter et al.) rolls a joint and considers a cut-up of Goethe by one of the Baader Meinhofs and how to wangle some travelling scholarships; at Stewarts Hotel where the Office Bar is the seat of real power, fangs are sharpened as numbers are counted in a spiral of shouts. Then, some time after the appointed hour, the whole animal collects itself together and the first item on the agenda is delicatessen. Now fortified and refreshed, the Collective attends to the Minutes of the last meeting, often with incredulity and invective. A revolving secretariat could take liberties with the genre, priding themselves on adding colour to otherwise drab proceedings by elaborating dialogue, asides, character notes, etc. Brought to order by mild-mannered machiavel Max Gillies (impersonating a chair), the meeting moves through the Business Arising: the Administrator's right to purchase a costume, holes in teaspoons to foil the junkies, priorities for next year's grant and such, when Romeril, driven by his daemon, rises to deliver a Rave on a point of ideological order. The Rave is the aria of the meeting.

Aroused, Romeril has a formidable charisma. The noble brow, the piercing eye, the sunken cheek, the lantern jaw, the floppy lock—a bastard Byron from the bush, Heathcliff in thongs, the *poète maudit* from Muckleford to whose fatal allure many can attest. These features twist into astonishing masks, roguish, shifty, ironic, angry, admonishing by turn. Opinions vary about Romeril on the boards. Romeril on the floor of a meeting with a head of steam and a cause is an unquenchable performer. He develops a voice. He produces great effects of pitch (pause) and resonance and revels in them, swooping from the heights of indignation to vaudevillian insinuation. Marcuse as shop steward, hunched and venomously intense, transforms into a gangling mime. A clown right out of the 'Stop laughing, this is serious' cartoon, whispering raucously behind his hand, choked with guffaw: 'Cop a load of this prick?!' In a flash he's back into the Eisenstein heroic mode, or maybe it's Graham Greene, some whisky priest crossed with a blighted revolutionary. Spellbinding! Mulletstunning!

The diction of a Romeril rave derives from an exotic conflation of *kunst*: Berkeley (Cal.) cut with Oz underworld slang, sparks of Marx, Brecht, bits of lit. crit. Mystifying at times but the *gestus* of the contradictions in the dialectic is always clear, that of one man against whatever perceived bullshit happens to be going down. You could be rapt by a Rave and go 'right on Bro!' or you could kill for a joint and groan for the hook and some petty 'bushwah' liberal common sense. Profanity is the auxiliary engine of the Rave, 'kin' oath it is, and Romeril's oratory is peculiarly phutatorial. The *gestus* here, of solidarity with the fuckin working class, has upon occasion pissed some persons right off. I remember a eurocentric, authoritarian, gay theatre worker alleging that the abuse of the Anglo-Saxon rooted words, the resort to scatology, was that of a macho Anglo-Celtic lefty avant garde defending its cultural dunghill. He won a secondment to the Arts bureaucracy. There is aggression involved in such profanity, but repetition works a largely comic effect on it, after the manner of Roy 'Mo' Rene in his Blue period. Anyway when Romeril got up on his hind legs, sometimes he gave the shadow a run, as his scaly raving peer Phil Motherwell was wont to say. More often one noticed how firmly his feet, with their dirty great gnarled and workcloven big toes, were on the ground.

He has the energy to cheer up the spirit of a show, odd for a materialist, and if he gets down you know you're in deep trouble. But he doesn't. He goes on vibing up the action and the characters, suggesting traumatic cuts and volte faces, canvassing the options, staying up all night and appearing at rehearsal like the Ancient Mariner with 30 typed pages of the final option. Again.

Unlike many theatreworkers who abhor the term theatreworkers, Romeril applies himself to the business of invention energetically but unsentimentally. He doesn't coddle ideas. He picks them up, whacks them into something else, discards them without a backward glance. The crux of the collaborative act is to box on. He is harsh on himself and does not suffer wankers gladly. He took me to the edge during the third draft of the attempt to quintesce Clark's *History of Australia* into a form of popular theatre. At that stage *History* was not yet a musical. Running at over 200 pages it was opening with Manning as a boy on Phillip Island. He was playing Noah's Flood with his mates Kitty and Donga, pissing on an ant's nest, playing God:

Manning: Woe unto the cities of the plain!

We were lost in the interleaving of personal and national history somewhere near Mount Despair. Romeril had been hired to kick out the jams. Sort of creative editor with no veto and buggerall money, bummer of a gig. He picked up our jaded spirits and was going great guns with his newly acquired Mac Classic. At the time Don Watson and I were still devotees of the typist and photocopier. We overcame the problem of

The last rave of Les Harding. Bruce Spence in *The Floating World*, Front Theatre 1974. (Peter Corrigan)

stasis and ran into the problem of flux. Scenes were dizzyingly transposed, characters and their allegorical transformations kept shifting, it seemed, with the mindset of each day and its alteration. Gender and race came into question more insistently. Captain Cook was a woman. Manning should be played by a Koori. We sat around a table doing the epic in different voices, driving ourselves crazy until the Musical genre looked like a safe haven.

Romeril is a collaborator parfuckinexcellence. He sees theatre as a collaborative act, in a way a microcosm of an ideal social organisation. The playwright works among equals to make the play work. A lasting image of Romeril for me is him tapping away at an almost neutralised ribbon, working up a draft of *The Floating World* from diggers' journals, the samizdat of the camps of the Burma Railway. He is sitting in the dust of a two-storied mudbrick house of his own half-building, set on very stony ground, communing, collaborating with dead soldiers.

11 ★ The Circus Way Round

THE HOUSE WAS ON A PEAK in Thornbury next to the railway track, girt by a narrow moat. I crossed a little rounded bridge redolent of old Cathay. The front door was ajar and I entered to find Tim Coldwell alone in the kitchen, ruminant. He was perched against a dresser made as if from the wreckage of the *Pequod* by Bob Daly. A recently opened bottle of red wine was on the table. Tim pronounced it sour in a worldly manner and offered a glass. He suggested the living room. We moved through a hallway with sealed doors to the other half of the house in which another elder of Circus Oz, Alan Robertson, lived with Eve Glenn, though whether they were in or out he had no idea as he was not presently on speaking terms with them. In the living room a totem pole, bought on a sojourn to Bathurst Island, leaned against the wall, out of scale, in uneasy transit. Also uneasy, as ever in transit, Tim put on a old favourite Prez Prado LP, much louder than his customary *sotto voce*, and began to unspool his life. A man of few words, for whom doing is the best philosophy, he was not his dry, droll self but crossed in love, obsessed, the full Pagliacci. Talking his way, unaccustomed as he was, through 20 years of life in the circus, seemed to help. He wanted Her to know all he was telling me. It tumbled out in a compulsive, chronological progression, a dowry of data for the beloved who didn't want him, didn't know him.

We had known each other since Devil's Elbow days, student days at Flinders. At a tender age my daughter Pome pronounced him Timclown. The last time we had met was in the Melbourne Zoo to try and talk up a novel scenario for yet another show, but nothing much had been said. All I remember is him observing stoically that: 'There needs to be jokes,' and the toucan screeching. Nothing came of it. This evening in 1994, he was keyed for this encounter, however, in the mood to unburden. To the strains of *Patricia*, us two old Tims shifted about to find the right spatial relationship the one to the other, like two old dogs settling. We felt

Timclown traverses tent top with teacup, Tallahassee 1910.

foolish, interviewer/interviewee, side by side on a small, sagging sofa. Finally, after grumpily subduing Senor Prado, Timclown limped to a rotting behemoth of an armchair and rubbed at a recently snapped achilles tendon. I sat at his feet and said to myself the APG is dead, long live Circus Oz.

Tim might have taken exception to this sentiment. He was not one of the raft of ratbag ex-APG personnel that impressed upon the Circus Ozling a radical, democratic temper and its rough and ready, Aussie bias. Very much part of its genesis, indeed he claims to have come up with the name, he came into the fusion of fools another way round. Brought up vaguely hillbilly in a Ringwood that was still orchards and pinetrees away from the highway, Tim was a lad who could take the gearbox out of the Humber and put it back again. He was a Boy Scout for the flying foxes and bridgebuilding, he learnt how to sail. His Mum was a school librarian who told him he couldn't spend his whole life playing with motorbikes and trucks and packed him off to Monash to do science and become an engineer like his dad.

He became a dopesmoking, demonstrating drop-out, a footsoldier of the revolution, Albert Langer urging him on. After a season of soft riots he tired of the lumpen life and dropped further out to Adelaide where the dope was cheaper and his girlfriend had enrolled in Wal Cherry's new Drama course. He worked down the hill from Devil's Elbow for my neighbour, a Mr Pound:

> Funny bald guy from Dorsommersetshire with the dogs. Living with the dogs was vile. There was some weird Rosicrucian connection. He had a roomful of books but they may have been his wife's. His wife had just left him. He was mad and more into dogs. Had a couple of tractors, did rotary slashing. I tipped a tractor of his over backwards on top of me once. Fell in a hole. Fuckin' lucky. I was going to Flinders to find out what this Drama thing was about. I picked up on the idea of Popular Theatre that George Anderson was spouting—sending students off to Church, Football, discussing it as theatre. And there was the Circus—a form of Popular Theatre that was alive and well, just needing a kick up the bum.

The state of carnival up the road, the yawp of electrified Toads, the smoke from revels attendant on Flinders student productions, attracted him. He may even have seen my productions of Buechner's *Wozzeck* (sic), 'apocalyptic clownmare', or Beckett's *Endgame* or *The Truth About the Protection Racket*, a vaudevillian doco on censorship, I do not know. I was about to ask him as I, semi-recumbently, filled my glass and knocked it over. I arose and went to the kitchen in search of salt.

Timclown went prousting on solo, his brows knotted in recall, a touch of the debauched cherub about his barely moving lips, recounting how he met up with Mick Harbison, roaring boy, golden-maned and melancholy Jack Daniel, a natural Auguste, and David Black. Dave was

A form of Popular Theatre. (Barry Dickins)

a Law student who wanted to be a clown, counterweighted by a mum in Menindie with other ambitions. They started to skill themselves circus-wise—unicycle, juggling . . . Mick's idea of a good time was making expeditions into the desert in very old trucks. When got his degree he straightaway ran off to Ashton's Circus. Philippe Petit, unicycliste, juggleur, buskeur and equilibriste extraordinaire, showed up at Flinders after the Nimbin Aquarius Festival. He was an inspiration. He had walked over the Harbour Bridge the hard way; he showed how high the game could be lifted and was a master of the art of stroking up a crowd to remove its small change.

Tim signed on as a tenthand for Ashtons where a posh yet stentorian voice had already recommended Mick to Dougie, the Patriarch, as ringmaster material. They both learnt more about trucks, lots about putting tents up and circus lore from the likes of Frank Gasser, Mervyn and Dougie Ashton, Jonas Salenkas (the Man with the Iron Jaw) and Fanny Espinosa, the lion tamer. Fast Alf Jones floated off on a sabbatical to Sole's and Tim became the Elephant Boy for a couple of weeks:

> Nearly got killed, Abu nearly got me. Abu had killed someone before, killed a couple of people since and is still alive, being a very valuable elephant.

And then there was the Theo Zucchini Trio, musical clowns, a formative influence, he remembers with affection:

> Theo Zucchini, dirty old man, fantastic little Italian clown. Lewd. Lewd but he could get away with it because he was 70 years old and played the fool. Phillip—I think he was actually an adopted son—who was incredibly cool in patent leather slap shoes and tuxedo who also worked the elephants. They played these three trumpet things with metal reeds and a different bell for each note and a strange valve system, like a lot of horns stuck together. A melody one that Theo played and bass ones for Georgie and Phillip. Phillip also played sax, sometimes two at once, and Georgie the accordion. They had one of those little shaker things that whistle. We use them a bit in the circus now. Like a saw with springs, you shake it—ger-doyngadoyngadoyng!—and it sets up a vibration that whistles. Theo would announce: 'And now I sing!'
> > Giorgio: You don't sing here!
> > Theo: All right, I sing over here.
> > Phillip: No, no, no, you don't sing here!
> Mouthful of flour. Pffff! Theo spits out flour at the audience, goes off in a huff and farts flour out of his bum.

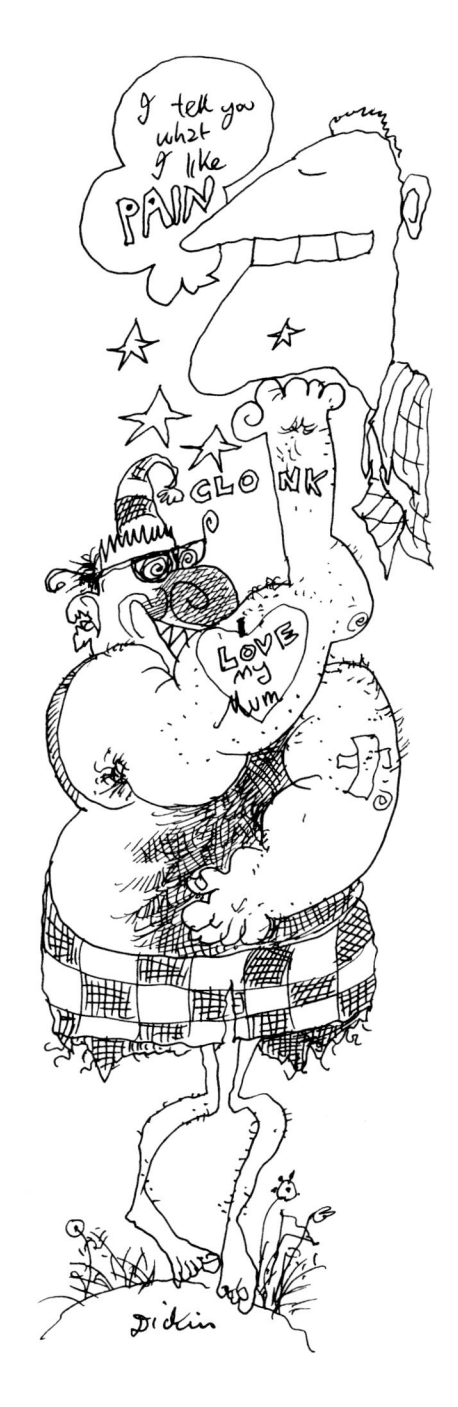

Men with Iron Jaws. (Barry Dickins)

Six months with Ashtons, and the Elephant Boy and the Ringmaster were established in the feudal world of the old circus—and wanted out. The new retainers did not want to become the old retainers they worked with, the characterful stuff of clowns. They wanted to become a new circus with their young selves in control, taking what they were learning

New Circus at the Adelaide Show in 1974. L–R: Mick Harbison, Tim Coldwell, David Black, unknown. (*Advertiser Newspapers Ltd*)

and loved about the old colonial/European tradition and do their own thing. With cool bravado they got their acts together. Mick volunteered to swallow a sword, Tim to ride a unicycle across the highwire and Jack said he'd learn to juggle five balls. They practised and practised and practised and exhibited themselves at the Royal Adelaide Show. Look Ma! Rude native saltimbanques! The Authorities moved to throw them out but relented when somebody who was organising a wine festival came up and invited them to perform for the duration.

> $640 comes to mind as the fee for the whole operation. Seemed like smart money at the time. We made this little show—got the truck painted up, put a little box at the back of it, got an old piano on it, made a high wire that came out over the top of it. Buzz Leeson came along as Musician, kind of MC, sat on the box at the back of the truck and shouted out instructions. We'd come on and do a series of acts as different troupes from different parts of the world. I did a sort of standard highwire but in a pierrot costume—dunno where that came from.

As they bluffed their way towards mastery, the legendary Frank Gasser was at the peak of his career doing six acts—two and a half somersaults, hand-to-hand balancing, head trapeze, platespinning—a circus in himself. He too was ambitious and wanting his independence. Circus Royale split off from Ashtons and the proto-New Circus went with them. A star- and Tim-struck Sue Broadway joined up, eager to find her own feats; Don Martin, a jongleur from California, turned up. They did the clown gags with Sonnyboy Gasser (out from Switzerland), the ringmastering and the rigging for another six months then struck off on their own in the summer of '74. The six of them in the old truck with a set of side walls, a bunch of chairs and an unreasonably high high-wire did shows around Adelaide. The spirit of pragmatic derring-do prevailed:

> We all had to make up a few more acts. I thought I can do a handstand—I'll do a chair balancing act. I went up to the garage and made a set of chairs, started doing a chair-balancing act. It was a straight pinch, a standard circus act. Albert Perry did a version of it, fairly straight. I must have seen pictures of other ones, Chinese ones. I started shouting back at the audience. I was Pepe, one of the Christiani Brothers.

The New Circus went on making itself up for another year, wondering which way to go, how to develop their bag of tricks, with an artistic and testosteronic rivalry growing between Tim and Mick that ended up in a fight in the best sawdust-and-tinsel tradition.

A new bond formed between the neophytes and Jim and Pixie Robertson, who had worked with Circus Royale after Tim had left. Pixie had worked in circuses in Europe. Jim knew the ropes backstage in theatres like the Princess and had a certain renown as the smaller Threequarters of the *One & Half Man Show* with Gary Patterson. These dynamic hobbits were fierce traditionalists, great believers in the neverending story of the Circus, sticklers for the good old ways and means. Pixie inducted the young Ms Broadway into the mysteries of the Web, an aerial act on a twirled rope.

At the Flying Trapeze cabaret in Melbourne Tim had met spheroid, circomanic John Pinder, the Aristide Bruant of Brunswick Street, whose showmanly ego, balls, cheek and dollar-spinning eyes were looking beyond the tiny Flytrap to the great hall of the Last Laugh. Told the New Circus had the show of his dreams for his new place, he chose to believe it. *Waiter, there's a Circus in My Soup* opened in May of '77 and ran till Christmas. It was the right place for the right show and light years from Ashtons and bred confidence and big ideas. After 150-odd shows Timclown began to think of himself as a performer. The increasingly cocky polymath of the little big top detested mere actors and saw that over two or three metres up in the air, they were unnecessary. The most desultory of performances was magically transformed when it defied gravity and the reflex of self preservation.

Circus Oz at the Last Laugh. Unicyclist: Tim Coldwell. Suspendees: Stephen Champion and Jon Hawkes (from ladder), Jack Daniel and Robin Laurie (off bandstand).
(Ponch Hawkes)

> I'd hardly ever seen a show in my life—except circuses—hardly ever been to the theatre. I thought we were doing something different to what actors do. I've been trying to analyse the difference between the way reality and the show fit together in the theatre and the way they do in the circus ever since. The connection between what's real and what the audience perceives. When you go to circus you see people really do things, really do impossible things. When you go to the theatre you see people pretend to do impossible things. You know that, you accept that they're pretending. When you go to the circus you're not supposed to know if they are or not, that seems to be the basis of it—real fraud.
>
> I'd been to the Pram Factory a couple of times. Saw the Popeye Puppets do Brecht's *Elephant Calf*, the one where Tony Taylor was a tank, Hellen Sky was the elephant and Graeme Isaac was the moon. Very taken with that, I was. I'd seen *The Hills Family Show* in Adelaide and didn't like it. Searching for a sort of pure . . .

I broke the thread of Timclown's manifesto returning from the kitchen with the Saxa to absorb the red, elephant-shaped stain from the carpet and insert a spot of memorialising in parallel.

By 1973, some members of the APG, Towerchildren in the main, had begun to take a jaundiced view of *mimesis* in the theatre as a tired old game. They also thought there were other, better ways of performing than pretending. Their best idea of theatre was to get out of it, shrug off the burden of running a venue and try and pack a political punch beyond the Carlton ghetto. Whitlam's dismissal stoked the fire in the political belly that the Whitlam years and Arts Council Grants had dampened down. The view from the Tower by the mid '70s was that the work of re-establishing Australian plays by Australian playwrights was done. It was time was now for a Great Stumble Forward towards a politically correct Australian Circus.

Jon Hawkes had no illusions about his own acting talent. He felt no chagrin about this. It was his opinion that Max Gillies, for example, simply had a box of tricks for doing plays and he didn't. Consequently, when in 1974 the Hannans proposed a Mobile Theatre Troupe Project to go out after an ethnic audience, using the popular Italian form of Canta Storia, he was into it. So were Laurel Frank, Alan Robertson, Carol Porter, Michael Price, Robin Laurie, Greig Pickhaver, Richard Murphett. They were tired of doing straight plays. They wanted to develop new skills, physical, musical and political. There had been considerable traffic between the Tower kitchen and the one shared by two interconnecting houses in Greville Street, Prahran. Here the Conway Bros of the Captain Matchbox Whoopee Band were holed up, looking for a life beyond psychedelia, nostalgia, cult status and Malcolm Fraser. Mick Conway and Graeme Isaac fell into musical cahoots.

These people got very fit, and after a juggling gestation of about six months, the Mobile Theatre Project had become Soapbox Circus and put on *The Timor Show*. They toured the pubs and clubs of the rock 'n' roll circuit and proved the veracity of Alan Robertson's First Law of Performance: That power comes out of the horn of a 300-watt amplifier. Performing in drunken venues, they also proved that if you stand on someone's shoulders and juggle three balls, people may listen to what you say and are less inclined to throw things. New Circus had run into Soapbox Circus in Adelaide, 1976. There was an instant rapport between them and some interaction in performances. Both sides saw their opportunity but were not unanimous about the direction a merged, new New circus might go. Timclown, as is his wont, had reservations:

Soapbox Circus. L–R: Carol Porter, Hellen Sky (in elephant), Robin Laurie. Beneath: Jon Hawkes. Behind: Matchbox with Ric Ludbrooke on guitar. (Ponch Hawkes)

> While New Circus was not deep in the lore of the traditional circus we were still trying to do something with it, rather than denying it. Maybe I didn't really think Soapbox were for real on the circus side of things, or were going to work hard enough, or learn enough. Soapbox were doing political numbers with singing and juggling. I could never quite wear the juggling, the way they did it and they juggled a lot. It was a bit ponderous and its connection with the story of East Timor was tenuous. It didn't seem popular, directed enough towards the masses. I had the sense that was what circus was about at that stage. Also I had a notion of how the circus

had been before and could be again: a respected, high-class family entertainment. Soapbox Circus seemed a bit cerebral, designed: 'We'll do circus because it's popular and we'll play rock 'n' roll venues because that's where people go, then we'll force unpopular bits down their throats.' So they got 'mooned' at.

Soapbox Circus, non-didactic for the nonce, was doing a slaphappy version of the medieval interlude *Gamma Gurton's Needle*, entitled *Smackinthedacks,* as a Christmas panto at the Pram towards the end of the Last Laugh season. Inevitably there was a deal of rolling up and raving in the Tower kitchen and also at Pinder's house in Drummond Street. However wary the parties, none could deny that New Circus had the tricks in the air, Soapbox had a few on the ground plus the APG space and funding potential, Pinder had the hip capitalist *savoir-faire*. They merged under APG auspices and in 1977 screeds of figures began to appear in Jon Hawkes's fair italian hand. A hiring company called Circus Australia P/L was set up which offered to hire the APG a circus tent. With Pinder as chief negotiator Moomba and the Melbourne Drama Festival, drawn on by a dazzling, non-existent show, agreed to provide the serious money for the APG to pay for the hire of a tent plus rehearsal in full, up front. The APG contributed some of its General Purpose grant as well. A nice bit of legerdemain but they went one better.

Something like a sparkle came to Timclown's lovelorn eyes, the steady drip from the old sour mash of his memory began spill into a flow of delight, almost, as he recalled the Astonishing Fabrication of the Tent.

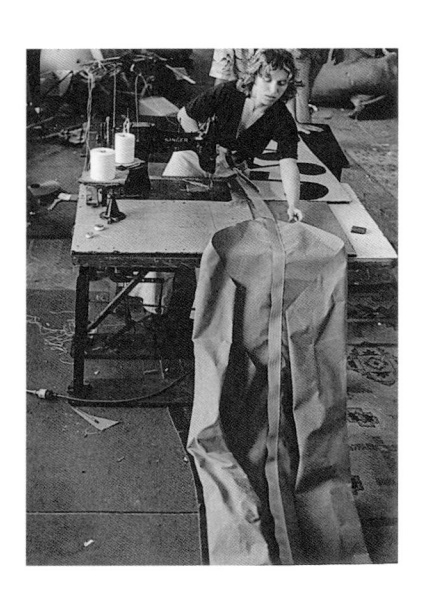

Sue Broadway sewing a big top.
(Ponch Hawkes)

We were going to hire a tent from Frank [Gasser], then Jim and I sat down and thought: for that money we could just about make one of them ourselves! I ran around chasing up people I knew on the circuit who'd made tents or could tell me about them, old showies like Lester Quay. And we said: 'Fuck it, we'll make it.' We had the nerve to believe that we could actually make a circus tent in the Pram Factory Basement. Me and Sue and Jack and Laurel Frank did most of the sewing. Sometimes Pixie but she'd just had a baby. And Jim and this Chilean guy, who had just walked in off the street, a political refugee. He was a welding instructor and he couldn't get a job and here were these people in this workers' theatre building this circus tent.

'I can world for jew', he said.

And with Jimbo, who had done a lot of welding, he helped build the poles while we were out the back sewing the canvas. Every now and then we'd get everybody in, drag it down the park and spread it out. With free labour, no design fee and materials scrounged at cost, we did it. Upstairs at night, *A Mad World, My Masters* was on and a character with a mechanical phallus was forever coming down to the basement to make running repairs. This was the only part of the show I saw, except for Kerry Dwyer who'd occasionally pop down undressed as a stripper. We'd go up for a coffee at interval completely green from the canvas.

★ The Circus Way Round ★   137

Raising the king poles for the first time at Princes, sorry, Optus Park, 1978. (Ponch Hawkes)

Below: Unicyclical, mustachio'd triumph, Carlton Gardens, 1978. (Ponch Hawkes)

The tape ran out. Expecting to draw discourse from Timclown as blood from a stone, I had only brought the one. After a brief agonising over the relative value of those in the house collection, he proffered Jimi Hendrix's *All Along The Watchtower* and his oral annals spooled over it, a symbol of all the fusion of circus and rock 'n' roll that happened in the '70s.

Putting on the Show was a piece of piss after making the Tent. The music component took a quantum leap. Circus Oz played Moomba and the Adelaide Festival with acclaim in the summer of '78 with 30 people on the books. Then the whole thing stopped. The band decided to go off and be a rock 'n' roll band called Matchbox. They got a gig in the Pram Factory Picture *Dimboola*. The others stayed and did a school show. At the end of the year they did workshops and put a show together with the VCA, pitching the Tent in the backyard of the National Gallery with Albert Hunt over from England directing. Stephen Champion and Jane Mullet joined the fold.

At the end of '78 they did another show at the Last Laugh. Jim and Pixie had left because they couldn't believe the circus was hanging about in town and not going On the Road with the Tent, forthwith. They travelled via a short circuit of circuses to Albury, there to raise children and initiate the Fruit Flies into the mysteries and traditions of the circus.

Timclown in *fin de siècle* Melbourne, pacing, sighing, groaning, for the first time shows signs of mnemonic stress, turns up a screaming Cuban trumpet. The dimensions of the room expand tenfold. Through the window hurtles a man in bright orange overalls, leather flying helmet and goggles. He springs up to the light depending on chains from a crumbling plaster rose on the ceiling. He swings wildly above our heads. The rose wilts alarmingly.

'Special Robert—Away!'

cries the antic aviator and flies off the light to smack into a wall. He sticks fast. It's Geoff Toll, back from the desert, believing on the power of the Velcrose! He devised the stunt in 1982 for a show in Canberra. He had obligingly adapted it to re-enact the attempted suicide of Henry Lawson, when I was impersonating Manning Clark in an early trial of *History of Australia*, before it was a Musical.

'Special Henry—Away!'

he'd sung out and ridden a long, wild pendulum arc across the Melbourne Concert Hall auditorium and splat! there he was glued to a panel, twenty metres up. He was one of the Comedy Cafe bunch, part of *The Razzle Dazzle Revue* with Rod Quantock and Co., and came to Circus Oz with a desire to become a show drummer, the Ringmaster as drummer, preferably working upside down. I get up to help him off the

Coldwell plays his version of 'Alone, all alone, on a night that was meant for love' for a rapt Ginny Pinder and publicity.

livingroom wall and he pads off back into the future on feather-shod feet. The Epiphany of St Geoff had done the trick. Timclown was upside down on the ceiling, adhering by his feet, in full retrospective spate once more:

> I introduced the roof walk for the second Last Laugh show. First the idea was a waiter who walks up the wall, across the ceiling and down the other side but I figured that walking on the ceiling was the easiest way to get maximum effect in that space. OK. How? You can use magnets or you can use suction cups but these things sounded pretty hightech. Then I

thought: who givesa . . . you slide along and no one'll notice. Pinder, who'd had worked on a lot of magic shows—Sam Angelico, Ross Skiffington—said no, it won't work, you'll be able to see how its done. You'd see the trick, not the illusion. I was convinced that it would be illusory enough for the punters. I worked out I could put hooks in a pair of boots and put tracks on the roof. Did the Yellow Pages, rang up people that made anything that sounded like that. Found a couple of steel sections and made some wheels, bought some hooks and made a pair of boots, a couple of short lengths of track and hung it up somewhere; figured I could walk two steps on that, fine, bought the full lengths. I got onto Peter Hill (setbuilder at the Laugh):

'We need two bits of fourbetwo and whack on some masonite to make a "floor". Leave the two tracks open down the middle and paint it the same colour as the ceiling, crawl up there, make holes in the roof and drag the whole thing up in six foot intervals. Cool school.'

Then I got up and did it. Dress rehearsal. I remember being terrified the first time. As we were putting it up, I'd kept wondering what I would do on it, with no idea what was possible. I went for the musical clown image, got a euphonium and put it up there on a hook. Cardboard box around it so the lid flopped shut, put a music stand in it. First time with an audience I hung there in the spotlight and tapped my foot. *Weird* laughs. People picked up on it in a strange way, a slow, creepy sort of thing. Someone's hanging upside down from the roof! I just tap my foot for a while, then start walking.

'Fuck he's walkin'! He's fuckin' walkin'!'

High hoots and shrieks of nervous sporadic laughter. Nobody knew how to relate to it and when I was hanging over the people sitting downstairs, it'd get sort of hysterical. Audiences loved it. I go to open the box and they'd piss themselves. I'd get the music stand out and kind of stand it on the 'floor' and did some business with the music, then pulled the euphonium out and played *Alone* from Alan Jones's *Donkey Serenade*:

'Alone, all alone on a night that was meant for love.'

I put the stand back in the box and slid off. It was a hit.

After a couple of months of that he got a headache that wouldn't go away and when they went to the (now demolished) Paris Theatre for a Sydney season he gave the roofwalk to Toll. Geoffrey bought a little drum kit and bolted it on to the apparatus. At first he was a beatnik, Cheech and Chong style, smoking an enormous prop joint with Jonno:

Geoffrey: I'm gonna get high, man.
Jonno: You gonna get high?
Geoffrey: Hang loose.

Bells once belonging to the act of the nineteenth-century touring campanologists, the Lynch family, four of a large set last played in *The Hills Family Show*, recycled again by Shirley Billing, Tim Coldwell, Julie McInnes and Derek Jones. (Ponch Hawkes)

Goes up the ladder, tracks along ceiling and plays drums with great fervour. Bored with this routine and into Carl Sagan at the time, he subsequently became an inverted astronomer. Tim went back up to regenerate the act with a scripted, Raymond Chandler pastiche.

After Sydney the circus went international for the best part of a year—to Papua New Guinea, to Holland, touring the *Staatschouwburgs*, fitting the show into proscenium arch spaces. They did a season at the Roundhouse in London, which might have been built for them, and then the Chichester Festival. They came across a punk a cappella group called Furious Pig. Sue Broadway fell in love with one of its members, Stephen Kent, a lean, elegant loon who could fold himself neatly into a suitcase. Sue carried him back to Australia.

Back home in February of 1981, Circus Oz did nothing for a spell, except exercise its grantsmanship. They wanted to work with a couple of crazy, cosmic Catalans, Juan Baixas and Teresa Calafel, who had come out with their richly visual puppet show, *La Claqua* (costumes by Miro), for an Adelaide Festival. Communication between collaborators was on a surreal footing. Juan suggested the Australians take as their theme 'The Cows of the Universe'. Puzzled, they went along with the notion and only later, better able to penetrate his accent, did they discover that Chaos was intended. A show was commissioned by the next Adelaide festival director, Jim Sharman. The creative process became

The cows of the universe hop into their cossies designed by Juan Baixas and Teresa Calafel of La Claqua, the Catalan puppetshow company. (Ponch Hawkes)

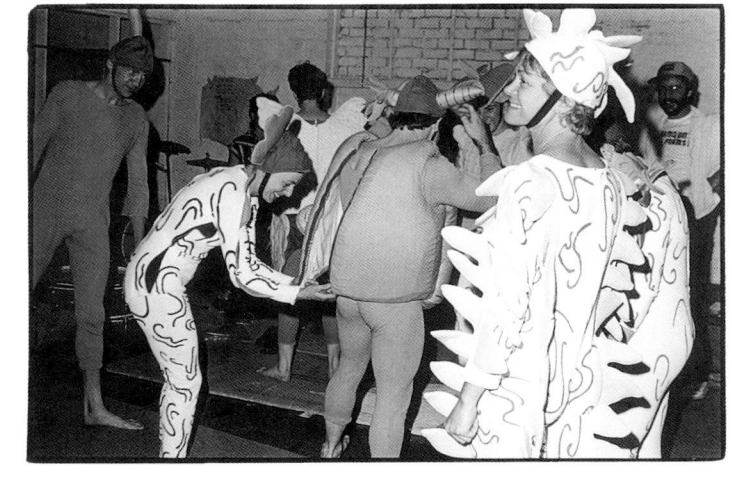

tense. Jonno, for one, was not on the same wavelength as Juan and Teresa and put up resistance, arguing about what they could and couldn't do. He was under stress, raising money with Pinder, and muttered darkly: 'Fuckit. I'm not going to perform, I'll just do the books.'

Timclown sojourned in Sydney a while, happily domiciled with Kerry Dwyer and her kids, dickering with designs for transportable seating for the Tent. His fellow clowns put ads in the Melbourne Age:

'Circus Looking for Home Base.'

Michael Leunig's mother replied and they all moved on to her property in Daylesford and camped there for a couple of months. They built the seats, bought a whole lot of trucks, tried to sort the Chaos of the Universe and set off on a tour round the south coast to Adelaide. They opened in a gale at Port Fairy. Rehearsal was all to pieces due to their preoccupation with infrastructure and frazzling internal ructions. Helen Garner panned their efforts with faint praise:

'Never mind the show, feel the seats.'

By the time the show got to Adelaide whatever ideas had come out of Juan and Teresa had worked through some rough, magical filter and developed into a brilliant, ecstatic piece of theatre.

A rot set in during the following season at Wentworth Park in Sydney. The Vibe was bad, everyone got sick and things began to fall apart. Professionally submerged differences, divisions, aggressions boiled up and became irrevocable. A bit of silly business that went sour exemplifies the low state of affairs. One evening, appearing as Alphonso Spagoni, the strong man, Jonno was doing the rope trick he got from Max Gillies. Timclown came on as nasty Uncle Jack and stood behind him, trying to tear a telephone book in half. People started laughing. Alphonso didn't twig to what was going on till he was done and there Uncle Jack was still madly tearing upstage. Jonno burned with a cold fury. Tim could only feel disappointed he hadn't ripped through the L to Z in time. This marked a parting of the ways. In the spring of 1982 Jonno went off to be the strongman of Community Arts with the Australia Council. Robin Laurie left. Stephen Champion left and Tim Coldwell left.

Sue Broadway, Jack Daniel, Geoff Toll, Angela Seaweed, Don Rosella, Stephen Kent, David Houghton, Jane Mullet and Alan Robertson soldiered on. Jenny Saunders came in to replace Jonno as administrator. Timclown began to hamlet about whether to be or not to be a performer:

> Circus Oz kept being on and off, on and off. As the '80s wore on we weren't doing a lot of work in Australia and that was what I wanted. I never liked the touring aspect. I hated hotel rooms before I'd even stayed in one. And they didn't get better. If I missed a Melbourne show it felt like I really wasn't part of it.

★ The Circus Way Round ★　　143

Coldwell on the set of *Molly the Singing Dog*, with the quondam Captain Matchbox, Mic Conway, who reclines on the constantly recycled tumbling moon, originally designed by Graeme Isaac for *Mary Shelley and the Monsters* in 1975.

The collective was difficult but it worked. Things didn't happen exactly how you wanted them to but that was interesting. I liked that aspect of it. If I had had to start from scratch it wouldn't have been half of what it is. Combine ideas and totally different ideas come out. I don't think the didactic intention was as prominent early on as some people say. A lot of it was learning how to do circus, finding out what made the powerful bits really work, the basic formulas. Nobody knew what might come up next.

We were going for a form but no one was sure what it was. Some things were absolutely there but there was a feeling always of something missing. But that's what you do. You work and something comes out of it. What's important is doing it and not necessarily getting it right. The idea of perfection . . .

Enter Mr Lu and Mr Yang riding into Albury on the Dragon of Instruction. Mr Yang dismounts, folded umbrella held up in one hand, bottle in the other. Throws bottle up in the air. It comes down neck first onto the umbrella spike. Mr Yang presses secret button and water pours out of bottle.

Mr Yang: Is raining!

Attendant inscrutable musclemen begin counting in mandarin. Timclown, Sue Broadway and forty or so Fruit Flies stand on their hands against the wall. They go down, up, down, up, in time, for three minutes—pause—begin again. Jack Daniel commences 2000 push-ups. Pumped-up Chinaman laughs scrutably. Jack disappears. Children form human pyramid, dive wailing through hoops and are soothed with gobstoppers and goanna salve by Pixie Robertson. Derek Ives, a punk prodigy from the Rock 'n' Roll Circus in Brisbane stands facing the wall, perfectly still. So do Judy Pascoe and Tim Tyler (aka Mr Pipi). They each have a chopstick balanced on their head. They stand there for an hour and a half, every day for three weeks. Mr Yang smiles approvingly. He balances a chopstick on his head. He balances an egg on the chopstick. Calls for another egg. Balances it on the egg on the chopstick. Calls for another egg. Same business.

Tim did hand balancing with Lu Guang Rong, developing quite a close relationship with him, given Lu spoke no word of English. He showed him the chair act. The response came through the interpreter:

'Mr Lu say he understand why you make joke on chairs.'

Trained to an Olympic level in the Chinese circus of the absurd, Timclown found himself in L.A. with some of the Circusozzies, playing the Olympic Arts Festival. High times. In Hollywood he taught some guy to do the chair act for Circus of the Stars, deluxing dourly with Judy Pascoe, who got to do the Chopstick and the Eggs on the show, live from Vegas.

Back home things swung on just fine for a few years but by 1988 the Old Guard collective didn't really exist any more. The anarchic, collective past was looking down the barrel of a commodified, corporate future. The words 'hire' and 'fire' entered the lexicon. Titles made their appearance for the first time—Artistic Co-ordinator, Production Manager—that failed to define the complex roles the Old Guard was used to playing. After Ponch Hawkes stopped doing the lights, for example, someone else was hired and they just did the lights, not the lights *and* the photography *and* business *and* personnel management. Timclown was adamant:

> It doesn't work. I don't do only one thing. And I can't accept the notion that you set up a theoretical construct to run something like a circus and then look for people to fit the jobs that you've defined. It's absolutely arse-about in any organisation but the circus has always been the other way. You define people by what they can do, what they're good at, what they want to do. The job's defined by the person.

A new Administrator was appointed and a bitchy power struggle was joined in the office while Jonno and Pinder, back with visions of a Big Show renaissance, were chasing money from the Bicentennial Authority. The Big Grant failed to materialise and they pulled out again. It was the end of the road for nearly all of the Old Guard. They were worn out. Ducking and weaving through *scheissenkriegen,* Robin Laurie was directing the actual show with Emil Wolk (from *People Show*, the eternal hippie, British theatrical troupe, who had trucked on for over twenty years through *People Shows 2, 3, . . .*). A new generation of performers came in.

Australian youth being instructed in the ancient art of jumping through hoops by Mr Zhu Fusheng on the right.

Bridges were built, blood flowed under them, audiences flocked and the overseas circuit got stronger. Circus Oz became a mature operation playing Melbourne and Sydney and either Brisbane or Adelaide every year, a bigger show, longer seasons (three to four weeks), to 700 people every night.

In 1990 Archaos came to Melbourne and catalysed a last radical hurrah that went wrong. Timclown had met up with these dangerous French freaks in London and they were the best thing he had ever seen in his young life. They had taken the classic circus and subverted it, post-apocalyptically. A Circus of Cruelty. Raw. Riven with sex and death. Full of mad laughter. Foul with the stench of gasoline and brimstone. Isabelle did the cloud (ropeswinging) act screaming with rage. Stephan, gun bikeboy in leathers, revved up the role of the liberty horse, riding around the ringboxes on one wheel. Ascent was by chainsaw, adapted with winchdrum and cable. Crazy Parisian arab clowns threw fireworks. Patou and Pierrot wore crash helmets and sheets of corrugated iron on their backs, hit each other on the iron with sticks, screeching with laughter, elemental slapstick.

The Circus Oz show for the Swan Street season at the end of 1990 was clearly under the influence of these diabolical pranksters. It was darker, had lost its usual Austral innocence. For other reasons but equally clearly, it was not together, did not come together and people stayed away. It lacked, in the Board's opinion, artistic quality, was not good enough and had lost too much money, so the Board pulled the plug on the Sydney tour. Timclown, uneasily wearing the hat of Artistic Director, was outraged. No matter how passionately he argued for the miracles that can happen through work and perseverance, positive support and organic growth (Remember the road from Port Fairy to Adelaide!), the Board remained negative:

'Nuh, it's not working. We're going to restructure the company. We're getting George Fairfax in to write a report.'

Thus Globo, Equilibrist of Balancesheet and Bottomline, got billing over the hapless pierrots on the high wire, management ruled over the mysteries of the circus organism and Timclown began walking backwards into a nervous breakdown.

He scored a Keating fellowship. He just had to help whack a little country tour together and he was free to recharge for a year when suddenly the Administrator announced:

'We're off to Edinburgh and a tour of England!'

It was hard. They were not prepared. Accidents happened. People began to flip out and the day before opening night Anni Davey fell off the pole and broke her neck. They had perforce to stagger on. The Melbourne season was locked in as soon as they got back. There were machinations, grandstanding, *grosse scheissenkrieg* as the new structure was implemented. There was to be a three-person Executive. As Artistic Director, Timclown was to be on it but he'd had enough, he needed to get out. The Board insisted he had an Obligation, the Restructuring required it, the Money depended on it. Why should he be the one free to skip off? The warring between Artistic License and Administrative Control flared up again. Resentfully, Timclown climbed back into his trench, held out briefly, then he lost it.

He walked out into the desert. He wanted to think about circus and the Aborigines but found he was incapable of thought, full stop. Off he went to Europe to do a few festivals, check out what was new and powerful. Over there he got a flurry of faxes. He had been denounced as a destructive element and replaced *in absentia*. The Administrator was away with the economically rational pixies and Sue Broadway had been appointed Artistic Director.

He got to the end of the Fellowship money. The circus was going to South America and the One he loved had signed back on. So, bereft of confidence, did he. There had been a lot of company turnaround, and displaced from the centre he felt he was working back from the ground again. It was, he reasoned, something to do with a process of recovery in his head that was keeping pace with Anni's neck, coming to terms with the responsibility of nearly having killed somebody. Given time, given love . . . but then he busted his Achilles tendon in the bike act.

He had exhausted the battery in the recorder and the memorialist but not his spiel. In playback he can no longer be heard as he goes on like Socrates at the Symposium, his words lost in a snoring static, touching on mysteries no one can hear—Real Fraud, the possibilities of crosscultural circus, the Mexican Day of the Dead. And love. The next day he was flying out to Tel Aviv. He gave me the address of an hotel he wasn't sure he'd be staying at, or for quite how long.

When I last saw him perform, years after our interview, he was high up in the roof of the Melbourne Town Hall, among the lights. He had made it to the Circus Oz 21st Birthday show and was now about twice the age of almost everyone else. Bare-assed with wings on, covered in white powder, he was perpetrating himself as a plaster Cupid. He was very still and centred, waiting patiently for the corporate sponsors to finish their promotional speeches. When his cue came, the chunky, somewhat simian godlet of Love let fly, but in a workmanlike manner, a flaming arrow of desire, on a wire. It connected with big, pretend candles on a big, cardboard cake down below. The gratuitously dangerous, transparently artificial illumination was the source of real delight.

So we the audience struck our palms together, producing noise and warmth and communion.

The chair act at the City Square for the greening of Swanston Street. Coldwell, above, tips his lid under the upside-down, Raymond Chandler, gumshoe shuffle. Judy Pascoe sulks, disinclined to assist, below. (Ponch Hawkes)

Appendix 1: A Chronology of Productions

1968

APRIL

Brainrot, an Evening of Pathology and Violence, Love and Friendship (Jack Hibberd) includes *This Great Gap of Time, One of Nature's Gentlemen, Just before the Honeymoon, Jack Juan* (music by Stuart Challender), *No Time like the Present, O* and *Who*. Directors: David Kendall, Graeme Blundell and Brian Davies. At the Prince Philip Theatre, Melbourne University.

JUNE

The Soul Seeker (Kris Hemensley) at La Mama.

JULY

One of Nature's Gentlemen (Jack Hibberd) at La Mama
The Audience's Audience (Bill Garner) at La Mama

SEPTEMBER

First Actors Workshop at La Mama.

NOVEMBER

First Workshop Performance Season at La Mama. Improvisations around *A Nameless Concern* (John Romeril) and *One of Nature's Gentlemen* (Jack Hibberd).

DECEMBER

Actor/writer workshop (John Hooker *inter alia*) at La Mama.

1969

JANUARY/FEBRUARY

Seven plays over six weekends at La Mama: *Who* and *O* (Jack Hibberd), *Escape* (William Wood), *Calm Down Mother, Keep Tightly Closed* (Megan Terry), *Orison* (Fernando Arrabal) and *The Carpark Event* (David Minter and John Romeril).

MAY

Mayday Street and Guerrilla Theatre on the Yarra Bank and *Mr Big, the Big, Big Pig* (John Romeril).

La Mama Arts Festival Season. Thirty performances in ten days.
>   *Commitment, Who, O, No Time like the Present, One of Nature's Gentlemen* (Jack Hibberd), *Calm Down Mother, Keep Tightly Closed* (Megan Terry), *Mr Big, the Big, Big Pig* (John Romeril), *The Elephant Calf, The Exception and the Rule* (Bertolt Brecht) and *The Birth of Space* (a non-verbal event by Clem Gorman and the Australian Free Theatre Group).

JULY
The American Independence Hour (John Romeril). *Dimboola* (Jack Hibberd).
The English Lesson (Barry Oakley). A season with Tribe's *Programmes A and B* at La Mama
The Exception and the Rule and *The Elephant Calf* (Bertolt Brecht) at La Mama and Melbourne University.
Mr Big, the Big Big Pig (John Romeril), factory tour.
Norm and Ahmed (Alex Buzo) at La Mama and the Melburnian Reception Rooms.

AUGUST
Dimboola (Jack Hibberd) at the Melburnian Reception Rooms.
In a Place Somewhere Else, street theatre for the Australian Labor Party Prahran election campaign.
Norm and Ahmed (Alex Buzo) at the Australian National University for the University Drama Festival.
The Kitchen Table (John Romeril) at La Mama.

SEPTEMBER
Season of plays at the Arts Lab in Sydney: *Comings and Goings* (Megan Terry), *Red Cross* (Sam Shepard) and *O* (Jack Hibberd).

OCTOBER
I Don't Know Who to Feel Sorry for (John Romeril) at La Mama.

NOVEMBER
Preparation for the Perth Arts Festival.
APG factory tour under the auspices of Australian Metal Workers Union, *The Developing Story of Mr Big*.

DECEMBER
Christmas pageant.
Whatever Happened to Realism? (John Romeril) with the band Semblance of Dignity in the La Mama carpark.
Work in progress and revival season.
The Audience's Audience (Bill Garner) at La Mama.

1970

JANUARY
Perth Arts Festival: *White with Wire Wheels* and *Who* (Jack Hibberd), *The Front Room Boys* and *Norm and Ahmed* (Alex Buzo), *The Man From Chicago* (John Romeril) and street theatre at Beatty Park Aquatic Centre and King's Park.

MARCH
Perth season revived at La Mama and the Prince Philip Theatre, Melbourne University.
International Women's Day: improvised play at National Mutual Centre Theatrette.
Pot and Peace Miracle Play (John Romeril). Outdoor pop/peace show. Washed out.

MAY
Pot and Peace Miracle Play, Open Day Melbourne University.
Dr Karl's Kure (John Romeril), May Day on Yarra Bank.
Customs and Excise (Jack Hibberd) at the Guild Theatre, Melbourne University. Two-week, lunch-hour season.
Street Theatre for the Vietnam Moratorium.
Dr Karl's Kure at the first meeting of the Melbourne Arts Co-op.
Customs and Excise at La Mama. Three-week season.
Dr Karl's Kure at Footscray Institute of Technology (sponsored by the Let It Be Agency).
Customs and Excise at Footscray Institute of Technology.
Factory tour of an adaption of *Dr Karl's Kure* (sponsored by the Amalgamated Engineers Union).

JUNE
First meeting of a six-month actors/writers workshop at the Ballet Guild, Bouverie Street, Carlton.

OCTOBER
Customs and Excise tour to Flinders University, South Australia.

DECEMBER
Marvellous Melbourne workshop production (Jack Hibberd, John Romeril and the actors). The first show at the Pram Factory.

1971

MARCH
Marvellous Melbourne re-worked version. Four-week season.

APRIL
Brother Dave (John Romeril). Tour for Union Arts Festival.

MAY
Brother Dave lunch-hour performances at Melbourne University.
Street theatre events developed in Tony Taylor's street theatre workshop, performed at various locations, 29 May – 30 June.
Workshops conducted by APG with actors from Portable Theatre.
    Secondary Factory for inner suburban kids each Tuesday at 4.30 with Kerry Dwyer and Claire Dobbin. Puppet Factory, Saturday mornings with Kerry Dwyer and Tony Taylor. Children's Creative Workshop, Saturday mornings with Christine Mearing.
There were also workshops for the Victorian Association for Teachers of English, Melbourne University and Swinburne Institute of Technology.

JUNE
Chicago, Chicago (John Romeril). Originally entitled *The Man from Chicago*. Directed by Max Gillies at the Pram Factory.
Dr Spock Play (group-created with John Romeril) at the Moorabbin Town Hall.

JUNE/JULY
Magnetic Martian Potato Play for schools developed by Kerry Dwyer and Graeme Blundell.

JULY/AUGUST
Christie in Love (Howard Brenton) and *Mrs Thally F.* (John Romeril) at the Pram Factory.
Christie in Love/Mrs Thally F. Lunch-hour season at the Guild Theatre.
Christie in Love/Mrs Thally F. Lunch-hour season at Monash University.

AUGUST/SEPTEMBER
Don's Party (David Williamson), directed by Graeme Blundell at the Pram Factory.

OCTOBER/NOVEMBER
The Feet of Daniel Mannix (Barry Oakley), directed by Graeme Blundell at the Pram Factory.

DECEMBER
10 Years of Film-Making (Arthur and Corinne Cantrill).
Poetry reading with Chris Wallace-Crabbe, King Hippo's Poetry Band, Stephen Gray, Garrie Hutchinson, John Romeril, Marc Radzyner and others.
The Feet of Daniel Mannix (Barry Oakley). A fund-raiser at $20 per head.
Concert by George Dreyfus.

31 DECEMBER
Rock concert.

1972

JANUARY/MARCH
Betty Can Jump, a feminist show, group-created in conjunction with the Carlton women's group.

MARCH/APRIL
A Stretch of the Imagination (Jack Hibberd). Peter Cummins as Monk O'Neill, directed by Jack Hibberd.

APRIL/MAY
Sonia's Knee and Thigh Show, a group-created political revue.

JUNE/JULY
The Compulsory Century (Bill and Lorna Hannan).
Hackett Gets Ahead, a group-created daytime show for schools.

AUGUST/SEPTEMBER
Bastardy (John Romeril), directed by Bruce Spence.
A Stretch of the Imagination (Jack Hibberd) with Peter Cummins, directed by Jack Hibberd, a new production.

SEPTEMBER
He Can Swagger Sitting Down (John Romeril).

OCTOBER
Joss Adams Show (Alma De Groen).

NOVEMBER
Brumby Innes (Katharine Susannah Prichard).
Turn his Bones to Silver and Gold and *Give Me Air* (Bill and Lorna Hannan).
The Tempest (William Shakespeare), Performance Syndicate, directed by Rex Cramphorn.

DECEMBER
A Night in Rio with a Few Stupid Mexicans and Other Bummers. Group-created rock 'n' roll cabaret in collaboration with Tim Robertson and John Romeril.

1973

JANUARY/MARCH
Beware of Imitations (Barry Oakley) with Max Gillies and Bruce Spence, directed by Bill Hannan.

FEBRUARY
Captain Midnight V.C. (Jack Hibberd), a Melbourne University student production, directed by John Smythe.

MARCH
The Bob and Joe Show. Mime and modern dance with Bob Thorneycroft and Joe Bolza.
Season of Hibberd and Romeril plays to open the Back Theatre: *One of Nature's Gentlemen*, *O*, and *Just before the Honeymoon* (Jack Hibberd), and *Mrs Thally F.* (John Romeril).

APRIL/JUNE
Dimboola (Jack Hibberd). A licensed theatre-restaurant show at the Pram.

JUNE/JULY
The Dragon Lady's Revenge, group-created by the San Francisco Mime Troupe.

JULY
The Ride across Lake Constance (Peter Handke), production by Tribe in the Back Theatre.

JULY/AUGUST
Come out Fighting and *Milhouse*. Films by Nigel Buesst.

AUGUST/SEPTEMBER
Bob and Joe Show II. Bob Thorneycroft and Joe Bolza.
Mechanics in a Relaxed Manner, directed by Jane Clifton in the Back Theatre.

SEPTEMBER
Who (Jack Hibberd) and *The Dumb Waiter* (Harold Pinter), directed by Charles Kemp in the Back Theatre.

OCTOBER/NOVEMBER
Earth, Air, Fire and Water Show, group-created revue (Jack Hibberd, John Romeril and the actors).

NOVEMBER
One of Nature's Gentlemen (Jack Hibberd) and *The Independent Female* (San Francisco Mime Troupe). Tour of Tasmania.

NOVEMBER/JANUARY 1974
Waltzing Matilda, a National Pantomime with Tomato Sauce. Group-created with Tim Robertson and John Romeril.

1974

JANUARY
Africa, a Savage Rock Musical (Steve Spears), directed by Lindzee Smith in the Back Theatre.

JANUARY/FEBRUARY
The Architect and the Emperor of Assyria (Fernando Arrabal), directed by Lindzee Smith.

FEBRUARY/MARCH
Women's Weekly Vols I and II. Group-developed and the origin of the Women's Theatre Group. Back Theatre.
Street theatre for the Australian Labor Party campaign.

MARCH/APRIL
On Yer Marx (John Wood)

MAY
Out of the Frying Pan. Women's Theatre Group Festival, including *Love Show*, documentary theatre, poetry readings and music.

JUNE/JULY
Peggy Sue (Jack Hibberd), directed by Kerry Dwyer.
White Nigger (Phil Motherwell, adapted from Brecht's *Jungle of the Cities*).

AUGUST
The Floating World (John Romeril), directed by Lindzee Smith.

SEPTEMBER
Orestes Trilogy (Aeschylus). Theatre Projects production.

OCTOBER
The River Jordan (Michael Byrnes), directed by Tim Robertson.

NOVEMBER/DECEMBER
Bob and Joe's Revenge with Bob Thorneycroft and Joe Bolza.
Community theatre tours to schools, factories, prisons, hospitals, community centres: *The Sport Show*, *The Migrant Show* (group-developed).
The Owl and the Pussycat (Popeye Puppets).
The Floating World tours to Adelaide.

1975

JANUARY/FEBRUARY
Bedfellows (Barry Oakley), directed by Jack Hibberd.

MARCH
Bedfellows tours to Adelaide.
Mary Shelley and the Monsters (Tim Robertson and the cast), directed by Alan Robertson.

MAY
Add a Grated Laugh or Two. A show about women and madness by the Women's Theatre Group.

JUNE
The Hills Family Show. A group creation.

AUGUST
The Les Darcy Show, One of Nature's Gentlemen (Jack Hibberd) and *Mrs Thally F.* (John Romeril). Tour of New Zealand.
The Mother (Bertolt Brecht), directed by Lindzee Smith.
The Elephant Calf (adapted from Bertolt Brecht), group-created by Popeye Puppets.

OCTOBER
Hills Family Show revival.

NOVEMBER/DECEMBER
The Golden Holden (John Romeril) in the Front Theatre.
On the Hazards of Smoking (Anton Chekhov) with Max Gillies.
The Second Rater (Ivan Turgenev) with Bill Garner.
Not I (Samuel Beckett) with Suarupo in the Back Theatre.
The Money Show. Community Theatre.
Toads Supper Show. Back Theatre
The Empire Builders (Boris Vian), directed by Charles Kemp. Back Theatre.

1976

JANUARY
The Golden Holden (John Romeril), revival.

JANUARY/FEBRUARY
How Grey was my Nurse? Group-created by the Popeye Puppets.
Yours for the Masking (Bob Thorneycroft and Joe Bolza).

MARCH
My Foot, My Tutor (Peter Handke) with Bob Thorneycroft and Joe Bolza.
Stasis, a group-developed show about Sylvia Plath, in the Back Theatre.
Pecking Orders (Phil Motherwell).

APRIL
Self-Accusation (Peter Handke).
Act Without Words (Samuel Beckett).

MAY
Sisters (Robin Thurston), directed by Richard Murphett.
Women's Theatre Group Supper Show.

JUNE
AC/DC (Heathcote Williams), directed by Lindzee Smith.

JULY
Waiting for Godot (Samuel Beckett). Theatre Projects production.

AUGUST
Knuckle (David Hare), directed by Alan Robertson.

SEPTEMBER/OCTOBER
The Overcoat (adapted from Gogol by Jack Hibberd with music by Martin Friedl), directed by Tim Robertson.

NOVEMBER
The Dudders (John Romeril and John Timlin). A theatre-restaurant show, directed by John Romeril.
The Young Peer Gynt (Henrik Ibsen and Stasis) at St Marks Hall, Fitzroy.

NOVEMBER/JANUARY 1977
A Stretch of the Imagination (Jack Hibberd), directed by Paul Hampton, with Max Gillies.
A Toast to Melba (Jack Hibberd) at the Adelaide Festival, followed by a season at the National Theatre in Melbourne.
Hills Family Show. Victorian country tour.
The Timor Show. Group-developed by the Soapbox Circus, APG and Matchbox.
Sylvia Plath Show (Stasis) tours schools.

1977

Nightshift made its debut in the winter with a supper show production, *Cowboy Mouth* by Sam Shepard, in the Front Theatre. Followed by *Five o'clock Shadow*, a season of plays: *Michie's Blood* (F. X. Kroetz), *Killer's Head* (Sam Shepard), directed by Lindzee Smith, and *The Local Stigmatic* (Heathcote Williams), directed by Richard Murphett. It toured Phil Motherwell's *Mr Bastard and The Surgeon's Arms* around town and represented the APG at the Atelier Internazionale degli Gruppi di Theatro. To Bergamo went Lindzee Smith with Motherwell's one-hander *The Fitzroy Yank*. It played in the cathedral. Peter Corrigan went along to shine a light as did Eugenio Barba and Jerzy Grotowski.

Domestic Contradictions, a group-developed radio serial, was transmitted for the first half of the year.

JANUARY
The Phoenix (The Dance of Life Company) in the Front Theatre.

FEBRUARY
Supper Shows on Friday nights with local bands including Hit and Run, Gulliver's Travels, Nudes.
The Hills Family Show, Adelaide tour.
Phar Lap—It's Cingalese For Lightning Y'Know (Stephen Mastare) opens in Perth.
Benefit night with Soapbox Circus and Stiletto.

MARCH/APRIL
The Hills Family Show, Sydney tour.
Phar Lap—It's Cingalese for Lightning Y'Know (Steven Mastare), directed by Paul Hampton in the Front Theatre.
Indian dance with Zamir Haroon in the Back Theatre.
Stasis schools tour.

APRIL
Old Kitbag (Barry Dickins) in the Back Theatre.

MAY/JUNE
The Hills Family Show revival.

APRIL/JUNE
Yesterday's News (Jeremy Seabrook and the Joint Stock Theatre Company), directed by Wilfred Last in the Back Theatre.
Soapbox Circus tours New South Wales and south-east Queensland in April/May.

JUNE/JULY
Antony and Cleopatra (William Shakespeare and Stasis) in the Back Theatre. Tours to schools.

JULY
Back to Bourke St (group-created) in the Front Theatre, transferring to Last Laugh.

JULY/AUGUST
A Stretch of the Imagination (Jack Hibberd), Sydney tour.
The Radio Active Horror Show (John Romeril with the cast).
Soapbox Circus tours Sydney in August.

SEPTEMBER
A Stretch of the Imagination, Canberra tour.

OCTOBER
A Stretch of the Imagination, Victorian country tour.

NOVEMBER
A Stretch of the Imagination, Tasmanian tour.

DECEMBER
Smackinthedacks (adapted from *Gammer Gurton's Needle* by Soapbox Circus).

1978

JANUARY/MARCH
Circus Oz at Moomba and Adelaide Festivals.
A Mad World, My Masters (Barry Keefe), directed by Wilfred Last.

FEBRUARY
News Supper Show, in the Back Theatre.
River, clowning and mime in the Back Theatre.

MARCH/APRIL
Back to Bourke St, return season in the Front Theatre.
Another Lady Sings the Blues, Frankie Raymond, in the Back Theatre.

MAY
May Day Supper Show Celebrations.
Louisa See Saw Players, directed by Peter Green in the Back Theatre.
A Dollar for the Autograph, George Dreyfus, in the Back Theatre.
Pre-Paradise (Sorry) Now (R. W. Fassbinder) in the Back Theatre. A Nightshift production.

JUNE
Troilus and Cressida (William Shakespeare), directed by Peter King.

JULY
English Fool Show (Chris Langham).
Every Night, Every Night (Ray Mooney).
Dimboola, the feature film, directed by John Duigan. Shot on location at Dimboola.
The Whittle Family Supper show, in the Front Theatre.

AUGUST
The Bitter Tears of Petra Von Kant (R. W. Fassbinder), directed by Kerry Dwyer.
Robyn Archer with Louis McManus, Supper Show.
Popular Theatre Group.

AUGUST/SEPTEMBER
The Fool's Shoe Hotel (Barry Dickins).

SEPTEMBER/OCTOBER
Island (Phil Motherwell) in the Basement.

OCTOBER
Dreamers of the Absolute (Phil Motherwell), directed by Lindzee Smith.
Voices (Susan Griffin), directed by Fay Mokotow in the Back Theatre.

NOVEMBER
The Ship's Whistle (Barry Oakley).
Light Shining in Buckinghamshire (Caryl Churchill), directed by Wilfred Last in the Back Theatre.
Grand Opening of the Panel Beaters Space with the Whittle Family, Jo Jo Zep, Stiletto, Paul Kelly and the Dots, Loaded Dice, Flying Tackle et al.
Nightshift presented a Design Season in the Back Theatre, in collaboration with RMIT and the Cantrills: *Red Love* (adapted from Alexandra Kollontai by Rosa von Praunheim), *L'Amante Anglaise* (Marguerite Duras) and *To End God's Judgment* (Antonin Artaud). At the Loft at 303 Smith Street there were Nightshift productions of *Saliva Milkshake* (Howard Brenton), *True West* (Sam Shepard), *The Ruffian on the Stair* (Joe Orton) and *The Fitzroy Yank* (Phil Motherwell).
Films by the Reel Women Film Group.
Carnage (Tim Burns), a Rusden College student production.
The Young and the Jobless, the long-running Unemployment Show. Three tours including Sydney and Canberra.

Productions for Radio went out through 3CR.
In Jan 1979 Suarupo and Jenny Kemp started their work on Grimm's fairy tales and toured hospitals.

1979

FEBRUARY
Garden of Delights (Fernando Arrabal), directed by Alison Richards in the Back Theatre.

FEBRUARY/MARCH
Mickey's Moomba (John Romeril) in the Panelbeater Space.

MARCH/APRIL
Concerning Poor Bert Brecht (Beverley Blenkenship) in the Back Theatre.
Self-Accusation (Peter Handke), *Rock Garden* (Sam Shepard), *Your Children* (Charles Manson), Skelta Theatre Company.

APRIL/JUNE
Traitors (Stephen Sewell), directed by Kerry Dwyer and Nano Nagle.

MAY
The Astounding Optimissimos (Tim Gooding) in the Back Theatre.
Circus Oz at the Last Laugh.
Campus tour with five-person troupe.

MAY/JUNE
The Floating World (Romeril), directed by Tim Robertson with Bruce Spence as Les at the National Arts Centre, Ottawa.

JUNE
The Case of Katherine Mansfield (Cathy Downes) in the Back Theatre.
Paradise Depression Style in the Back Theatre.

JUNE/JULY
Rosmerholm (Henrik Ibsen), directed by Jane Oehr.

JULY
What to Do about What. Bob and Nancy dance duo in the Back Theatre.
Give the Shadow A Run (Phil Motherwell) in the Back Theatre.
Rotten Teeth Show and *The Horror of the Suburban Nature Strip* (Barry Dickins) in the Back Theatre.
La Musica and *L'Amante Anglaise* (Marguerite Duras) in the Back Theatre.

JULY/AUGUST
The Woman (Edward Bond), directed by Aarne Neeme.

SEPTEMBER
Sheila Alone, Jealousy, or The Affair, written and directed by Jenny Kemp.
Self-Accusation (Peter Handke), directed by Lindy Davies.
The Point Isn't To Tell You, Jenny Kemp and Rob Meldrum.
Kinetic Dance Company, in the Front Theatre.
Role of Women, Women's Rollerskating Collective (Sydney) in the Front Theatre.
Angel of the Graveyard (Ray Mooney) in the Back Theatre.

NOVEMBER
Failing In Love Again (Jan Cornall).
Zastrozzi (George Walker).
Gentlemen Only at the Playbox.

Real Mighty Bonza Whacko Wimmin's Circus.
Cabaray with the Kevins, Jan Cornall, Di Duncombe, Rob Meldrum, Sue Ingleton and the Cabaret Cons.

DECEMBER
Role of Women, Women's Rollerskating Collective (Sydney) in the Front Theatre.
Everyman, Suitcase Players in the Back Theatre.
Women's Disco Band Supper Show.
Radio work continues (e.g. Radio Cartoons) on 3CR.
Nightshift was in New York doing *Men's Business* (F. X. Kroetz) and other things.
The Mobile Poetry Workshop (Eric Beach and associates) was out and about and in the Back Theatre.

1980

JANUARY/FEBRUARY
A Night with Venus, Shoestring Players, directed by Darryl Emerson.

FEBRUARY/MARCH
Carboni (John Romeril), directed by Bill Hannan

MARCH/APRIL
The Metaphysics of a Two-Headed Calf (Stanislav Witkievicz), directed by Roger Pulvers in the Front Theatre.

APRIL
Sister (Joy Wiedersatz) in the Front Theatre.
Manson, the Defence Testimony, Backstreets Theatre Company directed by Ian Campbell.
Kidstreets (Chris Dickins).
The Woods (David Mamet), directed by Jenny Kemp and Neil Gladwin with Rusden students.

MAY
Auction of Pram Factory Premises: gothick street theatre.
Artaud at Rodez (Charles Marovitz) in the Front Theatre.
Sore Throats (Howard Brenton).
Rezistor Routines, the Ensembles' first show, a group-devised cabaret on unemployment, outcasts and technology.

JULY/AUGUST
The Ken Wright Show (Barry Dickins).
Scanlon (Barry Oakley) and *The Hazards of Smoking* (Anton Chekhov) with Max Gillies at the Universal.
Cloud Nine (Caryl Churchill).
Banquet of Vipers (Alice Tierney), directed by J.-P. Mignon with Julie Forsythe.

DECEMBER
Kate Kelly Roadshow (Frank Hatherley) in the Front Theatre.
Circus Oz season at the Paris Theatre (Sydney).
Overseas tour to Pacific Arts Festival (PNG) and Europe.

1981

SEPTEMBER
The Bedbug Celebration (adapted from Mayakovsky by John Blay).
Savage Love (Neil Giles) directed by Alison Richards, music by Ash Wednesday.

1982 . . .

Circus Oz continues to tour nationally and internationally.

Appendix II: Who was Who

Allen, Micky Painter, photographer, designer and a power in the Women's Theatre Group. Spiritual seeker.

Anders, Doug Founding member and ex-Brisbane guru/spielmeister of Tribe, director and presently a genealogist.

Armiger, Martin An immigrant mod from South London. One of the initial intake of the Flinders Drama school. Unforgettable as Jewish-accented Nagg in *Endgame*. Founder member of the Toads, High Rise Bombers Bleeding Hearts and the Sports. Record producer, composer of music for theatre, film and TV and author (*The Waiters*, Text, Melbourne 2000).

Bailey, Paul Early eager workshopper at La Mama. Died much too early of heroin overdose.

Baker, David Film and television director known in the early days for his direction of many long-running television series e.g. *The Terrible Ten* and *Spyforce*. Later he directed *Squeaker's Mate*, a brilliant short film adapted from the Barbara Baynton short story of the same name, featuring Kerry Dwyer and David Mitchell. From Barry Oakley's novel *A Salute To The Great McCarthy*, he interred certain elements of the story in a feature film, *The Great McCarthy*, in which many APG members fleetingly appeared and which, according to many critics and the novelist, died quietly at quarter time. A later feature, *Neil Lynne*, was not commercially released.

Bell, Avril Singer with the Double Decker Bros with a voice that made her sister singers lose confidence. The girl most likely to succeed of 1972. Found her guru and is now Avril Bahkti, whereabouts unknown.

Bilson, Tony Cook who became a chef. Restaurateur and *grand fromage* of Sydney gastronomia while maintaining conversational gambits at his guests' tables.

Blundell, Graeme Actor–writer–director or director–actor–writer or writer–director–actor, boxed trifecta of talents. Formative ideas man of APG at La Mama and the Pram. Of Reservoir origin, now a seachanged Sydney-sider. Innumerable roles, stage, TV, film inc. *Alvin Purple* (directed by Tim Burstall), highly successful, politically unco sex romp. Resigned from the group in 1973 after a leadership tussle that made ALP faction fighting seem amateurish.

Bolza, Joe Euro-trained mime half of the Bob (Thorneycroft) and Joe mime/dance partnership. Currently a clinical psychologist.

Bren, Frank Performer/playwright. *An Hairy Man* (1967), *Have you Noticed Your Leg is Missing?* (1969) . . . perennial avant-gardiste of the European school and perseverant veteran of La Mama.

Brisbane, Katherine Sandgroper theatre critic of the *Australian*. Well-tiled promoter of new Australian drama. Co-founder of the Currency Press with her husband Philip Parsons.

Bryson, John Sometime barrister and author (*Whoring Around, Evil Angels, To the Death, Amic*), adventure capitalist, racing driver and the first APG Corporate Secretary. A tender to good causes, he was financially responsible for getting the *Gillies Live* omnibus on the road and providing many opportunities for others inside and outside the Pram Factory.

Bucknall, Jan A Triber who went to California and came back home again.

Buesst, Nigel Film maker, director and photographer from the iconic mattress-making family. Among his award-winning oeuvre are *Come out Fighting, Bonjour Balwyn, Jacka* and *The Loved One*.

Burstall, Betty Founder of La Mama, matron saint of alternative theatre in Melbourne, cunning midwife of the backyard renaissance in Australian drama.

Burstall, Tim Film director *1000 Weeks, Stork, Petersen, Eliza Frazer, Alvin Purple*. Lothario of Eltham, would-be Coppola of Fitzroy. Driving force in the '70s cinema revival.

Cantrills, Arthur and Corinne Hierophants of experimental film-making. 1970 made a feature length bio-pic *Harry Hooton* about the exemplary Oz *avant-gardiste*. Their doco *People Mix* (1971) has footage of APG performers at work.

Camillieri, Joe Malteser muso who made good co-founding or fronting the Double Decker Bros, the Black Sorrows, Hit & Run and Jo Jo Zep and the Falcons. Established his own Jazzhead record label in his own Woodstock Studios.

Carmody, Anna Early La Mama workshopper and performer. Married Peter (ditto), Beckett-loving champion of play making in the vernacular.

Cass, Fred Rock 'n' roll drummer with the Cassettes, dreamer of the rock 'n' roll dream.

Cerutty, Percy Barefoot shaman of track and field and the Portsea sandhills over which he ran his charges, mentor of '60s Olympian middle distance runners, and great contributor to the Aussie gold industry.

Charles, Jack A prominent figure in the emergence of an indigenous theatre. He starred in the Pram Factory productions of Jack Hibberd's *Dimboola*, John Romeril's *Bastardy* and Katharine Susannah Prichard's *Brumby Innes*. He also appeared in many television and film roles as well as for most of the major theatre companies in Australia. Managed to upstage Max Gillies.

Cherry, Wal Greatbeaked rationalist/enthusiast/inseminator. Founding director of the Emerald Hill Theatre Company. Founding professor of drama at Flinders University. One of the fathers of the drama boom in Oz tertiary education. Until his untimely death he was teaching and freelance directing in America.

Clancy, Meg Early La Mama workshopper, founder member of APG, siren and anarchist who now protects the nation from hard-core visuals at the Film Censorship Board.

Clayton, Syd Poet and prolific devisor of theatrical scenarios and events: *Evenings with the North Carlton Bicycle Club* and *Marcel Du Champs, The Man on the Left is Joe Bigger from Topeka* (1968), *Um Jum kun Aum Jum* (1969) etc.

Clifton, Jane Founder member of Tribe, BA (Monash)-holding, ruin-haunting, all-singing (*Stiletto*), all-dancing (has had tap training), ex-*Prisoner* celebrity, *belle-lettriste* and oral historian.

Conway, Mic 'Microphone' The Captain Matchbox of yore. Singer/songwriter, virtuoso of the ukulele and washboard, fire-eater and keeper of the flame of vaudeville. Currently fronting the National Junk Band.

Coppin, George (1819–1906) Comedian and entrepreneur, dashing and dodgy, who ran three theatres, four hotels, an amusement park (the Cremorne Gardens, Richmond), and a skating rink, and launched the St Johns Ambulance in Victoria.

Cornall, Jan Primary teacher drop-out, singer/songwriter. Founder member of Tribe and the Women's Theatre Group.

Corrigan, Peter Cosmo-provincial Melburnian architect (co-principal of Corrigan Edmond) and scold. National Institute of Architecture award for his work on identifying an Australian style with its locus in the suburbs. Best work exemplified by the Keysborough Church. Theatre designer in spaces grand and small, in cahoots with Barrie Kosky for the last ten years.

Crawford, Hector Mogul of Melbourne TV, whose productions (*Homicide, Sullivans* . . .) schooled a generation of directors, actors and crew.

Cummins, Peter Plumber, player, flautist, d.i.y. homebuilder, head-biter, runner. Still up and running.

Daly, Bob Tribe, APG, Circus Oz stalwart. Banjo-plucking muralist and cartoonist.

Dampier, Alfred (1847–1908) Actor/ manager, patron of a distinctly Australian brand of melodrama.

Davies, Brian A film enthusiast at La Mama. With Graham Blundell and Kerry Dwyer he was a motivating force in establishing the way of working which set the APG apart as a distinctive force in the new drama. He split to become a senior executive with an Adelaide pharmaceutical company and his life was tragically curtailed by cancer.

Davies, Lindy La Mama improviser and founder member of APG. Doyenne of Victorian College of the Arts, performance consultant and confidante to the stars.

Davis, Rennie Co-founder and mouthpiece of the San Francisco Mime Troupe by which he was eventually repudiated for vices of ego and politics.

Deling, Bert Counter cultural film-maker and collectivist superstar. Director of *Dalmas* and *Pure S.*

Dickins, Barry Raconteur, wit, playwright–performer, memorabilist, cartoonist, artist, comic sentimentalist, language conservationist and hack out of Dylan Thomas by Lenny Lower, whose innumerable credits include *The Foolshoe Hotel, Death of Minnie, Mag and Bag* and a seamless performance as Old Croft in *The Ship's Whistle* (Oakley) during which, one night, garrulous beyond the text, his teeth fell out and were ground to permanent closure by a huge, iron-wheeled traverse causing, among the audience, much alarum and delight, which the play itself, alas, did not.

Dobbin, Claire Impeccably fanged actress from the Bouverie Street stable of the Education Dept's Secondary Teachers' College which also gave us Max Gillies and Tony Taylor. Became a significant bureaucrat in the film funding business and is married to Dr Mal who dispensed pharmaceuticals and advice to many a Pram denizen while keeping an account with his camera. Currently an indy producer and script editor.

Dreyfus, George One-man show, composer, bassoonist, raconteur and serial autobiographer.

Drysdale, Denise aka *Ding Dong* Knockabout comedienne and TV personality who brilliantly parlayed top-heaviness into Melbourne celebrity.

Dufty, Dick Began acting at Melbourne University Law School, and after learning several musical instruments was engaged in the Pram Factory production of Hibberd's *Dimboola*, where he featured as Lionel Driftwood in the resonant musical group Lionel Driftwood and the Piledrivers. He has managed a successful legal career despite early stardom.

Duigan, John La Mama workshopper, aspirant actor appearing as shaggy dog anti-hero in Brian Davies's short film *Brake Fluid* and Nigel Buesst's *B*. Hotshot student of philosophy from Melbourne University and one of the early experimental filmmakers acting, writing, directing. *Mouth to Mouth* was the first of many *auteur* credits to win him commercial recognition. This was soon dissipated by his direction of the Pram Factory Productions feature *Dimboola*, panned by critics and rapidly expunged from his c.v. Despite this he has worked continuously in Hollywood, Australia and the UK and now has over a dozen feature film credits to his name including *The Year My Voice Broke*, *Flirting* and *Lawn Dogs*, and the mini-series *Vietnam*. He is also bankable as a punter during the Melbourne Spring Carnival.

Duncan, Mick Feral dance organiser and tenant of the Pram on a pro bono basis till he and his bull terriers took off for Northern beaches.

Dwyer, Kerry Founding member of the APG by way of university theatre and drama teaching. A rider of the second wave of feminism through the rips and shallows of chauvinism, she became disenchanted with the theatre and ran away with the circus. After a pitstop at Byron Bay, she followed the Goddess to Ireland, Italy and India.

Dyke, Peter Appeared at the Pram Factory as an aspiring actor of a philosophical disposition and was immediately hired as the group's accountant in which role he excelled at the theory and practice of double entry book keeping. He remained professionally calm through dozens of riotous meetings and protected the common till with great assiduity and moral purpose.

Faust, Beatrice Writer and a foundation member of the Women's Electoral Lobby, a notable polemicist and advocate of women's rights as well as being a champion of radical sexuality as long as it does no harm to others unless that's what they want.

Flannery, Ed Solicitor and member of the bar at Stewarts Hotel and later Percy's Bar and Bistro.

Flett, Dave Bass player with Lipp Arthur and Captain Matchbox. Genius designer and builder of recording studios.

Finney, Alan Robust workshopper. Excelled in 1972 La Mama production of Michael McClure's *Spider Rabbit* with Cathy Beavis. Now a major motion picture executive.

Fitzpatrick, Brian (1905–65) Independent radical journalist, historian, government adviser, defender of civil liberties and pillar of the Swanston Family Hotel. One of Australia's very few freelance intellectuals. Author of *British Imperialism and Australia* and *A Short History of the Australian Labor Movement*.

Frank, Laurel Costumier extraordinaire and designer of many ingenious puppets and coverings for the Pram, Circus Oz and the greater theatre and television world.

Friedl, Jan Actress and very gifted singer whose interpretation of Kurt Weill's music has taken her on world tours. Many major appearances at the Pram and for the Melbourne Theatre Company.

Gaden, John Quicksilver actor of the Sydney school who performed often for Nimrod and spread his talents to directing, including the challenging role of Artistic Director of the South Australian Theatre Co.

Gallagher, Carl Itinerant scribbler, painter, street man, sometime habitué of Stewarts fringeing on Nightshift.

Gantner, Carrillo Victoria's Disraeli, the sartorial and intellectual flying wedge of the Myer family, has been behind the counter in arts management for years and helped the Pram Factory wallet with some early grants when he was a Commissionaire at the Australia Council. Not totally retail, he jumped the counter and defended our culture at the Melbourne Town Hall, where he was a passionate councillor. He also embraced the Chinese as Australia's Cultural Attaché in Beijing, and founded the Playbox Theatre with ex-Prammers Blundell and Hutchinson

Gardiner, Geoffrey Early La Mama workshopper who later migrated to Canberra, where he helped run the Rt Hon John Dawkins during the Hawke/Keating years while keeping an arm free for some good times at the Lobby Restaurant. Former director of Melbourne Film Festival.

Garner, Bill Writer/performer and pansophist with mercurial and quixotic tendencies leading him, often as not, to adopt positions of advocacy derived from the institution he is animating at the time be that Monash University, APG, ABC . . . TV scriptwriter and editor.

Garner, Helen Writer and early functional feminist. Collaborator on *Betty Can Jump* and first secretary of the APG. Her novel *Monkey Grip* features some of its members. Shed the veils of fiction to exercise her gifts as a journalist. Currently growing a novel.

Gedye, Kelvin Imperturbable sound man whose life has been spent in the bio-boxes of this and other nations. Kept many shows at the Pram and Circus Oz in good hearing.

Giles, Neil Migrant from South Australia, persistent and percussive performer.

Gillies, Max Performer/politician frequently mistaken for somebody else. First elected Chair of the APG in the shuffle towards worker control. Many major roles and collaborative productions at the Pram Factory, MTC, Nimrod, STC, Australian Opera etc. and in his own shows, *A Night With the Right, The Max Gillies Summit, A Night of National Reconciliation,* from which derived the trail-blazing TV satirical series *The Gillies Report*. Still bearing the torch of satire to the arse of the rich and powerful.

Gradman, Eric Musician, composer, member of *Sharks, Flaming Hearts, Man and Machine*, currently lurking in Video-Paintbox-style advertising milieux.

Green, Peter Duntroon-trained performer and director, born to play the Good Soldier Schweik. Long time teacher of drama (at the Footscray Institute) and collaborator with Barry Dickins.

Hampton, Paul Escapee from the Bouverie Street Secondary Teachers' College along with Max Gillies, Claire Dobbin and Tony Taylor. A handy player, better employed as a director responsible for several of the Max Gillies shows including *A Night of National Reconciliation* at Kinsellas in Sydney.

Hannans, Bill and Lorna Known *en bloc* as 'the Hannans', they applied their intelligences to state education. Celebrated 100 years of it by co-writing *The Compulsory Century* for the Pram Factory. Introduced pure and applied democratic theory and procedural dexterity in the *coup de pram* which resulted, eventually, in the departure of Graeme Blundell.

Hartmann, Rivka Playwright around La Mama who turned to film, milking comedy from female Jewish *angst*.

Hawkes, Jon Swimmer, juggler, accountant, strongman, administrator and calligrapher from a good church background. Psychedelic bolshevist who smoked with Che, out-raved Fidel and performed mouth-to-mouth on Mao. Has been Director of the International Theatre Institute and is now a fixer for community music.

Hawkes, Ponch One of Nature's Den Mothers, photographer and communitarian.

Heald, Ted Strolling player from Chicago (via California) whose mom wanted him to be a teacher.

Hibberd, Jack Playwright, poet, novelist, quack (specialising in allergies) who has turned his hand to directing and criticism. Best known, perhaps, for *A Stretch of the Imagination* and *Dimboola*, he has maintained a creative stream of pieces, many remaining sadly unproduced. Occupied the Chair at the APG and was twice provoked to resign his membership. A member of the Australia Council's Drama Panel and Theatre Board.

Hill, Ted A prominent member of the Victorian Bar and a leading Communist after the war. His leanings in his latter years were towards the China faction and his group splintered from the official Communist Party in the early '60s.

Hines, Arthur Theatre Manager *manqué* who constantly rolled his own unperturbed by the crushing deadlines which the Pram Factory's conversational management style imposed on him. An escapee from the Melbourne Theatre Company's more traditional working platform, Arthur was responsible for lowering some of the heights of the APG's technical ambitions to saner levels.

Hoffman, Abbie Political joker and media mojo, one of the main organisers (with Jerry Rubin and Paul Krassner) of the Yippies (Youth International Party) at the Democratic Convention in Chicago, 1968. A yippie was defined as a hippie who had been hit on the head by a policeman. Wrote seminal revolutionary jokebook *Revolution for the Hell of It*.

'Horse trough', Harry aka *Davis, Harry* (1919–95) Vandemonian remittance man and *bon viveur* around Carlton. Emphysematically hustled pool at Martini's Hotel, outside of which stood a horse trough, whence his *nom de rue*.

Ingleton, Sue Performer/writer/healer, channelling adept of stand-up and the one-person show, with a stable of characters inc. Edith, the goddess manifest as rural crone and Bill Rawlins, the pregnant man. A principal in the experimental groupuscule Stasis.

Jillet, Neil Variously film, dance and theatre critic for the Melbourne *Age* after a long spell with the *Herald*, where he dealt mainly with theatre after a distinguished career as a foreign correspondent. Razor's stylish prose and pungent reviews won him the grudging respect of thespians not conferred on other scribblers themselves ambitious for theatrical fame.

Kemp, Jenny A director with the Stasis group, now freelance and a writer/adaptor with a potent theatrical *savoir-faire*. Her best work includes *The White Hotel* (1983, adapted from D. M. Thomas), *Good Night, Sweet Dreams* (1986), *Call of the Wild* (1989) for the Spoleto Festival (now the Melbourne Festival), *Remember at the Gasworks* (1993) and *Black Sequin Dress* (1996).

Kendall, David A founding member of La Mama, directed much of the original experimental work with Graeme Blundell, Brian Davies and Kerry Dwyer. Prominent in publishing circles, a renowned editor, he pursued acting studies in London. He later became Director of Melbourne University Theatre and is now the Senior Lecturer in Drama at Adelaide's Centre for the Performing Arts.

Koenig, John An absurdly gifted technician whose talents informed most Pram Factory productions through the latter half of the '70s. Probably his tour de force was the construction of a pre-Viagra mechanical erection worn by this book's author during Barrie Keefe's play *A Mad World, My Masters*. Neither its nor his like have been seen again.

Knappet, Bruce (1940–95?) An early kooka among the improvisers at La Mama. At Melbourne University his performance in *Krapp's Last Tape* inspired Beckett studies. A classical scholar, he also graduated in law and for some time practised as a barrister till retiring to the country, where he wrote several plays and taught drama until his untimely death.

Kramer, Danny Street man and Fosters longneck devotee with a proprietary feeling for certain salient Carlton benches. Intrepid and versatile conversationalist barred from most Carlton hotels for infelicitous behaviour when gripped by the product they sell.

Krape, Evelyn Performer (comical, tragical and physical, gutsy, ribald characters a speciality) in the feminist kick-off *Betty Can Jump*, in Dario Fo's one-hander *Female Parts*, as Astrid the flower girl in *Dimboola*, Granny in *The Hills Family Show*, Ginger in her own show of that name at the Playbox, the Nurse in the MTC's *Romeo and Juliet* and as Melba in Jack Hibberd's *A Toast to Melba* etc., etc.

Kuring, Jude Winner of a best actress Penguin for the eponymous role in *Coralie Lansdowne Says No*. Inmate of *Prisoner* during its halcyon years. Lost plot. With life-size puppet associates became the terror of the chattering, drinking class in Sydney.

Laurie, Robyn After mucking about with Tribe and dropping out of the Melbourne College of Education she longhauled through the APG, the Women's Theatre Group and the Great Stumble Forward to become a founding member of Circus Oz and the first Women's Circus, choreographing, devising comic and acrobatic material and playing the trombone angelically. She went on to work with the Fruit Fly Circus, the Rock 'n' Roll Cicus and the first Nanjing Acrobatic Project. She has devised and organised a babel of bilingual productions with Italian, Arabic and Aboriginal communities and directed with the Sidetrack Theatre, the Melbourne Workers Theatre and Theatreworks. She has indefatigably conferenced, chaired, inquired, consulted, taught and assessed at home and abroad. In 1990 she was awarded the Ros Bower award for her contribution to community arts. Currently she is the artistic director of Circus Oz.

Leeson, Stephen 'Buzz' The fourth Bee Gee and sixth Beatle. Singer/songwriter and teacher.

Leith, Graham The first electrician at the Pram Factory, took his life in his hands for the first six months till the wiring was nearly legal. He acted early on at La Mama and produced, with Sue McKinnon, the celebrated Passing Clouds vintages which go from prize to prize.

Maddison, Ruth Rangy photographer with a gift for catching people in the best of poses. Confidante of Bob Daly.

Marini, Yvonne Pocket Venus of Hellenic origin whose performing energy was turbo-charged. Became the unwitting centre of the Pram contretemps about salaries and triggered a *petit coup*. Grabbed by guru Maharishi from Timlin's loft at the rear of his house but later returned and married the good doctor Albert, a speed-witted medico.

Mastare, Stephen Playwright, poet and street man whose play *Phar Lap—It's Cingalese for Lightning Y'Know*, was performed at the Pram Factory and the Perth Festival.

McCaughey, James The man whose classical erudition brought his own translation of the Oresteian Trilogy to the Pram Factory. He now freelances as a director.

McKenzie, Ian A commercial photographer whose talents spread to lighting design and the construction of a famous dimmer board attractive enough to some Members for it to be co-opted to secure loans for dope purchases. His skill at fifty feet on the extension ladder drew audiences sometimes larger than attended certain Pram Factory plays.

McKimm, Barry Playwright/performer/experimental composer whose works include *Five Pages of Yapp, Mushrooms, Saturday.*

McSpeddon, Hugh Chief light-show head for the Too Much and Much More Ball-rooms and lead leaper with the Leaping McSpeddons. Still gives good light.

Meldrum, Rob An actor who took his acting very seriously and was part of the Stasis Group at the Pram where performance was a little more intense than delivered by the APG 'knockabout' style at which he also excelled. Still an unabashed experimentalist and freelance actor and director.

Milne, Geoffrey Sandgroper who joined the improvising *ur*-APG and sidestepped into academia. Now doubles as drama critic on Jonathan Shiers's ABC radio and is watching his step, which he first learnt to do as a lighting designer and erector for the Melbourne Theatre Company, the Pram and others.

Milne, Lorraine Member of top band *Semblance of Dignity* that gave same to APG rough-house in and out of La Mama. Composer and musical director for *Lionel Driftwood and the Piledrivers* in *Dimboola* and for *Marvellous Melbourne, Waltzing Matilda, The Hills Family Show.*

Mitchell, David Rivetting actor with the MTC, a dionysian Fr O'Shea in *Dimboola* at the Chevron Hotel. Mythologised by Barry Dickins in *Ron Truffle, His Life & Bump-Out* (Pascoe Publishing, Melbourne 1988).

Mokotow, Fay Tribe member, performer, director and one of the Chairs of the APG. First female director at the Nimrod Theatre, her career was stopped trag-ically short by a brain tumour. A leading figure in Melbourne Jewish theatre.

Molan, Phil One of the grand architects of the Pram Factory Constitution and a founding member of the Fitzroy Legal Service and the Victorian Aboriginal Legal Aid Service. He attended to much of the company's legal work and did a great deal of *pro bono* work for various members charged with possession of outlaw substances. He worked for the Institute of Public Advocacy in NSW and Legal Aid till appointed Coroner in NSW, where he died after a long battle with cancer.

Monton, Vince An outstanding DOP among whose credits is the great *Newsfront*, he turned to directing with possibly less critical success—*Fatal Bonds* and *The Sher Mountains Killing Mystery.*

Mooney, Ray Novelist, playwright. Member of the Melbourne Writer's Theatre. The film *Every Night, Every Night* is based on his play performed at the Pram and drawn from his own experience of Pentridge.

Moore, Rod A gifted distance runner who came straight off the track into La Mama with his running mate Peter Cummins. An elaborately handsome actor and teacher, he was diverted by few APG females because of a passion for other sorts of figures—the accounting at the Pram Factory. He also performed between balance sheets, including a season as a marsupial incarnation of Johnny O'Keefe. He rose above coups and counter coups and retired gracefully into academe where he teaches drama with a little English.

Motherwell, Phil Playwright, performer, novelist, member of wild-side groupuscule Nightshift. Regularly cast as a bad guy in film and TV where his work experience allows of considerable verisimilitude.

Mullet, Jane The flying member of the famous Left Wing Mullet family who supported her rise to the high wire at Circus Oz.

Murphett, Richard Thoughtful director and sage for various sub-groups of the APG. Now teaches thespian disciplines at the Victorian College for the Arts.

Nash, Margo Anarcho-Surrealist Insurrectionary Feminist and film-maker about the Pram. Moved to Sydney in 1978 and joined the Film-makers Co-op. Produced, wrote, directed, shot and edited award-winning docos and experimental films, including *Shadows* starring Robin Laurie. Her feature *Vacant Possession* was nominated for best original screenplay and best director in the AFI awards for 1994. Lectures in screenwriting at the University of Technology, Sydney.

O'Hearn, D. J. 'Dinny' (1937–93) A long-time friend of the Pram Factory and an adviser and confidant to many participants including Jack Hibberd, David Kendall and John Timlin. Sub-Dean of the Melbourne University Arts Faculty, he was a fervent champion of Australian literature. He was the co-presenter of the SBS Book Show, with Andrea Stretton. He died shortly after retirement, posthumously hosting one of Melbourne's biggest parties, as he had done when among the quick every St Patrick's Day.

O'Leary, Kim Joined the La Mama Company from the MTC's Saturday Morning Club where she had been nurtured by Malcolm Robertson. Of showbusiness stock (her dad was Geoff 'King Corky' Corke, Graham Kennedy's first 'second banana' co-host on the Tarax show, and her mum Val was the glamorous band singer), she flamed forth in redhead beauty but gave the performance game away.

O'Neil, Lloyd A senior figure in Australian publishing, Chief Executive of Penguin Books and F. W. Cheshire & Co. At one of the perennial financial submergings of the collective, Lloyd took on the role of White Knight as Chairman of the advisory board which raised many thousands to unblock the toilets and reconnect the power and thus enabled the Pram-saving production of Barry Oakley's *The Feet of Daniel Mannix* to put money into the passing plate.

Oakley, Barry Novelist, playwright, diarist, columnist. His plays have allegedly presaged the closure of two theatres: Emerald Hill—sadly—and the William Bates Memorial Theatre—thankfully. His satire on Menzies, *Beware of Imitations*, with Max Gillies and Bruce Spence, created a box office record at the Pram: 220 bums on seats. Most recently published his diaries *Minitudes* (Text, Melbourne 2000).

Patterson, Gary Clown and cinematographer. With Jim Robertson one half of the *One and Half Man Show*. The Cecil B. deMille of Super 8, video documentarian and archivist.

Pearce, Amanda Drop-out teacher and Triber who dropped back into teaching.

Phelan, Martin A former teacher and one-time gymnast who led the group in physical training around the Carlton Street park in preparation for street theatre. Short, stocky, feisty actor with a street sense about him and a slyness, shared by others of the ur APG, that caused them to lob at the Dwyer/Blundell menage around tea-time. He later teamed up with Al Finney to co-direct Williamson's *The Coming of Stork* at La Mama when the La Mama Company became the APG. Found himself a proper job and was lost to the mystery.

Pickhaver, Greig Joined APG after graduating BA (Drama) from Flinders. Drawn to community theatre projects (e.g. *The Sports Show*) and radio production.

Headstrong exponent of the rave and buff of rock 'n' roll and affiliated trades. Metamorphosed into H. G. Nelson and became world-famous for taking the piss out of the Olympic dream.

Pinder, John Hefty epicurean and hip capitalist. Proprietor of the Flying Trapeze and the Last Laugh (with Roger Evans).

Porter, Carol Founder member of Tribe. Performer, designer, graphic artist and tap dancer. Gravitated towards Nightshift and the shamanship of Lindzee Smith. Saw active service in the Women's Theatre Group.

Potter, Susi Overlanded from Flinders University to become an APG *ingénue*, jitterbugger (*The Dudders*), designer, macropod and mask maker (*Waltzing Matilda, The River Jordan, The Overcoat*). Dallied with the Women's Theatre Group and Stasis.

Presser, Lutz Tribe member, aquarian, artist and seeker.

Price, Michael Anarchist and traveller, man in the street theatre movement, in and out of Tribe and the APG and its sub-groups.

Pulvers, Roger Philosopher/playwright whose astonishing bouts of complexity were made even more dangerously arcane by a linguistic ability which propelled him into the further reaches of Japanese samurai dialects wherein mispronunciation could cost a limb. He was wondrous deft on the piano, and commanded a great repertoire of modern jazz. An American, he was not always comfortable with the sometimes brash Aussie dialectics of Pram Factory combatants.

Radic, Len Known in the '70s as Leonardo Radish from Jack Hibberd's play *Dimboola*. From the beginnings of La Mama and the Pram Factory Len was the drama critic for the influential Melbourne broadsheet the *Age*. From this roost he copiously noted the performance, direction and writing of the new Australian drama. He was often encouraging but more often perplexed by the group constructions and collective administration of the Pram Factory. He also is a playwright.

Radic, Therese née O'Halloran Joined in Holy Matrimony to Len. A graduate of Melbourne University's Conservatorium, she was long fascinated by composer Percy Grainger and wore her hair in a suspiciously long pig tail during the writing of her play *A Whip Around For Percy Grainger*. Said pigtail may also have led to, or been a gestatory by-product of, her play about Mr and Ms Mao and their ménage.

Rene, Roy 'Mo' Jewish stand-up radio and stage comedian who kept Australia alive through depression, war and prosperity by his spluttering wit and good-humoured mockery of the worst of our leaders and the worst of the led.

Robertson, Alan Left Anakie in the country for Anarchy in the town. Tribe, APG, Circus Oz stayer. Welder, rigger, inventor of theatrical machinery.

Romeril, John Playwright, poet and song-writer of amazing fecundity and imagination—over 60 plays to his name including *The Floating World* which has been translated into Japanese for performance in Japan and at the Playbox. Central ideologue and political theorist of the Left Bent with Asia much on his mind of late.

Shuv'us A natural Nightshifter who ascended from Tasmania to be apotheosed as a falling star in Helen Garner's *Monkey Grip*. Went forth into the wilderness with Lindzee Smith & Co for 40-plus nights and descended into Tasmania to keep shop on the waterfront.

Sky, Hellen Wonderfully silhouetted in John Duigan's *Dimboola*, she was the Pram mistress of dance and smart movement as well a more than decorative contributor to the performing artistry at Circus Oz.

Smith, Lindzee 'Dentist' Geelong Collegian, director and theatrical clairvoyant who acquired guru status after many trips. To California (MA (Drama) UCSB) and New York where he acquired the local twang and insider deals on Theatrical World Best Practice. Led the formation of the nihilist Nightshift which played NY as much as Carlton, financed in part by the bourgeois APG collective.

Smythe, John Performer and director whose contribution to the APG in the early days included directing the world premiére of Katharine Susannah Prichard's *Brumby Innes.*

Spears, Steve Playwright and garage-band guitarist. His *Africa*, a Savage Rock Musical (directed by Lindzee Smith) had a successful season in the Back Theatre, and *The Elocution of Benjamin Franklin* starring Gordon Chater won him international theatre renown and Gordon a comfortable retirement.

Spence, Bruce Performer, horticulturalist with a diploma in oenology. Iconic comic and character actor—from the eponymous Stork in Tim Burstall's film to the Gyro Captain in *Mad Max* and his towering performance as Les in *The Floating World.*

Starkie, Peter Lesser known brother of Skyhook Bongo. Some would say the better player with an ego inversely proportionate.

Stewarts, Hotel Carlton's one-time think and drink tank on the corner of Drummond and Elgin wherein various piffle and waffle was spouted. The management, Alf Morton (0.1% at the breakfast barrier; an improver during the day) and wife Val (Miss Victoria, 1952), was complemented by bartender Gino whose wife Dulcie became the dinkum Oz elocutionary model for the Canadian production of *The Floating World*. Another ornament was Kim, who worked her perfect posterior through law school at the bar in black micro-mini and fishnet stockings. Clientele were forever wanting something from the bottom of the fridge. Stewarts was destroyed by owner Grollo's renovation which involved a wall of mirrors, thus causing the mob to move on to Percy's bar rather than take a good, long, hard look at themselves.

Stocker, Dave Promising, prize-winning young film-maker who, over exposed to the light of Rajneesh, turned orange and disappeared.

Sumner, John Pommy merchant mariner and later stagehand who rose to the top of the Melbourne Theatre Co. wherein he discovered Ray Lawler, a little bit of Barry Humphries and quite a lot of Visy Board's Richard Pratt. John's production of *The Summer of the Seventeenth Doll* toured London and New York and was later to emerge as a film. He stocked the MTC with subscribers and mostly British drama which kept them in. He was mentioned in dispatches for supporting a $3000 grant for the first Pram Factory production and contributed finally a lot to the Australian theatre after the success of MTC productions of David Williamson's plays.

Symons, Red Tribe alumnus. Forsook math/science studies for rock 'n' roll stardom in Skyhooks. Sometime libertine and pantomime dame, now an arbiter of cool and media grump.

Talbot, Colin Author/metajournalist (*Massive Road Trauma, The Living Daylights, The Digger*), Carlton hipster, cosmopolitan punk and poetry wrangler (*Applestealers*).

Taylor, Tony Performer, occasional writer and parfit gentle soul oft disturbed by the violent rhetoric of collective meetings. More at ease in circumstances of group creation where he was always a primary source of energy. *Back to Bourke Street* and *The Hills Family Show* gave scope for his taste for nostalgia and *grotesquerie.*

Thompson, Dot Kept alive the tradition of the New Theatre, a lefty group which had its heyday before and after World War II in a small theatre in Flinders Street. In many ways it was the spiritual ancestor of the APG although much of its work was within the conventions of naturalism and social realism which then dominated left-wing theatre. Dot actually discovered the Pram Factory building and it was her initiative which brought the Group into the building. There was friction and the parties separated but by then she had made a major contribution to the acceptance of the new drama.

Thorneycroft, Bob Mr Bojangles reborn as Chesty Bond hoofing as modern dance half of the Bob and Joe duo. Until recently the charismatic organiser of the annual Mallacoota Easter festival.

Timlin, John A son of Footscray, a welder and mechanic who led the group creation of the monumental seating modules at the Pram and as Administrator bore a large part of the responsibility for getting bums on them. Responsible also, with Hibberd and Romeril respectively, for the theatre restaurant entertainments *Goodbye Ted* and *The Dudders*. Prefers Grange to grunge but Left to Right.

Tisdall, Billy Flitted in the shadows of Nightshift, appearing in productions in the Back Theatre, La Mama and elsewhere.

Tonto Steve Spears sidekick, good times promoter, patron of the Twins Hamburger joint.

Vaughan, Martin Appeared in the Brainrot season as Dinga in *Who* and Youth in *This Great Gap of Time*. Hung in and became a veteran, *Power Without Glory* and all that.

Wallace, Ian aka 'Pudding' Alto sax player with Lipp Arthur, Lipp and the Double Decker Bros, Niagara and a legend in his own bathroom. Scared shit out of everybody but particularly Joe Camillieri. Compered at Sunbury pop festival filling *longueurs* with readings of salacious bits from Carter Brown novels. Left to play sax in NY for ten years. Returned to condemn former associates as provincial dilettantes. Departed for Japan.

Weir, Peter Directed *The Cars That Ate Paris* which featured a few Prammies and then went, via *Gallipoli* and *The Year of Living Dangerously*, into Beverly Hills where he remains in high demand.

Westbrook, Eric Director of the Victorian Ministry of the Arts, personally responsible for persuading Bolte to build the National Gallery for hangings other than by the neck, an achievement that speaks of his considerable political skills. An artist himself, married to a better one, Dawn Sime, he had long ago swapped the bohemian temper for a knowing urbanity that did not always beam upon the Pram.

Whaley, George Engineer turned actor who for some time was Director of the Melbourne University Student Theatre. Later administered the Seymour Centre at Sydney University. Directed the Dad and Dave movie *On Our Selection* and has been prominent as an actor in stage, television and film for many a season.

Williams, Margaret Teacher and academic specialising in drama and theatre history with interests in drama and education, children's theatre and puppetry. Lecturer in drama at the University of New South Wales since 1973.

Williamson, David Australia's tallest and most popular playwright whose *Don's Party* premiered at the Pram in which there were small cells of malcontents unmoved by his work. These cells later divided and multiplied in the playwright's memory and became a Maoist plague on his *oeuvre* that forced him to retreat from Carlton to distant Diamond Creek, thence to Emerald City and the wide world.

Wood, John Wrote *On Yer Marx* which was produced at the Pram Factory. After a distinguished stage, film and television career, became Australia's best known cop in *Blue Heelers*.

Woodcock, Bruce Tenor sax with Lipp and the Double Decker Bros. Wrote most of the best tunes and then walked into the night.

Bibliography

Abehsera, Michael *Zen Macrobiotic Cooking*, Random House, NY 1964.
Alexander, F. *Matthias: The Resurrection of the Body*, Thames and Hudson, London 1989.
Artaud, Antonin *Le Théâtre et son Double*, Gallimard, Paris 1938.
Barba, Eugenio *Dictionary of Theatre Anthropology: The secret art of the Performer*, Center for Performance Research/Routledge, London/NY 1991.
—— *Floating Islands: Reflections with Odin Teatret*, Drama, Grasten, c. 1979.
Baudelaire, Charles *Les Fleurs du Mal*, Armand Colin, Paris 1958.
Beck, Julian and Malina, Judith *Paradise Now: Collective creation of living theatre*, Random House, NY 1971.
Brook, Peter *Empty Space* Penguin, London 1972.
Brecht, Bertolt *Plays* (trans. Bentley, Willett ...), Methuen, London 1966.
Brenton, Howard *Sore Throats*, Eyre Methuen, London 1979.
—— *Christie in Love*, Methuen, London 1970.
Brown, Norman O. *Love's Body*, Random House, NY 1968.
Burroughs, William *The Naked Lunch*, Calder and Boyars, London 1964.
Buzo, Alex *Norm and Ahmed*, Currency, Sydney 1976.
—— *Front Room Boys* in *Plays by Buzo/Hibberd/Romeril*, Penguin, Melbourne.
—— *Coralie Landsdowne Says No*, Currency, Sydney 1974.
Campbell, Joseph *The Masks of God*, Viking, NY 1959.
Castenada, Carlos *The Teachings of Don Juan, a Yaqui Way of Knowledge*, Ballantine, NY 1968.
Chaikin, Joe *The Presence of the Actor*, Atheneum, NY 1972.
Cheng and Smith *Tai Chi*, Tuttle, Vermont 1969.
de Chardin, Teilhard *The Phenomenon of Man*, Harper and Row, NY 1959.
Debord, Guy *The Society of the Spectacle* (trans. Donald Nicholson-Smith), Zone Books, New York 1995
Downing, G. *The Massage Book*, Random House, Maryland 1971.
Elam, Harry J. *Taking It to the Streets: The social protest theater of Luis Valdez and Amiri Baraka*, Universiry of Michigan Press, Ann Arbor 1997.
Escher, M. C. *The Graphic Work*, Hawthorn Books, NY 1968.

Evans-Wentz, W. Y. (ed.) *The Tibetan Book of the Dead*, Oxford University Press, London 1960.
Feldenkrais, Moshe *Awareness Through Movement*, Harper and Row, NY 1972.
Ferlinghetti Lawrence *The Coney Island of the Mind*, New Directions, NY 1958.
Fuller, Buckminster *9 Chains to the Moon*, Lippincott, Philadelphia 1938.
—— *Operating Manual for Spaceship Earth*, Pocket Book, NY 1969.
Garner, Helen *Monkey Grip*, McPhee Gribble, Melbourne 1977.
Garrison, O. V. *Tantra: The Yoga of Sex*, Julian Press, NY 1964.
Gelber, Jack *The Connection*, Faber and Faber, London 1961.
Goffman, Erwin *The Presentation of the Self in Everyday Life*, Allen Lane, London 1969.
Graves, Robert *The White Goddess*, Faber and Faber, London 1948.
Green and Gold Cookery Book, The R. M. Osborne, Adelaide 192?.
Grotowski, Jerzy *Towards a Poor Theatre*, Simon and Schuster, NY 1968.
Handke, Peter *The Ride Across Lake Constance and other plays*, Farrar Straus and Giroux, NY 1976.
Hare, David *Plays*, Faber and Faber, London 1996.
Hesse, Hermann *Steppenwolf*, Penguin, London 1965.
—— *Journey to the East*, Noonday Press, NY 1957.
Hibberd, Jack *Four Australian Plays*, Penguin, Melbourne 1973.
—— *Three Popular Plays*, Outback, Melbourne 1976.
—— *Dimboola*, Penguin, Melbourne 1974.
—— *A Stretch of the Imagination*, Currency Press, Sydney 1973.
—— *Peggy Sue*, Yackandandah Playscripts, Melbourne 1982.
—— *The Overcoat*, Currency Press, Sydney 1981.
—— *Marvellous Melbourne* (with John Romeril), *Theatre Australia*, vol. 2, no. 4 (1977), pp 29–39.
Hoffman, Abbie *Revolution for the Hell of It*, Dial Press, NY 1968.
Hofmann, Albert *LSD: My Problem Child*, Tarcher, LA 1983.
Huizinga, Johan *Homo Ludens*, Routledge and Kegan Paul, London 1949.
Huxley, Aldous *The Doors of Perception* and *Heaven and Hell* Penguin, London 1961.
Ishihara, A. *The Tao of Sex*, Shibundo Publications, Yokohama 1968.
Jarry, Alfred *Oeuvres Complètes*, Gallimard, Paris 1972.
Jones, Liz, with Betty Burstall and Helen Garner, *La Mama: The Story of a Theatre* McPhee Gribble/Penguin, Melbourne 1988
Jung, Carl *Man and his Symbols*, Doubleday, NY 1964.
Keefe, Barrie *A Mad World, My Masters*, Eyre Methuen, London 1977.
Kesey, Ken *One Flew Over the Cuckoo's Nest*, Viking, NY 1973.
Laing, R. D. *The Politics of Experience and The Bird of Paradise* Penguin, 1967.
Leary, Timothy *The Politics of Ecstasy*, Granada, London 1973.
Leys, Simon *Chinese Shadows*, Viking, NY 1977.
Linklater, Kristin *Freeing the Natural Voice*, Drama Book Publishers, NY 1976.
Littlewood, Joan *Joan's Book: Joan Littlewood's peculiar history as she tells it*, Methuen, London 1994.
Ludlum, Charles *The Complete Plays*, Perennial Library, NY 1989.
—— *Ridiculous Theater: scourge of human folly: the essays and opinions of Charles Ludlam*, Theater Communications Group, NY 1992.
Mao Tse-tung *Quotations from Chairman Mao*, Foreign Languages Press, Beijing, 1967.

Marcuse, Herbert *One Dimensional Man*, Beacon Press, Boston 1964.
Marovitz, Charles *Theatre at Work: Playwrights and productions in the modern British theatre*, Methuen, London 1967.
Marlowe, Christopher *The Plays* (ed. Leo Kirschbaum), Meridian, 1962.
McLuhan, Marshall *Understanding Media*, Signet, NY 1964.
—— *Culture is Our Business*, McGraw Hill, NJ 1970.
Meyerhold, Vsevolod *Meyerhold on Theatre* (ed./trans. Edward Braun), Hill and Wang, NY 1969.
—— *Meyerhold Speaks, Meyerhold Rehearses* (ed./trans. Edward Braun), Hill and Wang, NY 1969.
Neville, Richard *Playpower*, Paladin, London 1970.
Oakley, Barry *A Lesson in English*, Currency Methuen, Sydney 1968.
—— *The Feet of Daniel Mannix*, Angus and Robertson, Sydney 1975.
—— *Beware of Imitations*, Yackandandah Playscripts, Melbourne 1985.
—— *Bedfellows*, Currency Press, Sydney 1975.
Rabelais, François, *Gargantua and Pantagruel,* trans. Urquart and Motteux, London 1653, 1693, 1694.
Radic, Len *The State of Play*, Penguin, Melbourne 1991.
Reich, Wilhelm *The Function of the Orgasm*, Panther, London 1948.
Robertson, Tim *Waltzing Matilda* (with John Romeril), Yackandandah Playscripts, Melbourne 1984.
—— *Mary Shelley and the Monsters*, Yackandandah Playscripts, Melbourne 1983.
—— *A History of Australia: The Musical* (with Don Watson and John Romeril), Yackandandah Playscripts, Melbourne 1988.
Romeril, John *I Don't Know Who to Feel Sorry For*, Currency Press, Sydney 1973.
—— *Chicago, Chicago* (in *Plays by Buzo/Hibberd/Romeril*, edited by Graeme Blundell), Penguin, London 1970.
—— *Bastardy*, Yackandandah Playscripts, Melbourne 1982.
—— *The Accidental Poke* (in *Popular Short Plays for the Australian Stage*, edited by Ron Blair), Currency Press, Sydney 1985.
—— *The Floating World*, Currency Press, Sydney 1975.
Roszak, Theodore *The Making of the Counter Culture*, Anchor, NY 1970.
Schechner, Richard *Public Domain*, Bobbs Merril, Indianapolis 1969.
—— *Dionysius in 69*, Farrar Strauss and Groux, NY 1970.
Shepard, Sam *Seven Plays*, Faber, London 1985.
Schumann, Peter *Puppen und Masken, das Bread & Puppet Theatre: ein Arbeitsbericht von Peter Schumann*, Fischer-Taschenbuch Verlag, Frankfurt 1973.
Slessor, Kenneth *Five Bells: XX poems*, F. C. Johnson, Sydney 1939.
Southern, Terry *The Magic Christian*, Penguin, London 1969.
Stevens, Jay *Storming Heaven*, LSD and the American Dream, Flamingo, London 1993.
Spolin, Viola *Improvisation for the Theatre*, Northwestern University Press, 1963.
Terry, Megan *Viet Rock, Comings and Goings, Keep Tightly Closed in a Cool Dry Place*, Simon and Schuster, NY 1967.
Van Itallie, Claude *America Hurrah: Five short plays*, Penguin, London 1967.
Watson, James *The Double Helix*, Weidenfeld and Nicholson, London 1968.
Whole Earth Catalog edited by Stewart Brand et al., Portola Institute, California 1971.

Watts, Alan *The Way of Zen*, Penguin, London 1962.
Weiss, Peter *The Persecution and Assassination of Marat as Performed by the Inmates of Charenton Directed by the Marquis de Sade* (adapted by Adrian Mitchell), John Calder 1965.
Wilhelm, Richard (trans.) *I Ching. The Book of Changes*, Routledge and Kegan Paul, London 1951.
Williams, David *Collaborative Theatre: The Théâtre du Soleil source book*, Routledge, London 1999.
Williams, Margaret *Australia and the Popular Stage 1829–1929*, Oxford University Press, Melbourne 1983.
Williamson, David *The Removalists*, Currency Press, Sydney 1972.
—— *Don's Party*, Currency Methuen, Sydney 1973.
Wolfe, Tom *The Electric Kool Aid Acid Test*, Bantam, NY 1981.

Index

A

Abu, 131
Achren, Linda 92
Adshead, Soosi 92
Allen, Micky 37, 57
Anders(on), Doug 5, 14, 19, 21
Andersen, Andy 97
Anderson, George 130
Armiger, Martin 10, 92, 93
Ashton, Doug 131
Ashton, Mervyn 131

B

Bailey, Paul 3
Baixas, Juan 141
Bacon, Barbara 18, 19
Baker, David 3
Bain, Rodney aka Tonto 94
Ball, Barry 12
Balos, Rowena 83
Barr, Margaret 15
Beach, Eric 39
Bell, Avril 18, 19
Berkman, Chris 92
Best, Jack 95
Bilson, Tony 38
Black, David 130, 132
Blackburn, Steve 88
Blundell, Graeme 2, 3, 7, 10, 23, 26, 29, 32, 44, 46, 51, 57, 74, 77, 92, 107, 117
Bolza, Joe 17, 60, 62, 83
Bond, Graham 23
Bren, Frank 3
Brisbane, Katharine 6
Broadway, Sue 112, 132, 136, 141, 142, 143, 146
Brookes, Geoff 88
Brown, Penny 33
Bryson, John 57
Bucknall, Jan 15, 18, 20
Buesst, Nigel 3
Burstall, Betty 3, 5, 27
Burstall, Tim 25
Burstall, Tom 3
Button, John 95
Buzo, Alex 6
Byrnes, Michael 38, 98

C

Calafel, Teresa 141
Camilleri, Joe 18, 19
Cantrills, 3
Carmody, Anna 3, 117, 118
Cass, Fred 18, 19, 93
Champion, Stephen 133, 138, 142
Chapman, Eileen 100
Charles, Jack 26, 124
Cherry, Wal 7, 11, 54, 86, 123, 130
Clancy, Meg 3, 10, 11, 29, 49, 117, 118
Clark, Libby 109
Clark, Manning 126, 138
Clayton, Syd 5
Clifton, Jane 14, 15, 18, 19, 36, 37, 42, 65, 70
Coldwell, Tim 112, 128
Collins, Bill 'the Slaught' 10
Conway, Mick 134, 143
Cook, Peggy 3
Cornall, Jan 18, 20, 36
Corrigan, Peter 106
Cummins, Peter 3, 4, 26, 50, 53, 57, 69, 77, 109, 110, 116, 124

D

Daly, Bob 18, 37, 42, 97, 110, 128
Daniel, Jack 112, 130, 133, 136, 142, 143
Dave, Hollywood 38

Index

Davey, Anni 145
Davies, Brian 3, 54, 117
Davies, Lindy 3, 4, 49, 117, 118
Davis, Rennie 24
de Winter, Roz aka Suarupo 84, 85, 103
Delings, Bert 3, 18
Dickins, Barry 71, 72, 90, 101, 112, 113
Dobbin, Claire 29, 46, 70, 103, 104, 106
Dreyfus, George 88, 109
Drysdale, Denise 65
Dufty, Dick 57, 67
Duigan, John 3, 4
Duncan, Mick 30
Dwyer, Kerry 2, 3, 22, 23, 25, 46, 49, 54, 55, 57, 65, 70, 92, 93, 136, 142
Dyke, Peter 35, 100

E

Ellis, Bob 107
Ellis, John 23
Ellis, Lois 23
Espinosa, Fanny 131
Evans, Roger 111

F

Fairfax, George 145
Faust, Beatrice 3
Fields, Maurie 90
Finney, Alan 3, 25, 118
Flannery, Eddie 71
Flett, Dave 18, 19
Frank, Laurel 30, 32, 37, 81, 112, 134, 136
Fraser, Malcolm 134
Friedl, Jan 83, 86, 121
Friedl, Martin 109

G

Gantner, Carrillo 83
Gardiner, Geoffrey 3, 4, 118
Garner, Bill 2, 3, 7, 10, 11, 29, 33, 39, 44, 49, 65, 78, 80, 81, 87, 92, 110
Garner, Helen 37, 38, 49, 142
Gasser, Frank 131, 132, 136
Gasser, 'Sonnyboy' 132
Gedye, Kelvin 81, 105
Gelber, Jack 53
Gibb, Jillian 37
Giles, Neil 86, 92, 108, 112
Gillies, Max 29, 38, 46, 50, 51, 52, 55, 56, 57, 67, 74, 75, 77, 78, 79, 80, 91, 98, 109, 114, 116, 125, 134, 142
Glenn, Eve 128
Goffman, Erwin 43, 117
Grabowski, Paul 88
Gradman, Eric 19, 102
Green, Peter 3, 110, 112

H

Hampton, Paul 50, 54
Hannan, Bill 54, 57, 75, 81

Hannan, Lorna 54, 55, 77
Harbison, Mick 130, 132
Harrigan, Johnny 76
Harrison, Ursula 51, 70
Hartman, Rivka 40
Hawkes, Jon 3, 7, 14, 35, 37, 38, 42, 52, 53, 61, 62, 63, 65, 68, 74, 81, 134, 135, 136, 140, 142, 144
Hawkes, Ponch 37, 70, 144
Heald, Ted 35, 42
Hewett, Dorothy 90
Hibberd, Jack 6, 8, 26, 32, 44, 49, 53, 58, 63, 66, 67, 87, 89, 90, 95, 97, 100, 109
Hill, Peter 140
Hill, Steve 42
Hines, Arthur 30
Hooper, Helen 18
Houghton, David 142
Hunt, Albert 138
Hutchinson, Garrie 57, 93, 95

I

Ingleton, Sue 33, 70, 78, 80
Isaac, Graeme 58, 102, 134
Ives, Derek 143

J

Jerrems, Carol 37
Jillett, Neil 101
Johnson, Michelle 101
Jones, Fast Alf 131
Jones, Sue 110

K

Kaye, Norman 109
Kemp, Jenny 84, 85, 86
Kendall, David 3, 26, 27, 46, 118
Kenneally, Mary 88
Kent, Stephen 141, 142
Klooger, Jill 3
Knappett, Bruce 3
Koenig, John 30
Kramer, Danny 39, 72
Krape, Evelyn 27, 35, 53, 68, 69, 70, 77, 78, 80, 83, 95, 98, 103, 104, 110, 112
Kuring, Jude 15, 26, 69, 92, 93, 124

L

Lane, Charmayne 108, 113
Last, Wilfred 29, 46, 70, 98, 100
Laurie, Bain 36, 74
Laurie, Robin 3, 36, 42, 51, 61, 70, 77, 101, 133, 134, 135, 142, 144
Lazarus, Jack 40
Leuba, Robin 7, 11, 94, 107, 108
Lee, Bethany 3
Leeson, Stephen 'Buzz' 12, 78, 79, 81, 92, 102, 105, 108, 132
Leith, Graeme 28

Lilley, Peter 88, 89
Lindsay, Margot 7
Lu Guang Rong 143
Ludbrooke, Ric 135

M

Maddison, Ruth 37, 42
Marini, Yvonne 10, 11, 46, 57, 92, 93
Marinos, Lex 98
Martin, Don 132
Mastare, Steve 72
McCaughey, James 24, 28
McKenzie, Ian 28, 57
McKimm, Barry 15
McSpeddon, Hugh 18, 93
Mekas, Jonas 53
Meldrum, Rob 78, 80, 83, 84, 99, 101, 106
Meltzer, Larry 77
Miles, Andy 108
Miles, Bruce 110
Milne, Lorraine 74
Mokotow, Fay 15, 18, 65, 70, 78, 80, 81, 98
Molan, Phil 57, 110
Monton, Vince 3
Mooney, Ray 71
Moore, Rod 3, 7, 11, 49
Motherwell, Phil 62, 75, 112, 126
Muggleton, Amanda 111
Mullet, Jane 58, 138, 142
Murphett, Richard 14, 58, 70, 77, 87, 134

N

Nash, Margo 3, 36, 70
Neville, Sue 36
Norris, Terry 98

O

Oakley, Barry 17, 53, 60, 74, 75, 89
O'Hearn, Dinny 32
O'Leary, Kim 3
Oliver, Ken 100
O'Neil, Lloyd 57

P

Pascoe, Judy 144
Patterson, Gary 3, 133
Pearce, Mandy 15, 18
Perry, Albert 133
Petit, Phillippe 131
Phelan, Martin 3, 4, 7
Pickhaver, Greig 30, 37, 42, 58, 74, 76, 77, 92, 94, 101, 134
Pinder, John 17, 23, 111, 112, 133, 136, 140, 144
Podlena, Mr 30
Porter, Carol 15, 19, 20, 35, 36, 37, 42, 52, 61, 65, 101, 134, 135
Potter, Susi 84, 85, 92, 100, 101, 108, 110
Pound, Mr 130
Pounder, Betty 121

Presser, Lutz 15
Price, Michael 58, 77, 103, 134
Pulvers, Roger 32

Q

Quantock, Rod 88, 138

R

Radic, Len 88
Radic, Therese 46
Richards, Alison 108, 110
Rimbaud, Arty 9
Robertson, Alan 15, 18, 20, 30, 32, 42, 102, 105, 106, 128, 134, 135, 142
Robertson, Anna Pome 94, 108, 128
Robertson, Janet 113
Robertson, Jim 112, 133, 136, 138
Robertson, Matilda Bree 108
Robertson, Pixie 112, 133, 136, 138, 143
Romeril, John 6, 23, 25, 26, 30, 46, 49, 60, 74, 80, 90, 92, 93, 94, 97, 112, 114, 123
Rosella, Don 142
Rowe, Lyndell 3

S

Salenkas, Jonas 131
Saunders, Jenny 142
Seaweed, Angela 142
Sewell, Stephen 109
Sharman, Jim 141
Shuv'us, 42, 52, 74, 77
Simon, Lee 93
Sky, Hellen 58, 134, 135
Smith, Lindzee 3, 7, 35, 37, 42, 46, 60, 61, 62, 63, 65, 68, 73, 100, 101, 102, 118
Sneddon, Bill 95
Spears, Steve 65
Spence, Bruce 7, 15, 50, 53, 57, 59, 65, 75, 77, 102, 103, 106, 124, 127
Spence, Jenny 102
Stanislavsky, Constantin 46
Starkie, Peter 19
Starrs, Frank 18
Stewart, Wayne 100
Stocker, Dave 92
Suarupo aka Roz de Winter 70, 86
Sumner, John 26, 46
Symons, Red 20, 93

T

Talbot, Colin 23
Taylor, Tony 29, 49, 53, 54, 68, 78, 79, 82, 103, 106, 134
Terry, Megan 50
Thompson, Dot 26
Thorndike, Sybil 21
Thorneycroft, Bob 60, 62, 78, 81, 83, 110
Tillet, Rob 17
Timlin, Anne 54

Index

Timlin, John 26, 33, 54, 57, 66, 67, 73, 74, 91, 94, 97, 100
Tisdall, Billy 74
Tlacol, 12
Toll, Geoff 138, 140, 142
Tomasetti, Glen 46
Tonto aka Bain, Rodney 94
Topper, Cosmo 76, 88, 89
Triffit, Nigel 112
Turner, Ian 46
Tyler, Tim 144

V

Van Rosendael, Eddie 37, 38
Vizard, Steve 109

W

Wallace, Ian ('Pudding') 18
Ware, Alison 15
Watson, Don 126
Weiner, Jack 81, 82

Weir, Peter 23
Westbrook, Eric 95
Whaley, George 12
Whitlam, Gough 95
Wilkin, Catherine 111
Williams, Margaret 24, 44, 46
Williamson, David 32, 53, 74, 77, 89, 90, 95
Wolk, Emil 144
Wood, John 97, 110
Woodcock, Bruce 18, 19, 42

Y

Yang, Mr 143

Z

Zappa, Frank 8, 19, 93
Zucchini, Giorgio 131
Zucchini, Phillip 131
Zucchini, Theo 131